indexes

ANEURIN BEVAN

A BIOGRAPHY

By the same author

H. G. WELLS: A BIOGRAPHY

The Rt. Hon. Aneurin Bevan, M.P.

ANEURIN BEVAN

A Biography by
Vincent Brome

LONGMANS, GREEN AND CO
LONDON · NEW YORK · TORONTO

LONGMANS, GREEN AND CO LTD
6 & 7 CLIFFORD STREET LONDON W I
ALSO AT MELBOURNE AND CAPE TOWN
LONGMANS, GREEN AND CO INC
55 FIFTH AVENUE NEW YORK 3
LONGMANS, GREEN AND CO
215 VICTORIA STREET TORONTO I
ORIENT LONGMANS LTD
BOMBAY CALCUTTA MADRAS

First Published 1953

PRINTED IN GREAT BRITAIN
SPOTTISWOODE, BALLANTYNE AND CO. LIMITED
LONDON AND COLCHESTER

PREFACE

THE remarks of some contemporary politicians achieve a false immortality because an opponent finds it convenient to keep alive the unintentional overflow of a heated moment. It remains one of the greater hazards of the political life that any man born with the gift of eloquence and inspired by a responsive audience, may be carried away by words which haunt him for the rest of his days.

Applied to normal conversation, most of us would wish to retract half the words we uttered. In a sense, the biography of a living politician suffers from a similar shortcoming. It is too close to the contemporary scene. Yet much evidence which would be invaluable to future biographers can so easily die with the day, and here, in one sense with the dew still on it, is an offering to the writer of the future. It should also be remembered that ideally it is not only desirable to read Aneurin Bevan's speeches *in full*, but to *hear* them in full, since his personality can so transform the words he uses.

For the rest, this preface has one purpose: to thank some of the many people who so kindly helped me, over several years, in sifting, recording, analysing and checking the complicated mass of material from which this book was written. One stands out above the others. My biography of Aneurin Bevan could not have been written without the patient, devoted work of Angela Harling, who gave so freely of her time, skill and above all understanding. Amongst others to whom I am indebted are Frank Horrabin, H. W. Leggett, J. T. Murphy and Francis Williams. There are many other people who must, for various reasons, remain anonymous. I can only acknowledge their help at one remove. For the rest I am also considerably indebted to Jennie Lee's excellent book *This Great Journey* (American edition, Farrar and Rinehart, Inc. British edition under the title *Tomorrow is A New Day*, Cresset Press); and to two of Aneurin Bevan's own works, *Why Not Trust the Tories?* (Victor Gollancz) and *In Place of Fear* (William Heinemann Ltd.). Obviously I have had to draw considerably on Hansard and I am grateful to H.M.S.O. for permission to reproduce passages from many volumes.

I acknowledge with grateful thanks permission to reproduce passages from *Tribune*, the weekly Socialist periodical, and also to *The Times* for permission to quote from an Editorial article. Finally I wish to thank Messrs. Faber and Faber Ltd. for permission to reproduce extracts from two poems by Mr. T. S. Eliot.

V. B.

PLATES

In erecting such a Spacious and Various Edifice, the Spectator, at first view, will hardly conceive how much pains was bestowed in digging the Foundation, in railing Scaffolds, in finding conveying and fitting Materials, in contriving the Architecture, in removing the Rubbish. Other Builders consult onely their own Brains, and the Dead, (that is books) whereunto access may be had at all Hours. But in this Work, the Living, and the choicest among them, were to be advised with; whereof some were far distant, others seldom at leisure, some unwilling to Communicate their knowledge, others not at all affable.

However, if the Reader, reaping in a few Hours, the Fruits of many Months labour, shall receive any content, the Author will not only be satisfied for this, but incouraged for another like Enterprize.

EDWARD CHAMBERLAYNE
15th Edition 1684 *Angliæ Notitia*

I

IT was six o'clock of an early September day in 1947. Big Ben was a wraith and a luminous haze gave the Thames an air of reaching back into the centuries. Whitehall spread, solidly secure, traffic poured round Parliament Square and the Ministry loomed out of the mist, drearily functional. Up the shallow steps, through the hall into the Enquiry Room and a man in black who said 'The Minister? Yes—we were expecting you.' The message ran from point to point, 'The Minister—The Minister—The Minister.' Each person repeated the incantation and an unbroken chain conducted me smoothly into an ante-room where one of his secretaries—who wrote excellent poetry in his spare time— received me with that quality of shyness which belongs to the sensitive scholar. We had met before. We said it was a beautiful day. We said there was something perverted about London on such a day as this, and fell to talking of Ezra Pound, Day Lewis and Robert Frost as if, in some inexplicable way, these poets might restore London to its first beginnings. A sign passed, too subtle to detect, and suddenly he broke off. The Minister was ready.

There was a large desk, a wide window and a burly man with a big head, thick-set on massive shoulders, and blue-green eyes, who moved forward to greet me and at once settled back into the red leather chair again. When he spoke there were Welsh undertones in his voice and a hint of diffidence, as though, for a moment, confronted with a complete stranger, he was not altogether at ease. We began uncertainly, we touched upon small preliminaries and each measured the other behind the conversational screen, but soon sheer power of personality broke through. Presently we were launched into deeper waters. Somewhere the ghost of a stutter haunted his voice as he talked, and his r's tended to become w's, but the hint of a lisp was attractive.

Inevitably we spoke of democratic Socialism. We analysed what the Labour Government was trying to do, we examined the difficulties surrounding it, and then, suddenly, he defined Socialism in terms very different from the normal. Democratic

B

Socialism he said was an instrument for implementing the social conscience, and his case seemed to develop along these lines:— The social conscience expressed itself in thousands of families where children were taught the virtues of compassion and kindness and consideration for others. These beliefs were reinforced by Christian teaching which established fresh links in a long tradition of service as well as self, but when the child left the circle of the family, it found the outer material world largely uninterested in such attitudes. 'Economic necessity quickly frustrated the moral impulse. The very structure of society insisted on disillusionment which led to moral neuroticism. . . .'

'If you look at some of the points in the Labour Party programme you will see that they are, in a sense, tantamount to an attempt to let society "resolve its guilt anxieties"—or, putting it another way—to do the bidding of conscience. . . .'[1]

Many people sympathized with the sick person, everyone wanted the poverty-stricken mother to find a house for her children, but it was assumed by too many that the resolution of these difficulties was entirely the responsibility of the individual concerned. Under Capitalism poor people were thrust back upon their own limited resources and some encountered inordinate hardship. 'But if we do what the Labour Government is doing— transform all these thousands of personal and private headaches into public headaches—we can get something done. . . . To preach and not to practise, to be obliged by the structure of society to act inadequately or not at all, is to become a moral cripple. . . . It is to thwart instead of implement the social conscience. . . .'

There was much more in a similar vein. Slowly the talk shifted its ground and we delved back into contemporary history. Why was it that great events came as a shock to so many people? Why did a large part of the public, living in the midst of all the evidence, remain incapable of interpretation until events themselves forced the issue? Were people so caught up in day-to-day anxieties and details that the underlying patterns had to remain obscure? Could society be said to know where it was going?

Suddenly he said, 'Society only discovers its intentions retrospectively.'

We were silent a moment. 'Even with the Russian Revolution?' I said.

[1] Views similar to this are quoted in an unpublished pamphlet by Amabel Williams-Ellis.

He seemed to ignore my question, but went on something in this manner. . . . Some anthropologists say that social mutations are the results of the intermingling of people. One social group or force develops and becomes fully realized, but cannot go on developing by itself. It is broken into by a new force from outside. Progress is always a zigzag. A social group at one level reaches stalemate, is stimulated by the impact of another and may involve a third.

The Russian Revolution, he continued, was started in London and Berlin. It began when a group of thinkers created a revolution in a vacuum and first filled the vacuum with intellectuals. . . . If Western democracy assimilated ordered economic planning into representative institutions and reacted upon the Russians, world affairs might go better. But the thrust of the contemporary individual must find a way through to the Kremlin with its bigotry, its cold-blooded yet human concentration on distant horizons. . . .

Half an hour went by. A red and angry sun sank over the Thames, the lights came up, a discreet messenger slid a paper on to his desk and vanished. Still he talked.

I had come to meet the man some people regarded as a modern Danton. If I were patient some glint of the barricades would break through, some sign of authoritarian absolutism reveal the truth hidden in the thickets of his phrases. In debate, he decapitated his opponents with the ruthlessness, precision and wit which reminded some of the eighteenth century, but there was no hint of Danton or the eighteenth century now. There were moments when his pauses seemed more fitted to applause than silence. The rotund quality of the public speaker was there. But there was also wit.

'I once remarked that one big difference between the Russians and the English consists in the fact that we are slaves to the past and they are slaves to the future.'

Forty minutes and still the phrases came pouring in like Atlantic rollers, full, rich, measured. For a whole hour it went on with hardly a pause, hardly a word from me, and then abruptly he stood up, pleaded pressure of many things and escorted me to the door. The words continued to echo in my ears. Fine sounding words, florid perhaps, but redeemed by a certain grandiloquence.

I had witnessed one of Aneurin Bevan's "performances," which quite possibly was turned on for my benefit. The Bevan interested in philosophy, the man of ideas, fascinated by "intellectual" explorations, had broken out into what one close friend describes as "his turgid periods" and another as "eloquence." He may have said these things before. I do not know. He may have repeated phrases long tried and polished over a lifetime of dialectic, but much of it had a spontaneous ring, and it was most impressive. There was no doubting a brilliant gift for words.

Outside in darkening Whitehall where the mist threatened to become a fog, I blinked a little at the passing traffic. It was almost as if I had met the wrong man. Was this the person with a "constitutional ineptitude for objectivity," "the apotheosis of the agitator," a man so imbued with class bitterness it soured his whole vision?

Aneurin Bevan had come a long way. Far back in the 1930s he had released his anger against a Conservative Minister of Labour with a flash of the invective he understood so well, and himself become a Socialist Minister of Labour in the end. From political buccaneer to statesman was a long and arduous journey. Many people vigorously denied that Bevan had ever approached its completion. They regarded him as suffering from a permanent fixation with the agitator born in his youth. But no one in British politics over the last fifty years had excited quite such forthright attacks, no one except Churchill coined phrases whose echo still hung on the air, no one had so overwhelmingly won the support of the Labour Party's rank and file at its great annual conferences. His tendency to express himself in terms which shocked even the hardened susceptibilities of Winston Churchill invited the trouble which sometimes occurred. The famous description of the Tory middle classes as "vermin" had been embalmed amongst those examples of invective which characterized his bitterest moments. Bevan himself tended to get lost behind outbursts of this kind if he was not overwhelmed by the idolatry which the very mention of his name generated in special groups of the Labour Party. Nobody was neutral about him. He drove people to violent reactions one way or the other—a kick in the backside on the steps of White's Club or eulogies in private Left-wing salons. And it all seemed remote from Bevan the self-made scholar who liked to swop poetic declamations with close friends.

In his fifties he was a tall, powerfully built man with hair tumbling across one temple, inclined to stoutness but showing little of the diminution of drive which accompanies the middle

4

years for most men. He lived well, was to be seen sometimes in good London restaurants, drank and smoked, played an occasional game of billiards, had a Johnsonian delight in talking and could "toss and gore" his opponents in the perfect Mitre tradition. There was nothing of the Cripps puritanical Socialist about Bevan. Here was a lusty liver with an Elizabethan largeness of personality developed to the pitch where some of his friends felt him hopelessly alien to the mild ways of Anglo-Saxon England in the twentieth century.

He lived in a tall, narrow rather beautiful house of the Regency period at No. — Cliveden Place. It stood in a row of such houses off Sloane Square and was damaged by flying bombs in the Second World War. When his wife, Jennie Lee, M.P. for Cannock, called in an expert to look over it, the restrictions on building materials were still very severe and Bevan was then Minister of Health and Housing. 'You see,' said the expert, looking gravely at Jennie Lee, 'this house is strictly habitable. If it had been anyone else it might have been open to repair . . . but your husband being Minister of Housing!'

The living-room at No. — had polished parquet flooring, some easy chairs, a miner's lamp on the mantelpiece and one wall lined with books. Here were the works of George Eliot and Dickens cheek by jowl with American moderns like Stuart Chase and Dos Passos. Here were the works of H. G. Wells, a copy of John Morley's *Oliver Cromwell*, Trevelyan's *English Social History*, the collected works of Hazlitt, and two writers who meant a great deal to Bevan, José Rodó, a South American philosopher and Junius, the eighteenth-century political vivisector. The poets were mostly traditional, like Shelley, Burns, Keats, Byron. Several hundred books ranged along one wall in no particular order; they had been pulled down, read and pushed back again at random.

Sometimes, sitting curled up on the settee beside her husband, Jennie Lee would explain, 'I am a Socialist—but in my home life I'm a real Scottish Conservative. I believe that however big a public figure one may be, your private life should be your own secret—that is the main reason why my husband and I never speak on the same platform if we can help it—it looks too much like a circus. . . .' She called him Nye and he had been known to address her as Boy—a term used indiscriminately for certain M.P.s as well. They both liked ballet. They were attached to a Siamese

5

cat called Smoky liable to streak through the sitting-room at any
moment. They both regarded the stone-flagged garden with some
relief since gardening wasn't a very strong point, and it was
possible to find Bevan singing there with the full force of a considerable pair of lungs. It is also on newspaper record that Bevan
once gave a performance of O *Sole Mio* to a group of astounded
Italians on a Venetian canal, but his "career" as a singer would
have benefited if his voice had revealed as much quality as his
words. Where Morrison could sing verses from Omar Khayyám
in a rich baritone and Harold Laski rendered "Poor Old Joe" with
an intellectual quaver, Bevan practically talked an ancient ballad
he sometimes chose to sing.

He did not live the life of the ordinary family man at Cliveden
Place—does any politician? There were no children from his
marriage. An ineradicable streak of intellectual bohemianism
which showed itself back in the days when he shared a flat with
Frank Owen, then M.P. for Hereford, had brought him to live
on the borders of Chelsea, where his power to hold a circle of
friends by brilliant talk and his displays of dialectic continued to
delight the people now his friends or disciples, and some even of
his enemies. But only those with strong Left-wing propensities
could stomach the epigrammatic phrases which he appeared to
coin with supreme ease. . . . 'My dear,' he would say, 'commercial
insurance companies have done nothing but "hawk" on social
continuity. . . .' Or 'The Conservatives are searching for an
agreeable reason to explain the rule of the rich. They have
no lamps at their feet. . . .' Or 'The language of priorities is the
religion of Socialism.'

He could talk the night away once launched on a glowing sea
of language. He had no great regard for conventional habits.

'The most remarkable thing about Nye,' Fenner Brockway
M.P., wrote to me,

> is his ability not only to pierce the issue to its depths but the
> knowledge which he has to surround this insight. It is amazing to sit
> opposite him at a fireplace or at a luncheon party or in a political
> discussion, and to find how deep and dynamic and knowledgeable
> his thought is. For example, I was at a luncheon party with Socialists
> from France. He analysed their situation with a thoroughness which
> shook them. They had never thought out their own problems
> as he was able to indicate to them. Now French Socialism and
> French problems are not a priority in Nye's thinking—I suppose

6

they are more so in mine—but he was able to tell the French Socialists much that they had not realized.

There is a more remarkable instance of this in spheres which
one would regard as outside the ordinary ken of a Socialist politician.
Leslie Hale had for dinner, along with Nye, a leading Catholic who
may easily become a Cardinal. After the meal they discussed philosophy and theology and Hale said that it was absolutely fascinating.
Nye showed that his knowledge of theology and philosophy
could stand up to the arguments of this great Catholic
theologian. . . .

Confronted with that rare combination of knowledge special-
ized beyond his own, in one field, and a powerful personality, the
sheer wizardry with which he could bewitch so many people, was
sometimes challenged and, on rare occasions, confounded, but the
breadth of his knowledge in so many fields and the supreme
ingenuity and eloquence of his exposition, was the remarkable
thing.

★   ★   ★

At fifty-three his hair had silvered, the lines running to his jowl
deepened. Caught in a brooding moment there was a massive
melancholy about the head and the thrust of the jaw, but the
seer in the eyes peered at the mists encompassing the future as if
he might yet discern a worth-while world—Bevan's world. His
interests in philosophy had not perceptibly lessened. His struggles
with a "big book," a statement of his own credo were in full
swing, and about to astonish the world afresh. The realization of
intellectual superiority in some men led to humility and a deep
sense of duty towards less gifted people and the community at
large. Bevan had long set out to serve what he considered to be
the community, but humility sometimes wore on the public
platform, at fifty-three, the likeness of arrogance.

Two other characteristics in his own personality bore an odd
resemblance to those he was said to hate in others. He looked,
dressed and spoke as one of the middle classes, and his delight in
exploring ideas could hardly evade the label "intellectual." There
remained genuine *emotional*, temperamental and verbal links with
working-class people, and the power of memory when he spoke
of South Wales in the 1890s and the grey hell enforced upon
some of his fellows, continued to put bitterness and extravagance
into his words. But these were not consistently with him. The
book about to explode on a largely unsuspecting world had little

7

of bitterness in it. Yet other men like Jim Griffiths and Herbert Morrison had suffered in their youth without releasing recurring bursts of hate which scalded Bevan as much as anyone if only he had noticed. His bitterness had to be understood as something not settled and fanatical. He had abrupt alternations of mood like many Celts, but cold, possessed fanaticism did not belong to him. A note of gaiety, a gust of laughter, sheer full-blooded zest for living were more than capable of breaking in. It all depended where you met him and in what company.

The trade unions still regarded him with suspicion. Himself a trade unionist he had yet alienated half their members—'they are no longer agitators; they are courtiers,' he once said of their leaders. Sturdy common sense told them that his 'adolescent craving to swagger it as a lone wolf' (Francis Williams, *Public Opinion*, 1951) should not persist when national issues were at stake. They also suspected that a man who sometimes appeared to regard people differing from himself as either fools or rogues, might have in him a streak of egocentricity, antipathetic to the spirit of the trade union movement. Nor could they quite stomach hints which still haunted him from the past, of the Bloomsbury intellectual throwing off aphorisms over the broken coffee cups in a Left-wing, rent-controlled attic. There was, it could be argued, a certain rootlessness in Aneurin Bevan at fifty-three. He did not belong to Clement Attlee's group, he had sprung from similar origins, but violently opposed Bevin's, he was not part of the British trade union tradition in the sense that Jim Griffiths or George Isaacs was, and those three principles enforced by hard-headed experience—solidarity in times of crisis, political passions kept within reasonable bounds, negotiation and compromise, characteristics very strong in the Labour Movement—did not come easily to him. He seemed to prefer the stress and storm, and in the process vigorously asserted his working-class roots.

For him no small part of the stress inside the Labour Party emerged from his belief that Socialists must follow a completely Socialist policy and not compromise with Liberals, Conservatives or for that matter Communists. He saw some of the old world Socialists as modern Liberals. He fiercely believed in the rightness of his own interpretation of the Socialist Word. Indeed there were moments when he spoke as though its Revelation had been granted to him alone. That hopelessly simplifies what appears in all its complexities in later chapters of this book. At higher conclaves of the Party Executive, Mr. Clement Attlee was liable to say, 'Although we all know that Mr. Bevan is an excellent debater, we are interested at the moment in facts; perhaps it would not be too much for him to let us have a few.' It was characteristic of Bevan that he would then deliver himself of an intimidating array of facts, as fully versed in the groundwork as anyone else. He had no lack of facts.

Clement Attlee took a gamble when he appointed him Minister of Health. Whether it came off or not—and many believed it did —Attlee remarked that Bevan would have been a different man if he had fought a few hard constituencies instead of basking in the eternal security of Ebbw Vale. As Minister of Health, Francis Williams wrote of him: 'He finds it, I think, both personally pleasant and politically useful to persuade his friends, and perhaps even himself, that he still has a hand grenade behind the door, but what he really has there in these days is an electric refrigerator and a new type of mass-produced bath.'

After conference at No. 10 Downing Street he could stride about the room, laughing and talking with Falstaffian jollity. There was a biological robustness in some of his wit, and he could drop his eloquence for blunt, short Anglo-Saxon comment. In the National Executive of the Labour Party the intoxication of words exposed him to the greater tactical skills of Herbert Morrison, although for many years Morrison's policies were much more palatable to the Executive, the Policy Committee and the Parliamentary Labour Party. There were moments when he seemed distinctly impatient because the Parliamentary Party appeared incapable of absorbing the authorized version of his own thought. It was possible for him to lose his temper, although the ability to throw his whole self into whatever he was saying sometimes led outside observers to confuse passion with temper. 'The trouble is,' he would say, 'people cannot distinguish between a vigorous exposition and a provocative utterance.' There were times when he fulminated against a line of policy so ferociously as to convince everyone he would resign if they did not see the light, and then, some time later, accepted that course of action. But the boisterous Bevan who revelled in the sheer cut and thrust of dialectic, sometimes drove out his many other selves. It was the Bevan who, on the rare occasions when he visited the Press Club, gave someone a hiding at snooker, and departed in great good humour. He could be cheerful, happy-go-lucky, full of wisecracks. He treated his chauffeurs with great respect.

There were two sides to his character in the House. The *Manchester Guardian* wrote of him in 1950:—

Those who picture Mr. Bevan only as a monster of vituperation should watch him at work as a Minister in charge of a bill during committee stage and should come upon him at midnight or in the early hours of the morning—for ordinary mortals just the moment for impatience and frayed temper. At such times Mr. Bevan is a man transfigured. He is conciliatory without being weak, firm without being intransigent, and patient beyond belief.

Moreover, it is refreshing in the arid patches of night debates to listen to Mr. Bevan's voice, neither passionate nor forced. Indeed, there were moments this morning during the committee stage of the Medical Bill when Mr. Bevan showed all the refinement and gentleness of Sir Frank Soskice during an all-night sitting on the Finance Bill.

In another guise his magnetic personality always held members as he swung into his stride, eyes flashing, finger pointing, a man uncompromisingly alive with the fascination of the spell-binder. This rugged, piratical Bevan continued to shock the House of Commons and the country with his attacks, continued to challenge his own party's policy, flourishing in opposition. He had not so much mastered as brought to life within his personality every skill known to oratory. He knew every gradation of pause and just how long it could be sustained, his gestures were infinite, his sudden use of an exotic word—"those draconic decisions"— exciting, and he enjoyed a big word along with the scholars. His immense range of inflexion rose and fell like a coloured fountain. His stutter added the exhilaration of danger, the hope that perhaps this time he might at last break down. Even the Tories dropped the banter and laughter which preceded a speech in the House with the idea of disconcerting the speaker, to watch the spectacle of Bevan soaring higher and higher with verbal felicities, building up what appeared to be a eulogy of Churchill.

'I freely admit that the Right Hon. Gentleman is the most articulate Englishman that has ever lived. He has a gift of language, both in speech and in writing, and many of his spoken and written contributions are adornments of the English language. If there is anyone who has the gift of making himself clear, it is the Right Hon. Gentleman. It is a gift not shared by the Foreign

Secretary, who is able to shelter a very opaque foreign policy behind ambiguity of language. The Right Hon. Gentleman is above all men, clear. . . .'

They knew their Bevan of old. Something quite different lay in wait, and at last it came. 'How did it come about that (on Korea) he was so much misunderstood?' He established an empathy between an audience and himself. His pauses, his evocative language enabled them to participate. There was an ebb and flow. Fenner Brockway wrote: 'He has absolute dominion when he is at his best. Sometimes he is not at his best, but when he is, there is no one who can so completely silence his opponents and grip everyone.' Behind it all, he was the epitome of the calm, unshakable committee man, and at press conferences could remain imperturbable under great provocation, with many answers brilliantly at his disposal.

★   ★   ★

The American press characteristically spoke of him as "dirtmouth Bevan." Whether deliberately or not he had made himself the most controversial political figure of the day and no man could claim quite such a vicious brand of unpopularity among the middle classes. He had been at some pains during the war to reinforce certain of his enemies when they showed signs of liking him, and if some newspapers accused him of a sustained desire to avoid the mellowness which overtook distinguished politicians at the still youthful age of fifty-three, it was another of those dangerous half-truths which surrounded and obscured his personality. It would be a mistake to imagine him immune to the attacks launched upon him. 'It is sometimes believed by the thoughtless,' he said, 'that the political victims of press campaigns are cynically immune from emotional reactions. This is not true, as I know from my own experience. Indeed, complete indifference would argue an aloofness from criticism which would unfit one for public service.'

Francis Williams wrote in 1951, 'He is persuaded, and so are many of his friends, and some of his enemies, that it will not be many years before the limelight plays upon the Right Hon. Aneurin Bevan, Leader of the Labour Party, Prime Minister and First Lord of the Treasury. . . . To be Prime Minister is an ambition common to many politicians. Yet the mantle of Premiership does not always fall on those who have planned for it most—there is the career of Mr. Attlee, if of no other, to rouse a mild surmise in the mind of Mr. Bevan on those occasional moments when he finds it possible to see beyond the light thrown by his own star. . . .'

The light of his own star did not stop him, when he chose, from exercising a personal charm which wrung admiration from men who regarded him as poison incarnate. His vitality sustained him through sessions which broke the spirit of much younger men, and his gusty humour, half the result of an utter, perhaps conceited, confidence in his own powers, could be infectious. Intellectual arrogance was liable to break through, but he sometimes spoke of himself as just another emergent member of the working classes, part of the expression of deep historical forces. He resisted the idea of fierce personal ambition. 'If I do not stand I am accused of evading responsibility. If I do stand I am accused of being ambitious. I cannot do right.' But his attempts at self-effacement did not include the political martyrdom which attended anyone who finally refused to compromise with the Party line.

Many of his motives were probably mixed. Who knows what unconscious depths qualify the most completely rational of our actions? It might as much concern him to hold Socialism to its true heritage, to save Britain from disasters clear in his own vision, as to lead his own Party. Yet he was no innocent in manœuvre. And if he would hotly deny that he had any deliberate intention of leading any party whatever, the characteristic was ingrown in many politicians and did not necessarily debase. Teleological concentration upon the high places often led to corruption of thought and action; genuine awareness of underlying forces could as well carry a rebel to leadership with his integrity intact.

Whatever else was said there was no doubt that many in the British Labour Movement valued the presence of Aneurin Bevan in their midst. Some might regard him as a political pirate constantly disrupting the Party for his own ends. Others saw him as a great Socialist, and a brilliant orator. The intellectually blind respected him as a man who had taught himself to see and if his parricidal passion for attacking authority did not accord with the long tradition of Labour Party loyalty, John Strachey wrote in 1952: 'Aneurin Bevan carries with him the splendid cargo of his genius—a treasure indeed for the Movement which it is his life's work to serve. It is unthinkable that he should defy the party, when he can so readily and so profoundly influence it.'

In the outer world everything fell into contradiction. Some saw him as part of the tradition of Robespierre and Danton. Metaphorically heads would fall if he ever reached the ultimate places of power. The middle classes must become a subject breed, the upper classes fall into desuetude, the working classes sit uneasily as gods and the whole structure of British economy concentrate on putting power and privilege into the hands of "the people." At best it seemed we were in for the benevolent dictatorship of a British Tito. So the story ran.

At the other extreme, for many ordinary men and women he was the symbol of the potential in every child born to the harsh life of the mining valleys. He epitomized the emergence of the working class into the ranks of the ruling class. Some who knew him in the beginning said bitter things against him in his maturity, but they still admitted and admired the courage, resource and ability which had not only carried him into His Majesty's Cabinet, but made him one of its most turbulent and powerful members. Others saw him as the biggest brain in the Labour Party, the most inspiring personality the Left had produced, better equipped to deal ruthlessly with the troubles pressing on unhappy society than more moderate members of the Party— although the word ruthlessly bothered people not of their persuasion. For his disciples he was one of Nietzsche's sublime ones. He was born to lead mass movements, to issue aphoristic dogmatisms, to make evident his influence in his day and age, to bring about almost single-handed the Good Society.

Between these, many met him as an ordinary human being, a man who drank whisky or beer, talked common talk, sounded a good fellow, enjoyed billiards, and had a deep humanist interest in the fate of his fellows. They said he was at root a lonely man. Egocentricity, doubtful loyalties to the Party line, did not make him—from the official point of view—a very satisfactory member of a group, unless he led it, but the lonely are sometimes considerable people and Bevan's friends and enemies alike tended to agree that he was in several senses of the word a big personality.

*   *   *

Aneurin Bevan had come a long way. The cottages of Charles Street under the shadow of the pit heaps in Tredegar were half

13

a world away. But the days when they black-listed him in the mines, when he had no work for years and unemployment encouraged the seeds of bitterness which were to erupt so violently in later years, remained immutably part of his person. The days when mass unemployment threatened starvation, when he became an industrial dead-end kid, an agitator and strike-leader, when his father died of pneumoconiosis, when they arrested him one night as his sister lay dying; the days when massed ranks of unemployed marched over the Welsh hills singing *Cwm Rhondda*, when he first felt the lift of his own eloquence carrying him out on a tide of words, when the Right-wing press described him as 'an extremist . . . brilliant, bitter, proud, class-conscious, boastful of his ancestry and his family—a man anxious to tear down the pillars of society'; all this was inextricably built into his personality.

It belonged to the past now. So did some sides of Aneurin Bevan's personality. He was not quite such a revolutionary figure as he had been in his youth and the homely clothes he always wore at Buckingham Palace or Elvino's in Fleet Street had made concessions to smartness, the navy blue, pin-striped suit some-times revealing impeccably white shirt cuffs. Aneurin Bevan had come a long way but the dæmon in him was by no means dead.

'It is not easy to change basic habits at fifty-three' (the *Observer* wrote in 1951) 'but there is little doubt that Aneurin Bevan will be able to command and give loyalty—his blind spot—on the scale required of a statesman, only if he can escape from the egocentricity that his life story has induced. He will need to lose his feeling of being unloved . . . if he is to fit the modern scene. He has courage, resilience, and a touch of gaiety. And he has learned much in the years. Perhaps he can yet right himself and become properly adult.'

Properly adult? There were many ways of becoming properly adult. The *Observer's* idea of maturity would probably coincide with his idea of immaturity.

There were so many contradictions, some easily explained by his beginnings, some the result of roots which went right back to a father and mother who had reared a lusty brood of children in a very different Britain. It was not entirely fortuitous that the span of his life almost exactly covered what many considered a social revolution in the history of Britain. The year 1897 was more than half a century back and most people had forgotten what was happening in that decade.

*   *   *

It was a Britain where the telephone still seemed like sorcery, there was never a car on the streets and the tiny figure of Queen Victoria had acquired a saintliness from years of veneration. It was a Britain where tobacco was fourpence an ounce and whisky three shillings a bottle. The strange devices of nineteenth-century economics still envisaged some natural law at work behind the alternation of slump and boom, and as if to confirm what was tantamount to witchcraft, a long spell in the sun followed on the heels of a Great Depression. So far there were no signs of the shadow returning and solid British business men spread themselves spaciously, certain of their right to invest their money where they pleased and supremely unaware of any threat to their security.

It was a Britain of fine houses and grey slums, of broughams driving through gas-lit streets and some people walking four miles to work, of leisured men and women determined to preserve intact their ignorance of the social underworld, and working people who only dimly apprehended that God had not irrevocably cast them for their lot.

News of the Boer War ran across page after page of *The Times*, for the Boers were proving fighters dour beyond all expectation. A dispatch from *The Times* correspondent in the besieged town of Ladysmith read . . . 'The garrison are beginning to feel the pinch of siege life, suspense, sickness, shellfire and smaller rations. . . .'

London was distracted by diabolo, the occult had a growing place in the interests of fashionable ladies, there were long weekends in the country, hunt balls and banquets, and the incomparable Max Beerbohm in biscuit-coloured suit, dove-grey spats and cravat, was busy founding the cult of Max Beerbohm. . . . 'London is a bright, cheerful hell, but still, to my mind, hell. . . .' A letter to *The Times* said: 'Cannot the Treasury make a grant for the Flower Lovers' Society. . . .?' But the gentlemen of the Treasury continued to make calculations from a sub-human arithmetic which believed above all that the simple process of subtraction from national expenditure equalled prosperity.

Aubrey Beardsley had lately been dismissed from the Yellow Book at the time of Oscar Wilde's trial, young Mr. Wells was introducing science into romantic fiction, and Englishmen still curiously convinced that they were the Lord's anointed, that right would prevail even though their old Gods—Dickens, Gladstone and Darwin—were no longer in the ascendant. The staid mid-Victorian period had given place to the more restless late Victorian, the upper classes were living rather deliberately *fin de siècle*, the lower classes showing alarming signs of truculence. Dominating the scene stood the two so different figures—the dapper, frock-coated Joseph Chamberlain with an orchid more or less permanently in his buttonhole, and Queen Victoria celebrating her Diamond Jubilee with just the right touch of divinity.

The years 1890 to 1900 were years of Empire. The one-time Brummagem hardware merchant Joseph Chamberlain, stood shoulder to shoulder with Kipling. For all his gifts as demagogue and politician, Chamberlain was still at heart very much a business man and he set out now to make the Empire pay. He appointed a Royal Commission to enquire into the parlous state of the West Indies, he transferred Nigeria from the Royal Niger Company into the power of the Crown, he "reconquered" the Transvaal, federated the Australian colonies and laid about him energetically in many parts of the world.

The Parliamentary Committee appointed to probe the unpleasant business of the Jameson Raid heavily censured the conduct of Cecil Rhodes and his accomplices, and acquitted Joseph Chamberlain of all knowledge of the plot, without asking for any letters or documents which could have proved or disproved the case.

There was a large gathering of Empire potentates in the same year. Eleven Prime Ministers of self-governing colonies talked about a great Empire Federation, and Queen Victoria, with only a few more years ahead of her, drove to St. Paul's in an open coach down streets lined with Empire troops. The crowds received her rapturously. Wilfred Scawen Blunt recorded in his private diary '. . . she was in her old age a dignified but rather commonplace good soul, like how many of our dowagers, narrow-minded in her view of things, without taste in art or literature, fond of money, having a certain industry and business capacity in politics, and easily flattered and expecting to be flattered, quite convinced of her own providential position in the world and always ready to do anything to extend and augment it. . . .'

Blatchford's *Merrie England* had just sold a million copies. It revealed a smell of drains somewhere beneath the social scene. There was far too much squalor, poverty, hardship under the smooth surface. His message was still ringing through the country: 'I have kept as close to the earth as I could. I am only now talking street talk about the common sights of the common town. . . . I say that you, in common with all men, are responsible for the things that are. I say that it is your duty to seek the remedy; and I say that if you seek it you will find it. . . .'

The I.L.P., founded in 1893, was followed by the Labour Representation Committee in 1900. At a quite different level, the Fabian Society was trying to convert into a conscious principle forces which were then proceeding by blind instinct. They had no time for the Utopia of William Morris and in the person of H. G. Wells dismissed the social earthquake visualized by Marx for reasons which Wells made brilliantly paradoxical. Yet historical forces once clouded and uncertain were now gathering pace, and men and women in the trade unions, local government, co-operative societies and House of Commons, were part and parcel of that movement, if they themselves were largely unaware.

The Fabians set out to make them aware. Shaw startled the country with his verbal lightnings and threw off the lectures, *That the Working Class is Evil, Unnecessary and Should be Abolished* and *To Your Tents, O Israel!* He went further. He demanded an independent trade unionist party, a party fund of £30,000 and fifty Labour candidates at the next election.

The trade unions, still in their infancy, were not very bothered if the secretary of one union was Liberal and the secretary of another Conservative. It gave them strong levers in both camps. The idea of a Party of their own was something dramatically new, although the birth of the I.L.P. in 1893 had opened the door.

While a handful of men of invulnerable rectitude strove to find some better equilibrium between worker and employer, a considerable culture flowered beside industrial squalor. The "profit motive" was now enthroned to the exclusion of less ignoble ones, but other and equally profound influences were at work to set the aged frame of England moving towards a different way of life.

Into this scene, unobtrusively and with never a flicker of interest from the outside world, Aneurin Bevan was born.

2

LOOKING across the Welsh border towards the Black Mountains any summer night, one moment the crest was black and unbroken against the sky and the next a brilliant glow flared at its centre. It looked as though the mountain had suddenly erupted, but the phenomenon was very much man-made. It came when they opened the blast furnaces in Ebbw Vale and poured out the molten iron. It was a signal for half the countryside. It meant good going in the steel trade and that was a centre of prosperity which sent its ripples over many parts of South Wales from the towns to the remotest villages. There were times when the glow did not come, times when trade was bad and men and women knew, because the blackness remained unbroken, that trouble lay ahead.

Down behind Ebbw Vale, the miners of Tredegar knew about the signal in the sky. For their children it was fascinating and quite unreal: a great incandescence thrown out by the angry gods. Tredegar stood in one of innumerable valleys where the slag heaps overwhelmed trees and grass and flowers, pushing down towards the cottages obliterating everything in their path. Children played on the grey tips, laughing, shouting as cage after cage screeched along the cables from the pits, bumped to a stop at the tipping pier, and poured more dead slack on to the "backs." Another call on the hooter and another set of cages wobbled along. All day it went on, the green hills slowly replaced by the grey heaps. Some rivers ran black, smooth, spiritless. Fresh green shoots pricked through the heaps like hair struggling with obscene baldness. Rain came very often from the hills. But the colours it left were brilliant when the sun broke through again.

Tredegar was all sharp inclines and steep streets. A sprawl of cottages ran out from a squat clock tower picked out in brilliant vermilion and garish enough to have come from a Sultan's palace. It was a big landmark in Tredegar and became a big landmark in Aneurin Bevan's life. Beyond the tower and the cottages ran the great dead pit heaps, dump after dump, grisly evidence of a system of grabbing the quickest reward from the earth with little thought for the future.

Charles Street, when I visited it, was a row of aged cottages with cobbled fronts, threatened by encroaching pit heaps. Some of Bevan's family remember a very different street from their childhood. Beyond their house were green fields and Charles Street, less than half a mile long, ended at its northern end, virtually in the country. The river, where they lived, was clear and rippling, not the black snake which it became lower down the valley. . . . 'Charles Street cottages were not blackened— they were whitewashed, or pink-washed every spring. . . .'

At No. 32, Aneurin Bevan was born in 1897. One stepped through the front door straight into the main room, with a stone floor and big open range. Three other rooms were largely taken up by beds, two bedrooms upstairs, one with three beds in it, and another downstairs, all marked out by scrupulously scrubbed floors of white wood, decorated by rugs. In these four rooms the children were brought up and thrived. There is some doubt about their exact number. The late Mrs. Bevan herself told me that there were at least ten, of whom seven survived.

A lusty infant, with beautiful, wondering eyes, a source of considerable pleasure to his mother, Aneurin Bevan showed no signs in the first few years of that bright advancing edge of intelligence which was to mark him out later in life. Certainly he had a habit of watching with wonderment the pit heaps as the mechanical life within swelled their growth: certainly he picked up words with great facility and had from the start that true gift of the gods, an enormous vitality; little else was visible in the first few years.

A vivid hotch-potch of work and talk and argument, the family background was a healthy affair moving within simple limits, but with more than a dash of intellectual intensity. Family names Myfanwy, Arianwen, Iorwerth, Aneurin . . . came out of the mists of Celtic consciousness, and David Bevan, his father, seems to have dipped into the Mabinogion for fresh inspiration on the slightest provocation. Aneurin Bevan owes his name to the seventh-century North British poet well known in Welsh culture.

Phoebe, the mother, saw to it that her large brood of children was brought up as chapel-goers, and in the beginning Aneurin conformed. Sceptical gentlemen of Right-wing persuasion may find something significant in the fact that 'My Methodist parents used to say: "Have the courage, my son, to say no!"'[1]

One needed religion in the Welsh mining valleys of those days. The work-a-day world was a sweat-soaked business. Inevitably Mr. Bevan was a miner. On the day shift in winter months, he was lucky to see the daylight at all. He took his sandwiches and 'jack' out with him into the early morning darkness, caught the monstrous clanking train which took him down to the pit, and by the time he came to the surface again twilight was settling once more. In the stone-flagged kitchen before a coal fire he bathed sometimes to the delight of the children.

Mr. Bevan was a man to reckon with. A victim of pneumoconiosis—the terrible dust disease which hardens the lungs as though with cement until a man can no longer breathe—he contrived to do a heavy day's work in the mines, belong to Cymmrodorion (the Welsh cultural organization), read books and take a deep interest in the miners' lodge. Politically he began as a Liberal and became a Socialist. Later in life he was to leave the mines because of bad health and become an insurance agent, but now in Aneurin's boyhood he was highly respected by his mates as a "bit of a scholar" and for all the melancholy which overtook him whenever he thought of the way things might have been, he remained industrious, reliable, a man destined to win prizes at the local inter-chapel eisteddfodau. Aneurin Bevan was to win far more glittering prizes. For the moment nobody knew.

As yet, too, the outside world remained dim and unreal for him, a place where ogres lurked but with none of the old fairy-tale shapes. They were modern industrial ogres now. When children came to play in the streets, the rhythmic thum-thump of the pit ventilating fan was apt to be transformed into a monster with a vastly beating heart lurking somewhere up in the hills. There were other unseen presences. The Welsh have their own strange pool of mysticism. Aneurin Bevan did not escape it. Once he stood with a gang of children peering up a dark alley and one of them said, 'You wouldn't go up there, would you?'

'Wouldn't I?' said Bevan, trembling. 'Wouldn't I?'

He clenched his fists, stamped far up into the alley, and then walked back again. 'There,' he said, as he came into the light again. 'There's nothing there. . . .' Only the lamplight showed his face pale and taut.

[1] *Fabian Autumn Lecture*, 1950.

His mother Mrs. Bevan told me the story of these early days as she remembered it. At eighty-six she was still vigorous, alert with a considerable flow of talk and something almost regal in her presence. She remembered the winter mornings when by the light of an oil lamp, she stirred the fire, banked up the night before, cut the sandwiches for her husband, gave half her attention to the lusty brood of children and the other to washing, mending and cleaning, trying in the early days to make do on less than £2 a week, and helped considerably by the fact that the rent was only 3s. They had taught Mrs. Bevan to read and write at school but gradually she lost the faculty. When I knew her she said she didn't read or write at all. 'As the children came there was far too much to do. . . . I lost the knack.' Nor was bearing a family of ten children and rearing seven of them enough for this enormously vital woman who, in the early days, rose before dawn, had her household in order by 9 o'clock and began teaching four young apprentices dressmaking. Yet for all the work she did, strikes, silicosis and illness often ate into the family income until one day she burst out. 'If only I could have 30s. a week for certain, I could save out of it.'

Thirty shillings. . . . Sometimes less became a dream when it could buy desperately needed things. It became a dream in the great strike of 1898. Aneurin Bevan was less than a year old when the strike began and if its backwash did not directly affect him, it revealed characteristics in the mine-owners of Tredegar which the miners were never to forget. Long before any settlement was in sight many mining families were desperate, money gave out, food was exhausted, savings used up. Charity played its dubious part. Collections were made and a few families tided over the immediate crisis. Inevitably tomorrow brought another, until at last scores of men were driven to appeal again and again to the local authorities for what was known euphemistically as relief.

Richard Llewellyn knew what these strikes meant. 'My mother was dipping into our box to help women down the Hill who had big families still growing. Poor Mrs. Morris by the Chapel who had fourteen, and not one older than twelve, had to go about begging food, and her husband was so ashamed he threw himself over the pit mouth. . . .'[1]

A. J. Cronin knew too with his picture of pregnant women

[1] *How Green Was My Valley* (Michael Joseph, 1939).

21

drinking hot water for tea, scavenging for food, overcome with near savagery at the smell of new-baked bread.

But sometimes the end of a strike brought an extraordinary atmosphere. . . .

I looked at the smooth blue sky and the glowing white roofs, the black road, choked with blacker figures of waving men passing down the Hill between groups of women with children clustered about their skirts, all of them flushed by flickering orange lamp-light flooding out from open doorways and heard the rich voices rising in many harmonies, borne upward upon the mists which flew from singing mouths, veiling cold-pinched faces, magnifying the brilliance of hoping eyes, and my heart went tight inside me. . . .

And round about us the Valley echoed with the hymn, and lights came out in the farms up on the dark mountain, and down at the pit, the men were waving their lamps, hundreds of tiny sparks keeping time to the beat of the music.

Everybody was singing.

Peace, there was again, see.[1]

When peace came to Tredegar after the great strike of 1898 something remained simmering under the surface. It remained simmering at No. 32 Charles Street and in due course began to take effect on the subtle, receptive mind of Aneurin Bevan. . . .

* * *

By the time Aneurin went to school, William, his elder brother, had already entered the pits and he, too, now set off at dawn, and returned in the twilight a different man. Shut away in the small world of the cottage it was an inevitable part of the cycle of events. The mines were immutably the biggest thing in a man's life.

Then came a sudden rush of new experience—school, an unpleasant schoolmaster, books and a stutter—each following fast on the heels of the other, a world of startling new sensations. Yet as fast as books or a sudden glimpse beyond the world of Tredegar stirred his imagination, something seems to have thrown a blanket over it again; as fast as lessons promised to send him leaping over the horizons and away, the trace of a stutter made it difficult to ask the questions continuously re-forming in his mind. All the signs and portents pointed the right way, but often a clumsy schoolmaster or the stutter intervened. They were unhappy, introspective days.

[1] *How Green Was My Valley.*

If psychology means anything—and it obviously means a great deal—his schoolmaster's behaviour must have left a scar on Bevan's personality. For Mr. Orchard was remembered by Bevan's sister as red-faced and fat, with hard eyes, a man who stood at the school gate terrifying passing children and much given to using the cane.

There were at least three explanations why Aneurin Bevan developed a bad stutter, and still stutters today in moments of stress. One version says he disliked school, hated the cold stone building and its smooth asphalt playground, disliked entering the wooden door in the high wall, knowing he was cut off from any retreat, delivered into the hands of his master. In the end it dammed up half his personality so that books tended to lose their excitement, and from being struck dumb by Orchard inside school, he began to stutter outside—or so the story goes.

The second explanation—that he was born that way—his mother denied. Nor did she accept the shifted sinistral theory, which said that he was born left-handed, forced himself to use his right, and the process threw his whole nervous system into a disorder which finally found expression in the stutter. The schoolmaster, too, as the origin of the stutter, she swept aside. Mrs. Bevan had her own theory and it involved Uncle John.

Two bachelor uncles she said, went to live with the family at No. 32 Charles Street, one, Uncle George, a regular wage earner and a tower of financial strength. It had seemed difficult enough for the family to contain itself in the minute cottage before, and the addition of first one uncle and then another, with a third sometimes dropping in, led to further complications. The third uncle, John, a striking looking person, stuttered badly himself it seems, and such rich game for mimicking was not to be resisted. Whether it was Aneurin Bevan or his elder brother Will who did the mimicking whenever they visited him, remains obscure. Whichever way it went it was said to have produced a stutter in Bevan which gradually became more real than theatrical. For something deep-rooted in the mysteries of personality, it seems a superficial explanation, but his mother remained vehemently convinced that she was right.

She was equally emphatic that the Bevan family had not been "dragged up." Even "real poverty" she seemed to doubt. For if Mrs. Bevan had to contrive to feed, mend and wash for a giant brood in a matchbox home, if double, three-quarter and single

23

beds seemed to clutter up three of the four rooms, and there were sudden concentrations of people wanting to do quite different things at one and the same time, most of them fantastically energetic; when they pooled their finances the matter of simply paying for things became easier, and Mrs. Bevan had a genius for housekeeping.

In 1906, she said, when Aneurin Bevan was eight or nine, the whole Bevan family moved down the road to No. 7 and that was a step up the social scale. No. 7 had one modern fitment which set the Bevans socially on a level with the colliery manager and probably above him. They were the only people with a gas stove in the neighbourhood, and the colliery manager's wife—who lived opposite—was prepared to pocket her pride and come to cook her tarts on the stove. Nor was it just a matter of renting the house. This time they bought it, outright, for something like £130. It may have been that the family purse was much better lined as the family grew up and the uncles added their contribution, it is possible that Mrs. Bevan's memory had clouded or even, like most people, that she tended to romanticize early days in retrospect. But that was her story.

From No. 7, Aneurin Bevan continued to set out every morning for Sirhowy Elementary School, a round-faced eager boy, with large wondering eyes, black hair with a wave at the temples and little trace of the rebellious arrogance which life in the mines was so quickly to stamp on his face. His sister remembers him as a gentle child. But as his schooldays advanced and the stutter entangled every attempt at self-expression, while some of his schoolmates laughed cruelly at his crippled words, big things were happening under the surface, things which Mrs. Bevan said she sensed and which convinced her that Aneurin was different. Outwardly he plodded along at school, spent some of his spare time as a butcher's boy—1s. 6d. for three days' work—and read a long chain of *Gems* and *Magnets* avidly. He gave a giant concentration to these penny populars. Sometimes riding the butcher's bike he still contrived to read, and even when his nose bled—which it sometimes did—he seemed largely unaware of it.

His memory quickly revealed itself as remarkable and there were stories that he could repeat every sentence of the Sunday sermon as though it were his own. Soon his interests widened. They were interests picked up from many sources. Some from casual words dropped by his father, mother and brother, some from miners' talk, from schoolmaster and preacher. The Reading Room and Library paid for by workers' halfpennies was still something of a novelty. The Post Office had recently been moved and the inhabitants of Tredegar become the owners of a Recreation Ground. The workers were developing unified action at many levels, not least the cultural. For the moment there was still talk of the Old Queen very fine in her carriage, although she had died a few years before, of men striking across in the steel works ... Lloyd George and Liberalism. ... the stupidity of Londoners unaware of life in the pits. ... the Boer War, Syndicalism and what price freedom now. ...

The men of Tredegar remembered the poverty and squalor of the third quarter of the nineteenth century in certain South Wales mining valleys. Some spoke of the English gentlemen who took several millions sterling out of Merthyr Tydfil while colliers' wives walked a mile to get their water from a spring and sanitation hardly existed. Some spoke of the infant University of Wales struggling to find its feet without a word of encouragement from the coal-owners. They said few employers troubled about running water or proper housing, they remembered that the industrial strangle-hold had been crippling. In some mining towns 'The Company' had once owned the houses, the shops, the jobs, the whole machinery of life, and it was dangerous to speak your mind too freely outside the one corner of the community in which the miners could stake a personal claim, the Workmen's Institute or Chapel.

It all left echoes in the highly receptive mind of Aneurin Bevan. His stutter might drive him into quiet corners to read or listen while other people talked, but he missed nothing. Once his father took him down the main street and showed him three portly and complacent looking gentlemen standing at shop doors. Nodding at one he said, 'Very important man. That's Councillor Jackson. ... Very important man in this town.'

'What's the Council?' Aneurin asked, staring.

'Oh, that's the place that governs the affairs of this town. Very important place indeed.'

Some years later Aneurin Bevan was to say to himself. 'The place to get to is the Council.' Thirty-five years later he developed the theme in one of his most brilliant speeches in the House of Commons. For the moment, piece by piece, a crude picture of the outside world fell into place in his mind, helped by his own quick perceptions and his as yet rare bouts of reading. But it was particularly family talk which threw fresh light on the pits of Tredegar, the strange dislocation of life when father was suddenly at home for weeks, and men stood together in groups, or squatted on their haunches at street corners, talking.

At the age of thirteen Aneurin Bevan suddenly became more familiar with the ways of the Tredegar Iron and Coal Company. He left school and went to join his father and brother in the Ty Trist pit. There were the ceremonials of the boy becoming the man, of wearing white moleskin trousers—bought at no small cost by the family the night before his first day in the pits, and parading round very fine and proud and grown-up, but it did not last very long. The first few weeks could be hard, vicious for any beginner. . . .

Bevan has described it himself. '. . . There is a tiredness which leads to stupor, which remains with you on getting up, and which forms a dull, persistent background of your consciousness. That is the tiredness of the miner, particularly of the boy of 14 or 15 who falls asleep over his meal and wakes up hours later to find that his evening has gone and there is nothing before him but bed and another day's wrestling with inert matter.'

For one week's work Bevan received between nine and eleven shillings. But he had tremendous animal strength. It took a lot to tire him and for all his stutter and his tied-up nerves, working amongst men, away from school, had advantages in the beginning. Life in the pits quickly overwhelmed them. Presently he began to find compensations in reading, sometimes by candlelight, far into the night.

Soon he read omnivorously, everything and anything. In his teens he became a friend of Mr. Bowditch the Librarian at Tredegar Workmen's Institute Library,[1] and came back in the evenings loaded with books. They might be the romances of Hall Caine, Rider Haggard or the novels of H. G. Wells; he dipped into *She*, *King Solomon's Mines* and the *Queen of Sheba*, a row of authors recommended by Bowditch, or taken down from the shelves and read straight off as they came to hand. Gradually his reading widened into quite different fields. 'The volumes,' ranged from 'Nat Gould to Professor Drummond.'[2]

[1] A bust of Bevan stands in the Library in appreciation of his work.
[2] *The Tredegar Workmen's Hall 1861–1951*, D. J. Davies.

Long after the rest of the household had gone to sleep Bevan sat reading and gradually he pushed back the boundaries of the small Welsh mining town of Tredegar and entered with mounting excitement into the impossible complexities of a quite new world where men and women were not tied to the earth, conditioned by physical labour and countless small anxieties, but flashed away on the wing of ideas. Sleep did not gravely matter. The boy had immense reserves of strength. Half the night was sometimes out before he could tear himself away from *She* or *King Solomon's Mines*, and somehow he still contrived to catch the 5.50 train to the pits in the morning.

There was no touchstone for him in the teaching of an elementary school. He was forced to find his own way into his mind, but he had the advantage of others, when he could stay up half the night and emerge in the morning still with a light in his eye and a quip for the first of the family he met. Nor did the effect of his reading die with the morning. He carried with him down to the pits bubbling ideas from many books, and time and again the first tremendous impetus absorbed in the night carried over far into the day.

In these middle teens his mind was out of its shell and racing away and there were signs of that audacity which was soon to startle the whole mining community. It had shown itself first when he refused to swallow ready-made thought and shocked the prim Sunday school teachers by asking blasphemous questions about the eternal verities. God, Mammon and the Holy Trinity had been subjected to withering examination by the irreverent H. G. Wells, and disciples of Darwin had converted his message into a savage attack upon doctrinaire religion, but that did not invest young and stuttering "school-boys" with the right to challenge their elders and betters.

Cynical iconoclasm comes easily to adolescence and is as easily overlooked. This was said to be different. This was said to break into the cosy convictions of local ministers and leave them with the uncomfortable feeling that the boy knew too much, asked questions which were indecent in the young. Slogging Nonconformists, they could not face up to talk of Darwin, natural selection and protoplasmic birth. Bevan may not have posed these precise questions but he posed others which drove one Sunday school teacher to eloquent denunciation. It is said he threatened to leave Sunday school if Aneurin Bevan remained a pupil.

It was different with the colliers. Bevan now plunged boldly into their arguments, too, and said forceful things in his stuttering way. They never came amiss. True, the colliers were very ready to guy or gag him. When he began . . . 'I-I-I . . . don't . . . a-a-a-gree . . . with . . .' it was sometimes the signal for the men to shout—'Out of order, Bevan,' and drown the rest in laughter. He must have died a dozen sensitive deaths before he learnt not to mind, if in truth we ever, at root, cease to mind. Certainly he learnt to cover up, and the first layers of the mask which can settle into place so invulnerably today, began to appear. Simultaneously his passion for challenging anyone with powerful convictions, plunging into every street corner debate, grew. It must have needed high courage, tremendous drive. For anyone with a stutter, the shynesses of youth are magnified out of all proportion. It was a time of great emotional stress and great questioning.

His reading and widening experience threw up whole constellations of new ideas. What had once seemed fixed and eternal, the common lot of man in one locality, became flexible and capable of change; what the elders of the Miners' Lodge accepted as progress he now chafed against as compromise; what daunted the traditional leaders suddenly released in him a wave of energy, and back at Charles Street he argued with his father, one of the few men he respected, asked questions and threw bombshells gathered from his books.

There are many stories of this time. Of a flushed and heated Bevan with tousled hair and flailing arms making six separate attempts to get a hearing in a street corner debate; of the group dispersing until there were just two youngsters left and Bevan at last saying 'b-b-bloody fools—b-b-both of you!' Of Bevan walking through the gas-lit streets, with the shadowy line of the hills disappearing into the night sky, snow beginning to fall, silence coming down on everything, and the young man suddenly stopping to quote something under his breath which his companion could not catch.

Memories are very hazy of these early days. I spent some time in Tredegar talking to people who knew him then, and there was a marked tendency for some to be carried away by reminiscence. Others, in their eagerness to claim intimacy with a man now famous, produced highly apocryphal evidence with the air of revealed truth. One remembered him as a ruthless young

28

agitator. Another as an arrogant devil, out to have his own way. A third as an embryo philosopher, a Welsh Solomon who would one day enlighten the world.

'A king amongst men,' one old miner said with a glow in his eye, reflecting a widespread reverence.

'A dreadful one,' another with no glow.

Amongst it all this much is certain. Aneurin Bevan plunged into still more arguments, joined the local Council of Labour Colleges class and became active in the Mineworkers' Union. Anywhere where debate ran free or the events of the day came under fire, one was liable to find him preoccupied with overcoming his stammer and forcing himself to speak.

The events of the day were full of superficial similarity to many other periods of British history, but coming close now to a rare climax. The programme of the Liberal Government so glamorously unfolded in the year 1906 had worn very thin with the years. What began with such a shining light about it and brought to life National Health Insurance, was presently confused by the shadows of Syndicalism and Suffragettes, by a recalcitrant House of Lords, the trade unions demanding wages not neutralized by increasing costs of living, the Irish clamouring for Home Rule and a threat of war intangible but always waiting in the background.

In September 1910 a minor dispute over piecework prices in one of the pits of the Cambrian Combine had suddenly brought the South Wales miners out once more, and what began as a lesser trouble quickly developed into one of the most fierce and prolonged strikes the country had known. It lasted almost a year. It shook the owners badly. It revealed a courage and determination in the miners unmatched in any other industry.

This strike was symptomatic of the spread of Syndicalism, a far more alarming creed to the Liberal Government in those days than the "dogma of Socialism." The threat of revolution by industry looked much more real than the opposition of twenty-nine Labour M.P.s, returned to the House as a definite group for the first time. For the British brand of Syndicalism lacked the final cynicism which characterized the French, and had its roots in the far more realistic preamble of the American Industrial Workers of the World. . . .

'The working class and the employing class have nothing in common. There can be no peace so long as hunger and want are

29

found among millions of working people and the few who make up the employing class have all the good things of life. . . . These conditions can be changed and the interest of the working class upheld only by an organization formed in such a way that all its members in any one industry, or in all industries if necessary, cease work whenever a strike or lock-out is on in any department. . . . By organizing industrially we are forming the structure of the new society within the shell of the old. . . .'

From this the French had built up a whole philosophy which foresaw revolution occurring not from political pressure, but from a series of strikes of increasing intensity, gradually mounting to one widespread general strike which would end with every union taking over its own industry and forming a federation of autonomous industrial states. But there was a catch. The general strike, the French said, is only an "energizing myth." It will never in fact occur. Some British miners would have no truck with such subtleties. They believed in the general strike and less than twenty years later their faith proved not entirely mistaken.

For the moment Syndicalism spread throughout the country and South Wales became one of its strongholds. It entered deeply into Aneurin Bevan's outlook alongside many other growing beliefs. He saw very clearly what a powerful weapon the industrial unions could become if their possibilities were completely realized. Some members of the Liberal Government saw it too but they had many other things on their minds. The Suffragettes were the most sensational problem of the day, and on the surface presented clear-cut issues. They were prepared to go to almost any length—to chain themselves to railings, throw themselves beneath the hooves of Derby runners, to be forcibly fed in the most brutal fashion and suffer any humiliation, provided it led to women getting the vote. In fact, many Suffragettes would have been satisfied with the promise of the vote without immediate performance. The same contradictory duality ran through many events of the day. The great clamour for Irish Home Rule amounted then to nothing more than a demand for a "local" Parliament which would remain under the British umbrella, the Trade Union pressure for higher real wages might have been bought off at a very moderate price, but the Liberals could never quite bring themselves to make the concessions which would have eased the tension and saved the life of Liberalism for years to come. Instead they alternately favoured and frowned on the

30

demands of the Suffragettes, Home Rulers and Trade Unionists, until they forced them to greater extremes of action than they themselves ever intended. Not even a quite considerable array of enlightened legislation—The Trade Disputes Act (1906), Old Age Pensions Act (1908), Coal Mines Eight Hours Act (1908), Trade Boards Act (1909)—could quell the growing hostility. So it was that the Liberals soon faced a concentration of grievances all expressed in new and quite violent terms, but it was not their own behaviour alone which brought the fire down on their heads. The great Liberal era in England had reached its peak and was showing the first serious signs of decay. The apostles of Liberalism still stood by their ancient creed. They believed that change came about by compromise, by a slow, cumulative process never violent enough to cause upheaval, and always leaving the underlying system intact. There were others who said that the exigencies of the day were producing in Britain, and had already produced in Europe, growing doubts that the vital changes necessary could any longer be wrought along these traditional lines. Liberalism they believed was rapidly approaching an impasse.

Certainly the young Aneurin Bevan belonged to the forces which wanted that order swept away. He played a far more active part at miners' meetings now and whenever he saw the chance stumbled in, sometimes clumsily with the stutter, sometimes with a burst of sparkling words which astonished his audience.

Two things were fast becoming evident about his stutter. Driving himself to speak in public it appeared that once given up to the passions of debate, his nervousness slackened, and presently there were stretches when his stutter all but disappeared. It seemed to set the pattern for part of his political life, and whether consciously or not, in later years it was characteristic of him that he aroused fierce debate as though to forget himself in the stress of the moment. Simultaneously he was said to have taken to substituting synonyms for those words which paralysed his tongue. It might be a word beginning with S which broke the flow of a beautiful sentence and kept him stammering on the one sibilant until he slipped quickly into a synonym and the sentence completed itself. His brain worked with lightning speed. Today he thinks on his feet in the House of Commons more quickly than almost any other member.

Privately too the struggle against his stutter continued. Once, his mother told me, she came downstairs very late at night and found him addressing an imaginary audience in the kitchen. His friend Bill Hopkins recalls long walks while he listened to Bevan rehearsing a speech. All Hopkins ever said was 'Aye.' It is difficult to know quite what it cost him to master his stutter. He brought to it a singleness of purpose and bitter determination which would have carried him far in any field.

Total liberation was some way off yet, but as the words came more easily, his personality grew and very soon he was tilting at traditional cautions, moving in fearlessly where others were intimidated until he shocked and dazzled and infuriated, and the first murmurings against the impudent young cub who wanted to re-make the world over-night, gave place, in many, to grudging respect. It was wise to respect this "young agitator." He had a habit of flooring one with unexpected facts. There was still the stutter, but the mind had a knife edge. He was twenty-five before he conquered his stutter. 'During all that time I had to almost flog myself into speaking in public.'

* * *

Unconsciously Aneurin Bevan was following a path which had already absorbed Will Lawther, A. J. Cook, Arthur Horner, Jim Griffiths, and was later to absorb another group, a few years younger, represented by men like Morgan Phillips. It was a path which explains why there were so many young miners in the vanguard of British Socialism. The chances for any boy bred in a mining town were strictly limited to one of two alternatives. Either he went down the pit and remained a miner for the rest of his working days, or he studied in his spare time and hoped to become a manager or agent, in which case he might become a renegade from his class and automatically shift into the enemy's ranks. It was a dilemma which kept many able men tied to mining. They could more easily face the limitations of the miner's life than the scorn of their own kind, but there was another way out. It lay in the trade unions and beyond that, at several removes, in politics. Political issues were so clear-cut in the mining world that they deeply intensified the divisions between worker and employer, individual and trade union, and many young men threw themselves passionately into politics as a career. It carried their crusade a step further, it broke down barriers encompassing their lives, it gave them quite new purpose in living and added drama to what could be unspeakably drab.

Bevan then, was one of many, and if few of them were destined to wage the battle quite so bitterly, they formed together a group which has continuously sprung from the miners of Britain over the past fifty years and set the pace for both vital changes and prolonged feuds.

It is a peculiarity of many major movements in Britain that most people are unaware of them. Events reveal clear symptoms of fundamental change but they remain unidentified until they break right into the open. Certainly, at this period, a large majority of people believed that the miners were nothing more than a bunch of belligerent malcontents who must one day be put in their place, and completely failed to see that a new social tide was developing in the deep valleys of Monmouthshire, in the hills of Scotland and Durham and Northumberland and away in the villages of Yorkshire and Cornwall. And if it had no more power than a trickle as yet, it was moving under the surface everywhere, and sometimes the miners gave the lead.

Aneurin Bevan represented it in Tredegar. Ness Edwards, a valley or two away, strained at the same barriers, and Arthur Horner, deeper south, was soon to suffer for his opinions. Will Lawther looked at the grey pit heaps and read something which only miners could understand, and Morgan Phillips was following his father down the mines of Bargoed at the age of fourteen, with his mother's sermons on Socialism still ringing in his ears. Jim Griffiths, one of ten children of the local blacksmith, had a few years earlier joined the I.L.P. in remote Ammanford, and far away in the straggling village of Cowdenbeath, fast becoming a compact mining town, Jennie Lee was growing up in a two-roomed cottage, where the Socialism of Burns and the Bible, once an affair of the nobler passions, was eventually to give place to science and political economy.

3

THEY came one night to arrest him. Will, the eldest brother, answered the knock on the door and there were two policemen asking for Mr. Aneurin Bevan. Bevan came to the door, drew it behind him and stood in the street. 'You haven't answered your call-up papers,' one policeman said. Bevan motioned him to silence. Inside the stone-flagged sitting-room his sister, May, lay dying from a mysterious disease the origin of which they never traced.

Bevan considered the policemen a moment without answering. They did not relish the job. Will waited for his brother to give a lead, and Bevan, who should have been the least happy, stood silent, apparently quite self-possessed. At last he is alleged to have said, 'All right . . . I'll come. . . . But don't let her see you or by Christ . . .!' and he made a threatening gesture. They marched off down the road.

At seven o'clock next morning Will Bevan called at Tredegar police station and asked to see his brother. He brought with him a steaming hot breakfast carefully prepared by Mrs. Bevan, a very worried Mrs. Bevan. The "warder" said: 'Never known a prisoner like him before. Can't wake him up!'

This version of the story was told me by Bevan's brother. There is at least one other. Undoubtedly Bevan was arrested and almost at once released. Local lore has it that the quota of men called up from the mines was already exhausted, but the Government particularly wanted this young agitator in the Army out of harm's way. The morning following his arrest Bevan vigorously denied any association with conscientious objection and produced a certificate in court certifying that he suffered from nystagmus [1] a disease which made military service difficult. It was said that he gave a colourful address; that he spoke of choosing his own enemy, his own battlefield and his own time, when the real battle began, but there are many contradictions and although this part of the story was completely in keeping with the arrogance which

[1] Nystagmus is not easy to define. It is a condition rather than a disease, caused by eye adjustment to darkness. It is generally thought to have a psychological factor.

sometimes distinguished Bevan as a person, and his intransigence in the face of anything resembling authority, I have been unable to find documentary evidence.

Another story is told—apocryphal or otherwise—that he proceeded to Newport for re-examination of his nystagmus and on the door of the army medical depot was met by a tough ex-soldier who tried to dragoon him into army discipline a little prematurely.

'Who do you think you're talking to?' Bevan demanded and when the ex-soldier, looking even more ferocious, said, 'And who do you think you are?' he was answered, peremptorily, 'I'm Bevan.'

'Bevan!' said the ex-soldier, his manner changing. 'Do you mean Aneurin Bevan?'

'Yes,' said Bevan.

'Come this way, *Mr.* Bevan.' Instantaneous facilities of a highly unmilitary kind were said to have been offered. Such—if one accepts the story—was Bevan's growing reputation at the tender age of nineteen or twenty.

But the *Observer* wrote: 'While the great North Welsh rebel, Lloyd George was becoming the father of his country in its hour of need—taking confidence from the 2,000 years of Celtic peasant history behind him—the young Aneurin, watching him with something of the ideology of an industrial 'dead-end' kid, was rejecting the ways of his fathers. He felt he knew better what were the real needs of his like. . . .' His Welsh friends were more sympathetic: 'It was the fire that was in him, mun. It would not let him be.' Of course, but agitators are not very successful unless they express tensions already deep-rooted in society and Bevan, magnificently marrying Marx and Freud, was at this stage, as much the product of his environment as of his id.

The early days of the war had been disastrous. Appalling slaughter had quickly overtaken the British forces. 1914 almost wiped out the old Regular Army, 1915–16 brought the holocaust of the Somme and Kitchener's Army went the way of the Regulars. Then began the long, dreary, callous business of Passchendaele with whole battalions obliterated in a day. The troops read newspapers like the *Daily X*, tending to believe the picture of South Wales miners skulking safely in well-paid jobs, taking advantage of the vital need for coal to keep out of the war and squeezing every possible penny from the situation.

Outwardly Bevan had all the makings of a soldier. He was broad, solid and vigorous, he could outlast many men at the coalface and there was a brimming vitality about him which indicated immense reserves of strength. But the men of the mining villages could tell by his eyes—those wide, blue eyes which so suddenly blazed to fierce life—that here was another victim of nystagmus. The early pictures of Aneurin Bevan sitting in the Council of Labour Colleges class, show a lift about the chin, a challenge in the whole poise of the head which might belong to a man of destiny. From those very early pictures he looked like a person marked out to play a powerful part in whatever engaged his full attention, a person quite capable of breaking through the conventions and setting his stamp on men and events, but perhaps it was not entirely the result of innate character. The retracted chin, the challenge in the head, the crinkling of the eyes, might be in some part the reaction to nystagmus. Even so, there remained about the young miner's face something which showed quite clearly that here was no homespun agitator fallen a victim to his own eloquence. Here was a man, if not of destiny, then a man most heavily to be reckoned with.

*   *   *

In the late 'teens and early twenties, Bevan's name became known in a dozen mining valleys. His reputation for wit and audacity which kept any meeting he graced on tiptoe waiting for the next sally, the next crushing piece of logic, spread. His mind worked twice as fast as most of his opponents, and he had by now routed formidable champions even amongst his own people. One person after another had given up trying to contain him. 'Other people have let you have your own way,' one dour Yorkshire chairman informed him, with steam-roller certainty, one day, 'but you're not going to get it with me. I'm going to put my foot down.'

'If only you knew where to put it,' said Bevan.

It was repartee at a simple level but it brought a roar of laughter and laughter was more obliterative than anything. Often it went that way now. He could outwit, outstay, most of them. Despite the stutter he had become irrepressible and was such a born orator that dreary meetings were apt to come alive when he appeared on the platform. It all made him many friends and enemies, it left the elders of the Miners' Lodge shaking their heads,

36

it created fierce jealousies and feuds, but whichever way it took them, there was no gainsaying his gifts and in 1916, against all precedent, he was appointed chairman of the Miners' Lodge, the youngest person to get the job since the unions began. It took him further into the industrial battlefield and the same streak of arrogance, which had shocked the Sunday school teachers, developed. Bevan spoke his mind outrageously, made enemies with a cheerfulness which characterized friendships in other men, and lived continuously on a knife's edge. He was now seen by many as a dangerous firebrand, a man who asked 'why should we work our guts out to feed capitalist bellies?' His words were blunt, his manner on occasion intimidating, his courage immense. But he himself was presently engaged on something far more serious. Within the South Wales Miners' Federation, each pit had its own independent miners' lodge. Bevan set out to create combine lodges bringing several together to strike or negotiate uniformly, a much more powerful weapon to wield against the employers.

* * *

His growth through adolescence to manhood continued against a social background not calculated to appease his turbulent nature, a background which gave the Welsh colliers a grim sense of isolation if not disinheritance. The middle of the war found them still profoundly dissatisfied with every attempt to ease their lot. They regarded anything short of major legislation as conciliation more designed to keep the peace than change the social structure. Bevan belonged to a group which believed that the war against the Kaiser had little immediate relevance to the troubles of the miners. The war against the coal-owners was far more pressing and reverberations of these early attitudes echoed through his whole life. The struggle was between two Imperialisms in which the working class on both sides would suffer if the Imperialists determined the peace terms.

He now read two writers who left a profound impression on his mind, Eugene V. Debs and Daniel De Leon. Intransigent Socialists, it was ironic that America, the country thundering with a cannon pulse of capitalism, should have produced the writers who inspired no small part of Bevan's creed. De Leon's theoretical knowledge of Marx tended to be elementary, and some of the conclusions he drew and sought to apply through

37

the medium of the Socialist Labour Party were immature, but at this stage his exposition had a liberating appeal to many raw Socialists. 'In so far as I can be said to have had a political training at all, it has been in Marxism,' Bevan wrote later. '. . . When I found that the political polemics of De Leon and Debs were shared by so loved an author as Jack London, the effect on my mind was profound.'

An easy bridge between Jack London's *Iron Heel* and early Marxist books at once became evident. Mining valleys instantaneously translated intellectual theories into ugly facts, and the whole bitter story of the miners' battle against employer and environment fell into fresh place with 'the impact of a divine revelation. . . . The dark places were lighted up and the difficult ways made easy.'

Syndicalist thought was still very strong in Wales. 'Power, we were taught, was at the point of production.' Why then waste time trying to reach it through the House of Commons? As the unions grew and amalgamated they would command immense power over the whole industrial machine and the community could not work without industry.

It was unfortunate that in the event the unemployed were shown to have very little industrial power at all and unemployment was about to involve millions of men. For the moment some colliers in Tredegar thought in terms of industrial power alone. They regarded Tredegar as a company town and saw the directors of the various companies[1] as virtual dictators in their economic life. If they were out of grace with the Company, they were out of grace with the world. Other jobs were comparatively rare and it paid to keep on the right side of the Company, because the wrong side spelt unemployment, desolation and in some cases, they said, victimization. Within this small principality of 20,000 people the iron and coal companies were uncrowned kings, but there were elements amongst the miners who dearly wanted to force an abdication. The idea became part of Bevan's thinking alongside Debs and De Leon. It was to express itself dramatically in the next few years.

[1] Steel production in The Tredegar Iron and Coal Co. stopped in 1895. In 1898 the Ironworks were re-started but closed again in 1901. In 1907 the Whitehead Iron & Steel Company was formed.

4

A SHOWER of celebrations burst magnificently when the news of the Armistice came through in November 1918 and relief ran far over into December, when the greatest of all khaki elections, rapidly arranged by Lloyd George, swept his Coalition Government back into power again. Within a year the high spirits were dead, the elation evaporating and something more dangerous than disillusion beginning to overtake the country generally and what were to become known as the Depressed Areas in particular.

By the early days of 1919 the air was thunderous. The Labour Party had increased its votes from 500,000 to $2\frac{1}{4}$ millions, won fifty-seven seats and become the only opposition worth the name although it was an opposition without any glint of inspiration in its leadership. The throw of the electoral dice had defeated its pre-war leaders—Ramsay MacDonald, Arthur Henderson and Philip Snowden—and the responsibility fell on the not very adept shoulders of Mr. W. Adamson. There was a baffling wall between the Labour Party, encouraging its leaders to develop unbridled opposition in the House and M.P.s who reproduced the merest echoes of the Party's programme. True, the Party had now developed into something more than a Parliamentary committee of the trade unions, and the middle classes were directly entering its ranks, the last barrier dissolved by the 1918 decision to grant membership to individuals. But Sidney Webb, still the high-priest of Left-wing thinking, and a man who achieved the unique distinction of winning reverence from all parties, wrote: 'No philosopher now looks for anything but the gradual evolution of the new order from the old, with no breach of continuity or abrupt change of the entire social tissue at any point. . . .'

There were elements among the miners who flatly contradicted him. In the background the trade unions had consolidated their forces, $2\frac{1}{4}$ million affiliated members in 1913 had swollen to $4\frac{1}{2}$ millions, small-scale organizations were fusing into more powerful families and the Triple Alliance of miners, railwaymen and transport workers, planned in the early days of 1914, had become a reality, brooding powerfully behind the scenes.

Signs of trouble multiplied under the surface, demobilization began to drag badly, and millions of men numb and weary from years of discipline, danger and hardship were shocked to hear of another army drafted overseas to yet another war, this time the anti-Soviet war at Archangel. There had even been a police strike in August 1918, an unheard of desecration of democratic rights which produced outbursts of indignant rhetoric from every known quarter of the political compass.

Against this electrically charged background the miners found themselves in a strong position. Their union now had plenty of money, coal had never been in greater demand, and they were spoiling for a fight. They waited truculently for signs of the promised post-war land to materialize, and when it seemed unaccountably delayed, decided the time had come for action. The first significant flare-up came with a strike on the Clyde when the Riot Act was read to a demonstration sixty thousand strong in the city centre, the police attacked with batons and no less personages than David Kirkwood, William Gallacher and Emanuel Shinwell went down before them.

The miners next handed in strike notices and the Government suddenly realized that something must be done before things ran out of hand. A new world had been promised the miners after the war, a world of economic security, with rising standards of living and homes fit for heroes. If anything, it seemed rather more remote. A new world had been promised the ex-serviceman, a world of full employment, with widening horizons for everyone, and a great new purpose in living, but frustration, intolerance, and a crassly stupid lack of imagination intervened to produce political expediency in what was clearly a time for greatness.

The leaders of the Triple Alliance were granted audience by Lloyd George. Robert Smillie, the miners' leader, told Bevan the inner story of this meeting. It had very clear links with another and far bigger social upheaval waiting seven years away. Smillie said that they went 'truculently determined not to be won over by the seductive and eloquent Welshman.' But Lloyd George was disarmingly frank. 'Gentlemen,' he said, 'you have fashioned, in the Triple Alliance of the unions represented by you, a most powerful instrument. I feel bound to tell you that in our opinion we are at your mercy. The Army is disaffected and cannot be relied upon. Trouble has occurred already in a number of camps. . . . If you carry out your threat to strike, then you will defeat us. . . . But if you do so, have you weighed the consequences? . . . For, if a force arises in the State which is stronger than the State itself, then it must be ready to take on the functions of the State, or withdraw and accept the authority of the State. . . .'

'From that moment on,' said Robert Smillie, 'we were beaten and we knew we were.' [1]

Eloquently Lloyd George now came in with a plan for investigating the whole mining industry, on condition that the miners remained at work. It sounded, under the spell of his brilliant phrases, immensely sane and British and satisfactory, but the Sankey Commission has since gone down in British history as the Commission which voted for nationalization—even though the Chairman's vote alone produced the majority—and later had its conclusions ignored by Lloyd George. It has also become part of Left-wing propaganda for all time.

A stormy interlude with a strike in the Yorkshire coalfields which brought out the troops, was followed on 18 August by Lloyd George baldly announcing that the Government did not propose to carry out Sir John Sankey's recommendation to nationalize the mines. Mr. Vernon Hartshorn asked in the House: 'Why was the Commission set up? Was it a huge game of bluff? Was it never intended that if the Reports favoured nationalization we were to get it? . . . That is the kind of question the miners of the country will ask, and they will say, "We have been deceived, betrayed, duped."'

In the beginning the mining community of Britain did react in some such way, but away in Cowdenbeath and Tredegar, something far more bitter entered the scene, a sense of disillusionment which was to sour relations between miners and government in a new and acid way right down to the day when a Labour Government swept into power with a big majority, and Mr. Shinwell suddenly found himself confronted with a psychological legacy which came close to psychosis.

The dust of the dispute had hardly settled when Bevan moved abruptly away from the storm centre of South Wales, where he had spent the first twenty-one years of his life, to London. It was a scholarship presented by the South Wales Miners' Federation which brought him to that old-world seminary of Socialism, the

[1] *In Place of Fear*—Aneurin Bevan (Wm. Heinemann Ltd., 1952).

Labour College. It is said that the exigencies enforced on any scholar sent to London under these auspices were considerably softened by the Welsh colliers who subscribed £40 towards his living expenses. It did not work out quite as anyone expected.

In the early 1900s the Labour College stood in the drab backwaters of Earl's Court—a grey jumble of buildings calculated to depress many a buoyant spirit. In the first few weeks it may have inspired Bevan, but he quickly found limitations in some sides of its life which drove him back into himself again. Yet here, instead of the occasional person who read books, everyone read books, names like Rousseau and Marx were bandied about, everyone was politically conscious and if few of the students were brimming with original ideas, there were some quite prepared to argue the night away, and that he loved.

But the Labour College was no working man's Oxford. It had no dreaming spires in its physical or mental make-up. It was a solid, earnest place of learning, where young men from all over the country came to salvage educations lost in earlier years under the pressure of economic necessity. The unruly child of Ruskin College, Oxford, originally founded in 1896 to extend the privilege of university education to the working class, it had broken away from strictly academic circles under the leadership of Professor Hird, and moved to the good proletarian soil of Earl's Court where it was possible to teach the economics of Marx in preference to Jevons, with financial backing from the South Wales Miners' Federation and the National Union of Railwaymen.

In his early days at the Labour College Bevan met two men whose names were unfamiliar then to the outside world, but who were destined to become big people in the Socialist movement. Jim Griffiths was older than Bevan and married to a woman who served in a teashop in order to see him through his two-year course; Ness Edwards about the same age. Both had come from roots similar to Aneurin Bevan's. Many others then "up" have since given their lives to Socialism without achieving public distinction, but if Welshmen with the gift of tongues seemed destined to play a powerful part in the life of the Labour College —academic and social—it was not really made for men like Bevan.

It bore on its crest around a flaming torch the motto "Educate, Agitate, Organize." The method of Marx predominated in all the teaching. According to this, the key to understanding of the social phenomena must be sought in the productive forces, the state of which at any given time determined the relations in which men stood towards one another economically. In turn, they determined the legal, political and moral characteristics of any given society, and indirectly, the contemporary philosophy, science and art. The division of society into classes with different and in most cases diametrically antagonistic interests, sprang from the development of the productive forces, and gave rise to a struggle from which, ultimately, social revolutions arose. Whereas in the past those conflicts were fought out and social change achieved more or less instinctively, thanks to the higher development of the productive forces in capitalist society, it was possible for the working class 'to accomplish its historic action consciously.'[1] 'The difference between present and past upheavals lies precisely in the fact that now the secret of the historical process of change has at last been discovered. . . .' '. . . the objective external forces which have hitherto dominated history will pass under the control of men themselves. It is only from this point that men with full consciousness will fashion their own history. . . .'

Amongst the Labour College students and teachers, some as much doctrinaire whisky drinkers as they were Marxists, Bevan persistently clung to a belief in his own brand of Marxism which involved industrial unionism. On the evidence of W. W. Craik, then Principal of the College, Bevan scorned Parliament as an instrument for social change at that time. Of course he was still raw, unsophisticated, still badly handicapped by the stutter, but as Craik put it to me, 'there were many dust-ups on the stairs and in the Debating Society between Bevan and most of the rest of us' on this issue. Later Bevan was to change his mind, later Parliamentary democracy became the most powerful revolutionary instrument; for the moment he is said to have sworn by industrial unionism, pure and simple.

Life began in the Labour College with breakfast at eight. Lectures occupied a large part of the morning, there was a break in the afternoon and occasionally another lecture in the evening. A great deal of work went on between times in the single and double bed-sitting-room-cum-studies. Meals were frugal, a mug of tea and a hunk of bread and cheese sufficing for supper. Students cleaned their own rooms and every Saturday morning were

[1] This definition comes from W. W. Craik, then Principal of the Labour College.

supposed to rise at 6.30 to scrub the floors. None of the niceties of public school life came their way, but Bevan contrived to make immensely varied what might have been a dreary round, even if it brought complaints from one student that his intellectual life always had a tendency to flower when others were thinking of bed. Certainly he read far into the night. It is said that he didn't care very much for the schedules and regulations of the College. 'He never was one to take much notice of time.' Some shook their heads when one spoke of those days. Others tell of fresh attempts to subdue his stutter. He even attended elocution classes given by Miss Clara Bunn, who, on his own acknowledgement, helped him considerably.

Tom Ashcroft, a fellow student, wrote to me: 'Nye did not strike me as a serious student in the ordinary sense at all. He had, of course, something—a touch of genius—which not one serious student in a thousand possesses! It always appeared to me, quite mistakenly perhaps, that he learned what he knew from talking, discussion and argument, rather than books. . . . I seem to remember that he was a late riser! . . . He struck me as an extremely attractive personality with a quite astonishing gift of the gab—it seemed to me, I confess, that the great secret of his attraction as a speaker was his own evident delight in speaking!'

There were amateur theatricals. Frank Horrabin organized a production of Shaw's *Blanco Posnet*. A wonderful picture of the cast with broad hats, pistols, beards and cloaks shows Bevan in a soft white hat and tight-fitting trousers, a good-looking young man, still very much himself for all his garb. Bevan was one of the jury in the play. He would poke his head in at rehearsals, glance round, say 'I'll be there,' and vanish. He came through reasonably well at the actual performance.

Bevan spent many hours exploring London from the Labour College. The city fascinated him. He went down to the dingy places of the East End, into the alleys and courts of Fleet Street, into the by-ways of Billingsgate; he explored the parks, the bookshops in Charing Cross Road, and came to the House of Commons. But money was scarce and constantly brought excursions planned on the grand scale abruptly down to earth. There were occasions when his sister came up from Tredegar, bringing untold treasure which they promptly spent in a happy-go-lucky way. In four days they ran through money which Mrs. Bevan had expected to last a week, taking in *The Beggar's Opera*

—a great favourite with Bevan—*Pygmalion*, Pavlova, Hampton Court and half a dozen other plays and places.

★   ★   ★

Big things were toward in the London he came to know. In September 1919 the Trades Union Congress had considered the Government's decision to go back on the recommendations of the Sankey Commission and decided to compel '. . . the Government to adopt the scheme of national ownership and joint control. . . .' Fine words. Over the next year they failed to carry much weight. A "Mines For the Nation" campaign was launched in December, and still the Government remained unmoved. In March 1920 a general strike was abandoned in favour of 'political action in the form of intensive political propaganda,' as if they had not already run a large part of the propaganda gamut. Then the Labour Party Executive went into conference with the Miners' Federation, the conference wandered to an uncertain end and for the next month, while the dust accumulated on the massive blue volumes of the Sankey Commission's evidence, the life seemed to drain out of the whole dispute. Bevan followed it closely. It was the centre of argument amongst students of the Labour College and the subject of many fiery letters back home to parents and friends.

At the other, literary, end of the social scale, the *London Mercury* presently announced its belief in the birth of a new lyrical age, but T. S. Eliot came closer to the heart of the social scene with *The Waste Land* and one of the *Preludes*, which the wider public largely ignored.

> Wipe your hand across your mouth, and laugh;
> The worlds revolve like ancient women
> Gathering fuel in vacant lots.

Vacant lots. . . . There were far too many vacant lots in those days. Desolation marked too big a part of the social scene as was evident even in opulent, teeming London with its great inconsequent way of life at the centre of the modern world. Men turned from unemployment to the racing news, from strikes and slumps to Charlie Chaplin and *Riders of the Purple Sage*; the Jog Trot and the Shimmy had wider currency than the troubles of the Triple Alliance, and a treasure hunt craze was soon to attract more people than political meetings. Perhaps one was the inevitable complement of the other. Life was too much without trivialities.

In the Labour College there was deep debate about some of these things and Einstein's relativity was just about to burst on an uncomprehending world to keep some awake at night trying to fathom its implications.

There are many more stories of Bevan's Labour College days. Of one hapless tutor who challenged him, only to have him carry the debate beyond the tutor's depth, of the Labour candidates they decided to put up for the Kensington Council, one achieving a record low vote, and another coming close to beating his Tory opponent.

But two years at the Labour College in London did not seem to leave a very deep mark on him. Another layer of sophistication grew over, he widened and deepened his knowledge of history, philosophy and economics, and came to understand something of the mainsprings of big-city life.

Yet if he himself showed little sign of fundamental change it was a very different story with Tredegar. Presently he left the Labour College, the paralysis of a considerable slump brought large sections of industry to a standstill, unemployment was around the 2,000,000 mark and the feud between workers and employers in Tredegar entered a new and more bitter stage. There was no job waiting for him when he got back. He might be a first-class collier capable of getting more coal out per man shift than most others, but he was also a marked man, a known agitator, and now he was "deliberately excluded" from the pits. He joined the evergrowing ranks of the unemployed, and entered what must have been one of the bitterest periods of his life which was to run for some eighteen months and leave another scar no less permanent than the mines. He said of this period '. . . I don't suppose I earned more than 10s. a week on an average, but like most working class families we bore one another's shocks. I had to make up my mind whether to stay at home and stick it out or emigrate. After some weeks of indecision, I decided to stay and succeed in the place where success would mean most. . . .'

As more and more men fell idle and the time limit for drawing the dole expired, the local council in Tredegar saw that something must be improvised to prevent widespread privation, and an old scheme for laying new water pipes was revived. Bevan became a labourer. He dug trenches and laid pipes with gusto. It was said that however grey the outlook there were times when Bevan sent a gale of laughter echoing down the streets and when the pipe-laying involved Charles Street, his mother provided jugs of coffee, and the whole proceedings became convivial.

But schemes for improving the water supplies of Tredegar had their limits. Very soon more men were unemployed. Very soon the queue for the dole had lengthened, more men sat on their haunches at street corners, and the grey paralysis of unemployment deepened to the point where it seemed to hang like a tangible cloud over the whole valley. Presently, Bevan wrote, 'In parts of Monmouthshire whole townships were idle. . . . The poverty was appalling and the outlook black to the point of despair. . . .' And then one day the unemployed miners decided to march. In Tredegar they marched first on the Board of Guardians who controlled poor law relief. 'As this was in the beginning provided from the local rates the situation was ridiculous, for of course unemployed miners could not pay rates with which to relieve themselves.' They marched from Blaina, Nantyglo, Ebbw Vale and Tredegar and they marched on the workhouse at Tredegar where the Guardians were gathered, 'and I marched with them—at the head of them—for I was one of the leaders.'

According to Bevan they locked the Guardians in for two days and nights. Locally some say it was one night, and there are those who dispute that he was a leader. Whichever way it went, the Guardians were quite content. They loathed Whitehall as did the miners. There were long-drawn-out discussions, and one afternoon Bevan fell into argument with a man from Blaina, a person he regarded highly as self-educated, well-read and intelligent. It was a beautiful day with white clouds idling across a blue sky to the far distant Black Mountains. 'Aneurin,' the man from Blaina said, sadly and quite without bitterness, 'this country is finished. Come with me to Australia. I've sold my house and I can just manage to pay my debts and make the passage money. . . .'

The words moved Bevan. '. . . For he was a man for whom I had an affection amounting to love, and I felt my eyes flooding. "David," I said, "I hate to see you leave us, but if this is how you feel about it then you must go, and I wish you all the luck in the world. For myself, I am going to stay here and fight it out. You're an older man than I am." '

Bevan told his father when he reached home that evening. 'I

47

think you've made the right decision,' his father said. 'But it will be a long fight.' [1]

*   *   *

There were many harsh experiences. It was said that his early efforts at pipe-laying for the local council left his hands, soft from the years at the Labour College, raw and blistered. His attempts to get unemployment relief sometimes brought humiliations. . . . 'When I applied for benefit my sister was earning thirty shillings a week. . . . Because of her earnings I was refused transitional payment and my mother, my sister and I had to live on my sister's money. . . . I did not feel very kindly towards the gentlemen who compelled me to live on my sister's earnings. . . .'

But the spontaneous combustion of his own high spirits were still liable to take charge, and life was rarely dull at No. 7 Charles Street. It had an ever open door and a stream of visitors. His mother said Bevan now tended to find his company amongst men older than himself, amongst teachers and lecturers and trade union officials who came to Charles Street and sometimes stayed far into the night arguing. Mrs. Bevan learned to rue these arguments. Whenever debate became fierce—which was not infrequent— Bevan had a habit of picking up forks and spoons and twisting them into unrecognizable shapes.

There were occasions when he could have used his strength to other purpose. A tough, one-armed collier attacked him one night after a stormy meeting in the Workmen's Institute. Bevan put his hands in his pockets and stared poker-faced at the collier, circling warily, waiting for retaliation, and said, 'You can hit me again if you like. You can go on hitting me. You can hit me until I'm carried off to hospital. You'll still be wrong.'

*   *   *

A long fight, his father had said. It would be a long fight. Yes. It had already lasted over half a century. In that time the miners had built their own defence systems and, where they were officially lacking, social services—the Workmen's Institute and Library, and, far more remarkable, The Tredegar Medical Aid Society. Later to inspire some characteristics of the National Health Service, this microcosm of a new social organism flourished

---

[1] *In Place of Fear*—Aneurin Bevan.

48

in Tredegar. Every miner paid 3*d*. on every £1 earned towards a central medical fund, the rate varying for teachers, shopkeepers and other classes. Threepence in the £ eventually gave them the choice of five doctors, a surgeon, and a number of visiting specialists with a range of medicines free of charge. In the end 94 per cent of the population joined the scheme and it was controlled by a committee of thirty workers elected by the subscribers. Backed by the Medical Aid Society illness ceased to be a disaster in the miner's life, and Bevan saw it as an experiment in miniature. These small Welsh mining towns were sometimes looked upon as the test-tubes of Socialism, where controlled experiments of a limited kind could be carried out under special conditions.

Another experiment of a quite different kind needs closer attention. As much a battle as an experiment, it had its counterpart in towns and villages throughout the country, with one difference. It was a battle for control of the town of Tredegar and the difference lay in some of the methods used. For over half a century what Bevan regarded as conservative elements of one kind or another had held key positions in the local council and few had seriously challenged their power. As the years advanced trade union machinery had become more dignified and less violent, some of its leaders—now with a vested interest in their jobs—men counselling restraint and caution, men presently seen by the tougher colliers as decadent. They had accomplished many things, they had escaped the legal stranglehold which had threatened to extinguish them back in the year of Bevan's birth, and they were steadily growing, but the younger and more militant colliers— Bevan amongst them—wanted to force the pace.

The Query Club, as it was called, was one result of this. It came about as a result of endless talk and argument amongst a group of Bevan's friends, who wanted to overthrow the Conservatives and mine-owners' men, and win power on the local council, and other local bodies, for their own type of Socialism. There are three interpretations of the Query Club. One sees it as little more than a new and inspired discussion group for the enlightenment of local Socialists. Others say it developed into something quite different.

They remember the Query Club as a small-scale organization capable of concentration on a limited target, tactically fleet of foot, able to move swiftly where the trade unions lumbered. In the beginning membership was limited, but as more men were trained to influence the local authorities and trades council, they planned to develop.

Local legend has it that everyone spoke his mind. A handful of volatile Welshmen, imbued with similar ideas, but each with his own interpretation, inevitably produced moments of fierce debate. As inevitably Bevan was the dominating figure. When feeling ran high he was said to be capable of a statesmanlike calm which quickly restored the balance and then, as if to demonstrate his versatility, he would suddenly burst into rhetorical thunder with brilliant words and flashing eyes, reducing everyone to admiration. It was sometimes intense, usually enjoyable, and always they went into it with zest.

More normal routine consisted of the Query Club debating, every Sunday, the methods best calculated to bring about a change in the social life of Tredegar, agreeing upon nominees for various offices, drawing up agendas and resolutions. There was something schoolboy about some of its habits, as when they resorted to a secret sign language. Bevan wiping his forehead with his handkerchief probably meant "propose a resolution in terms of my next sentence." Evidence on the Query Club becomes very confusing, the third school seeing it not so much as a revolutionary or educational organization as a "ginger group" within the Left devised to rouse complacent trade unionists out of their lethargy.

The Welsh are an animated people. Take any bus from any village and the chances are it will brim with talk and quips and argument beside the implacable silence of a London No. 11. They pour this vitality into politics. A strong sense of community drives them to mass actions, to marching over mountains in great bodies, to singing hymns and performing at eisteddfodau. Biblical passions, politics and singing have a tendency to become inextricably mixed. Indeed it was the preachers who helped to bring the political passions of the Welsh miners into the open. The workers, protesting against their lot, looked around for intellectual weapons to justify their cause and turned to heterodox beliefs. The pressure of the working-class movement and the religious revival of the early 1900's were reciprocal forces, one helping to canalize the undisciplined energy of the other. Nonconformists had first called upon God to remedy the squalor and injustice they saw around them, and when God remained inexplicably silent had turned to men themselves, and so became a stimulus encouraging the gathering ferment. If the Query Club was one tiny fragment of these great social forces it lacked none of the vitality of its parents.

*　　　*　　　*

By 1922 Bevan's industrial activities, his battles in local elections, the Miners' Lodge and Federation suddenly crystallized dramatically. He entered the lists for the Tredegar Urban District Council and won. To the embarrassment of the Conservatives, the mine owners' men and the directors of the Tredegar Iron & Coal Co., the agitator, the black-listed collier, the erstwhile unemployed man, sat cheek by jowl with traditional councillors, fired by an audacity quite alien to them. For the first time he met what he described as "the bourgeoisie" in debate.

Ebullient, explosive, with a gift of tongues liable to carry him into outrageous statement, a brain which worked at enormous speed and no particular concern for the normal conventions, he must have seemed the devil incarnate. He was still gauche. He was still subject to bursts of overwhelming passion. His clothes were the work-a-day garments of his friends and family, his views revolutionary, but he was a brilliant debater.

'I started my political life with no clearly formed personal ambition as to what I wanted to be, or where I wanted to go. I leave that nonsense to the writers of romantic biographies. A young miner in a South Wales colliery, my concern was with the one practical question, where does power lie within this particular state of Great Britain and how can it be attained by the workers?'

He had found his first foothold. He won several battles on the Council. There was the battle of waste collecting when he demonstrated that no more extravagant way of collecting waste could be devised than the existing contract system. There were hospital committees, library committees and institute meetings, but local memory has a tendency to preserve the picturesque and when one talks to the people of Tredegar they usually recall the battle of the waste. Or they tell you of a sweeping generalization which Bevan delivered to the Council, followed by 'It's up to you to disprove it.' Or of moments of explosion with chin out-thrust, eyes blazing, indignation at the lot of his fellows overwhelming him. Or they describe how, some years later, he challenged and in one sense vanquished a local newspaper. In the end a local paper was banned from the Workmen's Library for alleged unfairness in its reporting. It was the beginning of a long feud against the Press which he finally described as the most prostituted in the world.

For the moment his reputation grew alongside notoriety. The name Aneurin Bevan became familiar in the great conferences of the South Wales Miners' Federation, was bandied in pubs and mine-workings, and repeated with horror by those convinced that his talk would lead to revolution. He was now a big figure in some parts of South Wales. Whenever he proceeded down the main street of Tredegar many people greeted him, he dispensed a word of advice here, a quip there, a greeting to everyone, and many there were who excitedly retailed the latest exploit of their brilliant young gamin threatening to shake the portals of a society far wider and more formidable than those of Tredegar. Many remember his councillor days warmly. 'Always working for us he was mun. . . . Always ready to fight for us, see. . . . Generous to a fault. . . .' Popularity grew with success.

Already Aneurin Bevan had fulfilled many rôles. He had agitated and organized strike action, taken a Council of Labour Colleges class which became highly distinctive, stimulated combine lodges, reached the local council, and was about to perform the rôle of Miners' Disputes Agent, brilliantly.

Throughout the country men who had shared his two years at the Labour College were playing similar if less spectacular parts. Trade union leaders were fighting desperate battles to reach the House of Commons, local councillors who began life as mill-hands were now nominated as Labour Party candidates, and many miners converging on Westminster. Already the names of some of these men were familiar to newspaper readers, but there was one person deeply involved in the silent ferment who was still unknown, who never went to the Labour College, who did not yet know Wales or London and certainly had never heard of the Query Club; a person destined to play a very considerable part in the Labour Party and Bevan's life.

5

NOBODY took any particular notice of the Scots girl standing outside Pringle's Picture Palace, Edinburgh, that dank Sunday evening, but she felt herself the cynosure of all eyes, and while she waited for the crowds to gather, she indulged a very unflattering piece of self-analysis. . . . What manner of "revolutionary" was this, dismayed by the thought of peddling a little literature at the kerbside, intimidated almost to tears by nothing more than a few hundred people made after much the same fashion as herself.[1]

Ten minutes before, other news-vendors standing around Pringle's Picture house had come to life and gone into action with their wares. The drab frontage broke into a brisk market place. It was definitely her turn now. At first it came out in a pale whisper which nobody heard. Then the whisper took on sub-stance, and at last to cover her nervousness completely she was shouting with unnecessary vigour, 'Rebel Student twopence! Rebel Student twopence!'

Miss Lee, still in her teens, did some good business that day. It was her first effort at selling Socialist newspapers and it was the result of a small crisis in the life of the fledgling paper Rebel Student, started to back Bertrand Russell, then nominated as Labour candidate for the Edinburgh rectorial elections. The students thought the paper a fine job, but the sales did not meet the printer's bill, and they sallied out into the byways and high-ways to beguile the citizens of Edinburgh into risking twopence on an unknown, doubtfully produced but very forthright news-sheet. In the end Jennie met with success. So did others. But while she gave her leisure time to riding this small crisis in a long forgotten corner of the Socialist movement, she tended to neglect her own personal and far more pressing troubles which threatened to bring her university career down in confusion.

Also the child of a miner, Jennie was born in the village of Cowdenbeath, Scotland, a straggling, haphazard place with all the characteristic scars and pit heaps inseparable from the mining

[1] *This Great Journey*—Jennie Lee.

industry. She was born in a two-roomed cottage which still stands today and she has recalled the bleak routine of those small years when the alarm clock rang at four in the morning, her father went off before five and her mother began the elaborate business of washing and dressing her babies. The daughter of a Scottish woman known as Grandmother Greig, she had no sooner finished putting the children right for the day than she had to hurry round to the restaurant-cum-hotel run by her grandmother, and start a hard day's work to help meet the appalling costs of rearing a family. Even when Mr. Lee put an end to this by insisting that they must live on his wages and nothing else, Grandmother Greig still brought the hotel linen round for her daughter to wash.

The strong tides of the early 1900's quickly reached the straggling village of Cowdenbeath, swept away the ancient hotel and forced Grandmother Greig to rent a brick structure set above the new Arcade. Cowdenbeath changed rapidly in these years and with it Jennie's childhood changed too. She saw the new tramway line run between Cowdenbeath and Dunfermline, watched the old familiar buildings come down and new ones go up, saw the village lose its local intimacy and develop the impersonal cohesion of a compact town. A vivid jumble of impressions poured in on her, and most of them went home deeply. She fell in love at five and was carried round on her lover's shoulder until one day he forgot to wave to her from the tram and a black pit opened and her whole world was swallowed up.

Then the Lee family moved from the but and ben into Grandmother Greig's hotel, and when Mr. Greig died took over the hotel in their own name. They paid rent to one of Mrs. Greig's brothers, but the promise of a new and more spacious way of life was not fulfilled. Alas, Mr. Lee had in him a puritan streak which wasn't calculated to warm the cockles of every traveller's heart. He kept the hotel dry. Instead of a drink he tended to offer visitors a copy of *Merrie England* or *Britain for the British*. Whisky in those days still sold better than Socialism and not all Mr. Lee's vibrant analysis of social evils could convert a thirsty traveller into a disciple of Blatchford. Not that he attempted to proselytize, not that he was pious or even, within the strict meaning of the word, an agitator, but a man who had started work at twelve in the mines and had seen the harsh things which happened in the life of Cowdenbeath could never quite forget that something was badly wrong with the society surrounding him.

While her father clamoured for practical action to relieve the poverty of Cowdenbeath, dispensed his copies of *Merrie England* and took a vigorous part in the local I.L.P., Jennie grew into a dark, wilful child totally unlike her gentle, retiring brother. She began reading very early and lost her identity with each new book. She put herself into the shoes of each new character, so that one moment she was tall and fine and haughty as the Count of Monte Cristo, and the next a swashbuckling tough, bursting into the saloons of the far north, word perfect from Jack London. There were other books, too, of a very different character, in Mr. Lee's small library, books like *Das Kapital*, Ingersoll's *Lectures and Essays* and *The Science History of the Universe*. Jennie read a passage or two, turned to her father for guidance and heard for the first time about strikes and lock-outs, without really registering what it all meant.

Very soon the Lee family had reason to be interested in these things once more, if they ever lost interest. Before Jennie was eight her mother found it tried even her remarkable powers to cope with running an hotel and rearing a family with no one to help. There was no sudden financial crash, no spectacular ejection from the hotel; it simply became too much of a burden and Mr. Lee preferred to go back to the life of the pits and live in a small house again rather than suffer the constant strain and dubious benefits of Grandmother Greig's legacy where the bills always tended to outrun income and it was a struggle to find the rent. It did not mean that they were suddenly stricken with poverty, nor were they poor by Cowdenbeath standards, but they were now forced once again to think of everything in terms of so many hours in the mines, and when Jennie's younger brother lost a boot in the burn one day it was a question of two days' work in the pit thrown away—a quite considerable economic crisis. They did not starve at any point, they were on the whole better fed than most children in the district, but every penny had to serve a set purpose.

It was one of her schoolmates in the elementary school who first set Jennie wondering about the peculiar dispensation under which the people of Cowdenbeath lived. She compared presents one Christmas with a meek little girl who never made much impression on anybody and invariably came bottom or nearly

55

bottom in class. The girl listened wide-eyed to the long recital of Jennie's presents and then told the story of her own. She had a penny, an orange and a handkerchief. That was all. It shocked Jennie. Then she made another discovery. There were other children without even the penny, the orange or the handkerchief, and that appalled her. She went thoughtfully to her father. She told him what she had seen and asked what it could mean, and then for the first time he launched into a long description of the forces which he considered kept the working man's life at such a low ebb in Cowdenbeath, for the first time he used terms like Capitalism and Socialism, and gradually becoming excited built up to '. . . There will have to be a Revolution soon. . . .' Jennie went solemnly away. Something sinister had touched the sweet security of her world. She saw a new significance in homes so much poorer than her own, in children who came to school in evil-smelling rags and men squatting idle in the streets.

The year 1914 and the First World War broke into far more lives than was at once evident, and for all her youth it influenced Jennie's deeply. Her parents were against the war and their attitude embarrassed her. All the children at school, all the mistresses, were filled with patriotic fervour and Jennie blushed for her parents' ignorance. Then she went one evening to an I.L.P. meeting and heard the talk of flags and valour and glorious death on the battlefield vehemently described in unromantic terms. The same week her history lessons dealt with the persecuted Covenanters who went into the hills to hold their meetings when torture drove them out of the towns. The I.L.P. meetings were held, by force of circumstance, away from the towns too, their members suffered the modern equivalent of the Covenanters' persecution and under the romantic spell of history Jennie came to see their gatherings in similar terms. It did not last long. Romance could not easily survive the harsh realities of Cowdenbeath.

Things moved swiftly after that, carrying her away from the mining town and the rickety hotel, on towards Edinburgh and University. There were more daring meetings of the I.L.P., preaching its anti-war propaganda at the very gates of military camps, with David Kirkwood speaking, and Jennie's father in the chair, until the soldiers arrived and threatened to throw them out. There were great battles between Jennie's grandfather, the Disputes Agent for the Fife Miners' Union, standing firmly against the war, and the rest of the miners' representatives all

belligerently pro-war. There were exciting week-ends when
I.L.P. propagandists stayed at the Lees' home bringing strange
new ways and talk into the set routine, when fascinating foreign
names like Neitzsche, Hegel and Marx were bandied about. And
then the discovery of Mr. Garvie, the blind bookseller, and Dick
Wallhead, the hard-bitten I.L.P. member and reading with him
the many volumes of *The Story of the Working Class*, bought
communally by the Cowdenbeath Socialists and kept in Mr.
Garvie's back-shop.

Through all this Jennie went steadily on with her elementary
schooling and became more and more imbued with the spirit of
Socialism, until she had little leisure left for anything else. The
Sunday school was a Socialist affair, Sunday evening usually
meant a public meeting, twice a week she collected I.L.P. dues
and on Saturday, one or other of the travelling agents came to
stay. By the time she was fifteen, Jennie decided that she did not
want to leave school. The thought of spending the rest of her
days typing, or selling stockings behind a counter, appalled her,
and that placed her parents in an awkward predicament. They
were more than prepared to give her every chance, to keep her at
school as long as possible, but where would the money come
from? The school examination results followed and the exciting
news reached the Lee family that Jennie had won first place in her
class. That decided Mrs. Lee. At any cost Jennie must go on. For
the next year the family cherished every halfpenny, forwent every
small luxury and carefully adjusted its whole way of life to leave
the door open for Jennie. The following year she sat for another
examination and this time came through rather lamely. The
reason was not far to find. Socialism had made more and more
inroads on her time and when she should have been studying she
was either collecting I.L.P. dues or lost in argument about God,
the Universe or Bob Smillie.

The time rapidly arrived when she had to make a choice. It was
a matter of Engels or examinations. No parental pressure was
brought to bear, but remorse suddenly overtook Miss Lee and
she swore that she would abandon this haphazard way of living
and concentrate on getting to university. She carried out the vow
with a determination which nearly broke her health. Night after
night she came back from a hard day at school, ate hurriedly and
buried herself in her books. No more reading of novels, no more
idle gossip, every argument which threatened to extend itself cut

short. In the end she took first place in the school and then, quite suddenly, a few days after the examination, collapsed.

It turned out to be nothing very serious but the warning was enough, and she determined not to overdo things in her first year at university. It did not prevent her distinguishing herself again. She collected a first in all the subjects she took except—paradoxically—economic history. In psychology she amassed a wonderful array of technical knowledge, and came through once again with flying colours, but she still had a tendency to be baffled by the presence of prostitutes on the street.

Then the crisis year arrived, the year of Bertrand Russell's nomination as rectorial candidate, the birth of the *Rebel Student* and the disturbing evening outside Pringle's Palace, selling Socialist literature to an audience which was far more interested in the explosive possibilities of the great Communist meeting which really brought them to Pringle's. Miss Lee's private circumstances were depressing enough. Her total living expenses were now 30s. a week, and that meant a main meal of soup and plum duff price 8d., or alternatively just plain meat roll price 4d. Her room cost 14s. a week. An occasional cinema, papers, fares and stores to provide breakfast and supper, ran away with the rest. Thirty shillings a week. . . .[1] It was not a lot of money but it put a heavy strain on the finances of the Lee family and in the *Rebel Student* period she was trying to face up to the fact that things were going badly at home, and for the first time wondered whether her university career might not come to an abrupt end.

Once again she was faced with an old situation in a new guise. Once again it was a choice between schooling or Socialism. Of course, in the long run, one would condition what she did with the other, but for the moment she underwent a Chekovian struggle with herself, and the realization that intrinsically it was not of cosmic consequence did not make the decision any easier. In the end came another burst of swotting. Somehow she must win a second scholarship.

The next few months were one long concentrated cram which took full advantage of a naive education system permitting anyone to fill himself to bursting point with the requisite facts, spill them out again on examination papers and collect yet another academic laurel. The result this time was a £100 prize in Roman Law and

[1] *This Great Journey*—Jennie Lee.

Constitutional History and Law. For the moment, the threat to her university career receded.

Life now divided itself between Edinburgh and Fife where her parents had just removed, and a curious inversion arose. Here was the university, all high, fine learning, and there was Fife, a bleak, dim mining centre. One should have offered intellectual excitements, the other a sluggish background, but it was just the reverse. The dreary formula of swotting and examinations which produced for the reasonably intelligent the requisite certificate at the right time, never seemed to trouble itself with the big questions about the social scene which were always at the back of Jennie's mind. It kept the shutters carefully down between school and society, but when term was over and Jenny went back home, here was a socialist movement asking questions which seemed to her challenging, about the events of the day, and sometimes far better informed than the university students themselves. Paradoxically it was a dull business going back to university.

For nearly five years this routine went on and Jennie Lee accumulated an M.A. degree, a diploma in education, a teacher's certificate and—"final flourish"—an LL.B., but for most of the students, Edinburgh University was not a place to add academic flourishes to one's name. Degrees meant the difference between drudgery and happiness, between a soulless mechanical job and individuality.

In 1924 she had her first taste of addressing a public meeting beyond her own locality. She was booked one day to speak at a mining village near Edinburgh, and the prospect alarmed her. Still a slip of a girl with a quick flood of words, a quicker mind and an impatience with the more solid social conventions, she was lamentably lacking in that grim earnestness which Scotland expected of its female reformers. She had a round face, a snub nose and tousled hair. Individually they were attractive enough features, but taken together they made her look even younger than her nineteen years, and when she arrived at the straggling wayside station on the day of the meeting she quickly singled out a rather forbidding collier and realized, with a tremor, that this was her man. His eyes saw and passed over her, combing the crowd. When the platform was almost empty she decided it was time to come out of her shell. She walked firmly up to him and announced her identity. He took one look down at the girl

beneath him and before he could stop it snorted, "Great God!..."
This was the person to crown a week's careful organization, to
control a "tough mass" meeting, to persuade people who might be
her grandparents that Socialism was a fine, dignified, inevitable
thing. The two words said a great deal more than that. They held
a whole range of hidden meaning and Jennie was not slow to
discover it.

By the time she reached the hall her mind was blank, she was
scared, and her panic-stricken impresario seemed somewhat
distant. Then a blaze of people, a great blur of faces and her name
announced. . . . 'Somehow I staggered through. When I sat
down I had not the faintest idea of what I had said. I wanted
only to escape.' For a fraction of a second she waited for somebody to whistle derisively, or laugh, or indulge plain unmiti-
gated ribaldry. Nobody did. The clapping began and continued.

For many years afterwards the words "Great God" came up
at the back of her mind whenever she was speaking in public and
had the effect of producing prematurely elderly ways in the young
girl, fresh from university. She must conceal her youth at any
cost. It was some time before men realized that the sight of a pretty
girl on the platform brought a quite new verve into the dour ways
of Scottish politics. The most puritanical audience had its baser
moments.

With her university career coming to an end, and a new
restlessness pulling at tautly strung nerves, the outer world
suddenly threw a bombshell into the social scene which had no
precedent in the whole of British history. It very nearly realized
the dream of the French syndicalists, and it came as close to
revolution as anything Britain had known, yet it was largely
spontaneous, and if its involuntary leaders had not been overtaken
with awe at the mighty thing they had conjured up, it might have
reached a different resolution.

The General Strike of May 1926 began when the owners
demanded wage cuts for the miners and increased working hours.
The subsidy granted by the Government in 1925 was exhausted,
the coal industry unable to stand on its own feet, and the owners
confident that their case against the miners was sound. But the
miners, faced with still further cuts in a meagre standard of living,
did not hesitate to accept the challenge, and what should have
remained a local dispute suddenly assumed quite different
proportions. They consulted the General Council of the Trades

Union Congress, they issued the slogan—"not a penny off the pay, not a minute on the day," and on Saturday, 1 May, came a dramatic meeting of all trade union representatives. The General Council asked for a mandate to strike and the answer came back overwhelmingly, 3,653,529 for and 49,911 against, with 319,000 "awaiting instruction." A great wave of cheering swept across the conference hall as the voting was made known. Ramsay MacDonald joined a vibrant rendering of the "Red Flag," and Ernest Bevin, with his infallible touch for the lofty moment said. . . . 'We look upon your "yes" as meaning that you have placed your all upon the altar for this great movement, and, having placed it there, even if every penny goes, if every asset goes, history will ultimately write up that it was a magnificent generation that was prepared to do it rather than see the miners driven down like slaves. . . .'

So at midnight on Monday, 3 May, a hush descended on the great industries and services of Britain such as this country had never known before, and people woke in the morning to a strangely silent world. They waited for the morning papers which did not come, went out to catch the trains and found the tracks silent, looked in vain for the usual fleet of buses, and finally, if they were not directly involved in the strike, walked to their jobs, or hitch-hiked or gave it up and stayed at home. Heated debates broke out spontaneously at street corners. Young girls put on roller skates and made their way to work, flocks of bicycles appeared on the streets, some carrying sedate civil servants to Whitehall, one mounted by a Cabinet Minister. University students offered to run the trains, strike pickets invaded stations in ominous silence, there were great mass meetings, slogans were repeated and taken up by the crowds, minor clashes developed between strikers and police, and the B.B.C. broadcast reassuring messages with cathedral calm, until Mr. Stanley Baldwin saw fit to address the nation in something resembling outworn rhetoric.

Perhaps the sheer totality of the strike—as if a master switch had been thrown and the country's lifeblood checked—awed the men who controlled it; perhaps fear of Government action with troops and police intimidated them; perhaps the lack of a completely co-ordinated plan which left the local strike committees without effective orders once the die was cast, made them apprehensive of the whole thing getting out of hand and running into who knew what excesses; perhaps fundamentally the leaders

61

had not faced up to the fact, if indeed they saw it, that a general strike was tantamount to revolution. Whatever the cause, the first fine boldness of the General Council began to wilt within a few days, and within a week the leaders were already casting around for some way out of the stupendous impasse which they had themselves created. Not so with the rank and file of the workers. As the sweeping success of the strike became known, enthusiasm mounted, non-union members joined hands with the faithful, and meeting after meeting threw its cap in the air.

Away in Edinburgh, the battle had set Jennie Lee seething with excitement. She hurried down to the local trade union head-quarters and demanded some part in the strike however small. She was given the job of receiving and issuing orders for strike bulletins, and for the next few days helped to keep Edinburgh informed of what was happening in the outside world. There were many stormy meetings in the town, a few buses and trams driven by blacklegs were overturned, police broke up mass pickets and by the third day copies of a national daily with the headline 'Pistol at the Nation's Head' were publicly burned in Edinburgh, and some idea of what the strike was all about had permeated down to the surprisingly large number of politically neutral people who did no more than glance at the headlines.

In Tredegar the scene was equally tense. Bevan, elected a delegate to the national conferences, had supported Arthur Cook and Arthur Horner, and then rushed back to his own valley to take charge. The Councils of Action were highly organized in Tredegar, and it appears that Bevan aimed at complete "control" of Tredegar without violence and virtually achieved it. Away in another valley it was different. Things ran out of hand and there was fighting.

For nine days the strike ran on. For nine days British industry was at a standstill, and the world waited, wondering whether Britain was about to experience the first stages of a revolution which must in the end be bloody, or whether once again its genius for pacific resolution of the most passionate struggles would prevail. Then came news which startled the rank and file of the unions and shocked the local leaders. The strike was off. At its strongest moment, when the workers stood solidly behind the General Council and there was little sign of wavering, a mysterious edict came out of London announcing unconditional surrender.

A wave of bewilderment ran through the miners. In Fife they said their leaders had run away, in Tredegar some put it more forcibly. This to them was the final symptom of trade union emasculation, but there were sections of the workers who saw it differently. They had no stomach for a prolonged battle on this scale with the whole community paralysed, they were glad to come to terms, and the community for its part had long ago settled down to half-comic acceptance of the privations which the strike produced. Now, one section shrugged its shoulders and returned to conventional habits with something resembling a sigh, and another felt a flood of relief that the intangible threat of violence waiting in the background had at last dissolved.

For the miners it was different, and Bevan himself had very personal reasons for bitterness in 1926. The year before, his father had choked to death in his arms from the disease pneumoconiosis which cements up the lungs with coal dust until breathing becomes impossible. It is a horrible death to die. No one who has witnessed it ever forgets it. He was buried in the hill-top cemetery, Cen Golen—the hill of light—on the outskirts of Tredegar. 'No compensation was paid him by the mine owners; in those days it was not scheduled as an industrial disease under the Workmen's Compensation Acts,' Bevan said.

For Bevan it was typical of an indifference only relieved by spectacular upheavals like the General Strike. 'While the miners were striking in 1926,' Bevan wrote (*In Place of Fear*), 'a great many people were moved to listen to their case. Certain high ecclesiastical dignitaries even went so far as to offer to mediate between the mine owners and the miners. . . . For years these conditions continued. But were those high Church dignitaries moved to intervene then? Not at all. For them the problem was solved. It had never consisted in the suffering of the miners, but in the fact that the miners were still able to struggle and therefore create a problem for the rest of the community. The problem was not their suffering but their struggle. Silent pain evokes no response. . . .'

The rites of surrender in the General Strike were attended in London with what the miners regarded as something close to humiliation. How otherwise could it be, they said, when the leaders of an "unbroken army" were asked to admit defeat, and defeat without reserve or condition. The delegates of the General Council were kept waiting at Downing Street until Mr. Baldwin had appraised their real intentions. Then he refused to make any promises or concessions, but brusquely dismissed the Council with '. . . Now, Mr. Pugh, we have both of us got a great deal to do and a great deal of anxious and difficult work, and I think that the sooner you get to your work and I get to mine the better. . . .'

Obediently, as the master switch was thrown again, millions of workers poured back into their accustomed places, and vitality returned to all except one industry. The miners fought on alone. They had refused to accept the General Council's ruling, they had rejected point blank the owners' terms, and they were prepared to continue the battle when the community rose to condemn them. Editorial after editorial spoke of this deliberate attempt to embitter industrial relations and commentators produced sonorous indictments filling many columns.

Jennie Lee saw the strike collapse in Edinburgh and heard that the miners of Fife were holding out. She longed to break away from her university backwater and return to Fife, but big things were toward in the university and she had to fret and fume and glean what news she could from letters and local papers. Then in June term ended and she was back again. Fully qualified to find work at last, she found that Socialism exercised far more pressing claims and plunged into the strike battle, addressing one meeting after another, writing and distributing handbills, rushing from corner to corner of the coalfield 'wherever morale needed stiffening.'

It was a grim struggle which dragged on for months and led to great bitterness between the miners and the General Council of the T.U.C. A. J. Cook, Secretary of the Miners' Federation of Great Britain, wrote, 'It is quite evident that some of the T.U.C. were afraid of the power they had created; were anxious to keep friends with the Government, and not to harm the employing class. . . .'

There were other interpretations of the General Strike, but wherever the final responsibility for surrender lay, and whatever the difference between political manœuvring and constitutional caution, the miners fought on with a dourness and determination which surprised the Government fresh from its victory and very sure of its powers. Week succeeded week and still the miners showed no sign of wavering. In November, six months after the General Strike collapsed, the majority of the miners were still out. But the end was near. Plain starvation threatened some families.

The miners began drifting back, first in their scores and then in their hundreds, but the Communists, with their great gift for ignoring the inevitable, said that no revolutionary party could face such a defeat and the strike must go on. A few weeks later, when thousands were returning to work and the issue arose whether they should continue negotiations or break off and tell the owners and the Government to do their worst, Bevan told a miners' conference at the Kingsway Hall in London. . . . 'You have heard from district officials of district organizations of the Miners' Federation that there will be disintegration. . . . I come from strong men; my own men could stand until Christmas, but what is the use of arguing like that when this organization, as a whole, is hopeless and will smash our weak areas. There are areas in South Wales, and friend Horner knows it very well, there are areas where the poor law relief is stopped, and therefore what is the use of talking about an army when it is a paper one. It is no use disguising it. I am going to suggest that if I thought there was a possibility of augmenting our negotiating power with a further struggle, I would vote for it and fight for it. . . .' Instead he suggested that they should '. . . continue the negotiations in order to elicit what exactly are these national principles so that you can focus attention against the Government.'

When he was walking away from the meeting with Sydney Jones, an old friend of Bevan's, Sydney said . . . 'A damn fine speech Aneurin. . . .'

'You think so. . . .'

'Yes—but I wonder what you would have said if you had been on the other side.'

Later Bevan commented to me on those days. It ran something like this: We were facing chaos. We were encouraging a renaissance of company unions, of Spencerism, and if that had got a firm grip it would have taken generations to break it down again. There is always this dichotomy in Communist thinking. . . . For them a pedantic theory must work out word perfect in practice. It never will. And in his book *In Place of Fear*. . . . 'The defeat of the miners ended a phase, and from then on the pendulum swung sharply to political action. It seemed to us that we must try to regain in Parliament what we had lost on the industrial battlefield.'

Back in 1926 they were still far too close to see the situation clearly, but whatever Bevan or Horner or the miners said, the general feeling that the game was up grew rapidly in the later weeks of November. Six months before, when the miners were first left to fight alone, the Government put out a statement which began . . . 'His Majesty's Government have no power to compel employers to take back every man who has been on strike,' but vague promises of no victimization were made and now, as the miners' strike in turn collapsed, the same phrases were repeated.

Miss Lee's father was one who suffered after the strike. Mr. Lee was a fireman, and firemen were then in an ambivalent position in the coal mining industry. Whenever a strike broke out they were expected by the union to carry on their safety measures against gas and flooding, even though they were staunch trade unionists. Mr. Lee accordingly turned up at the pits in the early stages of the strike only to find that what was known as "blackleg labour" had taken part possession. He consulted two other safety men in his pit and they decided that they could not work alongside blackleg labour. They thereupon left to join the strikers.

When the strike collapsed Mr. Lee was at once singled out, and sacked. The manager said he wanted "reliable" men as safety men, from his point of view a vital necessity. Some months later Mr. Lee was offered a job in his old pit as a casual labourer and took it. Never particularly strong, his muscles had been softened by years of comparatively sedentary work as a safety man, and presently when he came home in the evenings, after a day's straight labouring, he was a broken man, hardly able to eat for tiredness and craving only bed and sleep. His wife and daughter watched the transformation with deep misgiving.

The year 1927 left a trail of disillusion and despair over the coalfields of Britain and brought great hardship to many miners, among them the Lee family. Jennie's father was finally blacklisted in the pits, and her brother had emigrated to Australia, which left the family dependent on Jennie's earnings as a teacher. In the early days of 1927 she had become a school-teacher in one of those grey buildings called elementary schools which are so easily mistaken for barracks. She took a class of forty-five children, all huddled together in one room. They were noisy, restless, underfed children, and from nine in the morning until four in the afternoon she struggled to keep some semblance of discipline and some show of interest, knowing that a family now depended on her success. It would have been easier in different surroundings. If the window had framed a view different from the coal dumps, if the walls had not been pale green with streaks of damp, if the heating arrangements had not left half the children cold and the children themselves had been better clad, she might have doubted the decision growing at the back of her mind. As it was, after six weeks in the job there were no doubts left. This was not her way of life.

These were days of reaction from the battles of 1926, days when the people of Fife had to find the money for food bought on credit in the lock-out and rent arrears allowed to accumulate under the stress of battle. All the old defiance was dead. Nothing seemed to move very much any more. The pits were sluggish, the shops poorly provisioned, men and women listless, and mothers for ever counting a small hoard of shillings to see whether another pound of potatoes could be squeezed into the weekly budget. The growing hopelessness drove scores of young men away from their homes to the South of England or the Dominions or America; anywhere where this grey blight which had settled on Fife did not sap your strength. Jennie lost her brother in the tide of emigration and the house seemed oddly silent afterwards. Women she had once known as vivacious young girls, she now came upon as sluts, forced into squalid habits because a brood of children could not be supported by an unemployed father. The inevitability of the transformation was the tragic thing. There was no gainsaying the compulsions of poverty.

She continued to plunge into political meetings, to carry Socialist propaganda into many new corners of Fifeshire. She knew now, with far greater certainty, that she was more at home on the platform than in the classroom, and if, in those days, she was still feeling her way towards a style which left the fire in her words and removed the ranting, the sheer freshness of her approach set off a spark in one audience after another.

In the beginning she prepared everything she said. She would carefully write out speech after speech with all the facts, wit and wisdom proportionately distilled—but it never worked that way. Once she confronted a crowd from the platform, all the manufactured phrases broke down and a flood of spontaneous words swallowed up the written speech. There were moments when she muffed a phrase or fumbled for a word. They steadily decreased as her reputation grew. In some places she was instantaneously successful, in others they took time to accept a young and pretty woman scathingly attacking full-grown men. It was not quite decent. Traditional Scotland expected its young women to be demurely domestic.

Her first big sensation came at the I.L.P. Conference in 1927. Under Maxton's chairmanship the I.L.P. had now become aggressively proletarian and socialist, its middle-class leaders were resigning or disappearing one by one, and in 1927 it was Ramsay MacDonald's turn.

A quick storm blew up inside the I.L.P. They did not insist on MacDonald's resignation, but they refused to send him as a delegate to the Labour Party Conference of 1927. This led to a bitter debate at the I.L.P. Conference in the same year. Emanuel Shinwell moved the rejection of the whole idea, in his most trenchant, downright manner, and then as Fenner Brockway put it, 'a young, dark girl took the rostrum, a puckish figure, with a mop of thick black hair thrown impudently aside, brown eyes flashing, body and arms moving in rapid gestures, words pouring from her mouth in Scottish accent and vigorous phrases, sometimes with a sarcasm which equalled Shinwell's. It was Jennie Lee making her first speech at an I.L.P. Conference. And what a speech it was! Shinwell was regarded as a Goliath in debate, but he met his match in this girl David. . . .'

When Fenner Brockway himself followed and read extracts from a letter written by Ramsay MacDonald in which MacDonald said he preferred not to be an I.L.P. delegate in view of differences within the Party, the day was won; opposition melted away. Maxton concluded by saying that 'the Movement knew and needed no giants.' But it wasn't Maxton's words, or Brockway's adroit handling of the situation, or Ramsay MacDonald's defeat, which remained in the minds of many delegates; it was a picture of the Scots girl with the flashing eyes and burning words.

By the early part of 1929 Jennie Lee was an established figure in the Scottish Socialist movement and the I.L.P., but for all the high recognition she had won and the academic learning she brought into the lowly places of Socialism, she was quite unprepared for something which happened the following July, and seemed like someone offering the moon.

A telegram came one day. Mrs. Lee opened it, saw nothing startling in what it said, and when her daughter arrived home

from school remarked casually—'Oh, there's a telegram for you.'
Jennie read the telegram and a look of incredulity, which her
mother quickly interpreted wrongly, spread over her face. Mrs.
Lee took the telegram again. 'Why,' she said at last, 'it's not
serious is it?' The telegram said: 'Labour Movement in Shotts
desires to nominate you for Parliamentary candidature of North
Lanark under I.L.P. auspices. . . .'[1]

[1] *This Great Journey*—Jennie Lee.

6

ANEURIN BEVAN and Jennie Lee both came from mining communities, and both brought something fresh and startling into the traditional ways of the House of Commons.

They became back-benchers of that ill-starred, timid, sadly misunderstood Labour Government which took office grandly enough in 1929, and reached out to reshape a social scene which dissolved under its hand. What might have happened if the financiers and industrialists had not convinced Philip Snowden and Ramsay MacDonald that the country was on the brink of an economic precipice, if the Labour Party had not relied upon the Liberals for their majority in the House, and a truculent House of Lords had not made things difficult for every piece of Labour legislation, it is idle to speculate. Beyond this there remained a bigger trouble still, a veritable thunderbolt.

When the Labour Party came to power the signs and portents were healthy enough. The American boom was still blustering along and if unemployment was high in Britain there seemed every prospect of getting it under control. Within a few short months the thunderbolt struck. The great Wall Street crash of 1929 hit millions of people in half a dozen countries and before its force was spent, threatened to topple the remote towers of the trusts and cartels themselves. In its wake a tide of despair and disorganization overran the world and protestations that economics were made to serve not bedevil mankind were lost in wailing and lamentation which seemed far more ready to believe that hidden forces would always erupt to defeat the ends of man whatever we did. One of the most bewildered figures stood out by reason of his handsomeness. There was no doubting the fine presence of Ramsay MacDonald as there was no doubting the programme of the Labour Party, but the programme had been conceived in times of comparative calm when opportunity abounded, and now, when it was three parts dead, there was no one swift or imaginative enough to shift the course of Socialism round another point, along a second and less suicidal track. No one that is, amongst the leaders. Amongst the rank and file there were at least two rebels who lost no time in bringing guns to bear.

Jennie Lee had been elected to the House of Commons twice for the North Lanark Division in one year. First the death of the Tory member in February 1929 precipitated a by-election, and Miss Lee, already I.L.P. candidate for North Lanark, plunged into a three-cornered fight. The Conservatives concentrated forces out of proportion to the immediate importance of the Division, because they knew that a General Election was imminent and here was a testing ground for the full scale show.

A final burst of meetings, handbills and canvassing and Jennie Lee was in with a 6,578 majority. The result delighted her and sent a stir through the whole Socialist movement. If this was anything to go by, here was the writing on the political wall. In the same year a General Election burst on the country and once more Jennie was returned, one of the 287 Labour members who formed a majority with 59 Liberals, against the Conservatives and Independents 269.

The story of Aneurin Bevan ran along very different lines. In 1929 when Aneurin Bevan entered politics proper a curious situation had developed in Ebbw Vale. Its details cannot yet be revealed but inevitably there was dissatisfaction amongst some sections of the population which strongly resisted the idea of returning a comfortable effigy to the House of Commons instead of a virile M.P.

There was much speculation about possible candidates. There were natural heirs in direct line of industrial descent, powerful trade unionists, types which emerged from working-class ranks, good, solid, out-spoken people with little time for intellectual subtleties. Next in the running came Bevan, as subtle as they were straightforward, and by now involved in every kind of local activity, a tremendous figure in Tredegar with a range of jobs from Urban District Councillor to County Councillor, but still a mere youngster of thirty-two. Four names eventually emerged, Evan Davies, George Davies, Bryn Roberts and Aneurin Bevan. In the end Bevan won the day.

The election was a three-cornered fight full of contradictions. Here was Mark Brace, nephew of the great William Brace, chief Labour Adviser to the Mines Department, surprisingly standing as a Tory, and William Griffiths, a Liberal school-teacher, alongside Bevan, the self-made scholar.

71

Bevan threw his whole personality into the fight and travelled and talked himself hoarse. Sometimes he prepared rough notes of a speech, sometimes he left it to chance. A friend recalls a system of sheets of paper each page with a single word at its centre which, once remembered, brought a whole mosaic of argument to his aid. For the friend's part he could rarely decipher the word. I have tried to trace in the files of the *South Wales Argus* the exact content of these speeches, but they appear not to have been reported. As one man in Newport puts it . . . 'Mr. Bevan was never very helpful to the Press or dependent on them. He was so confident of return that there was virtually no campaign. He had a walk-over. . . .' For all that, the general impression which his speeches left remains vividly enough in the minds of the men who took part in that election; it is a pity the actual records seem to have vanished. In the end, with a poll of 20,008 Bevan had an 11,164 majority over the combined total of his opponents.

So, from opposite ends of the country, and in the same year, Jennie Lee and Aneurin Bevan came to the House of Commons. Within a few months both of them were disgusted with the behaviour of the Labour Government and within a year both were asking difficult questions. Why wasn't the Government pushing ahead with its contributory pensions scheme, what had gone wrong with Land Utilization, where was the great slum clearance scheme and the Coal Mines Bill?

Now came Bevan's maiden speech. If the speech itself, read in retrospect, has none of the inevitability of a *tour de force*, there is no questioning its power, and the manner of its delivery alone was worth recalling. But it made no concessions to the traditions of the maiden speech. It introduced controversial issues and craved no indulgences.

> . . . I would not have intervened in this Debate, as this is my first effort, were it not for the fact that we have listened to some very extraordinary speeches from the benches opposite, and I think it is necessary to point out that this is the first example of what we are to expect in the form of collusion between the Tories and the Liberals in obstructionist tactics. The Committee will have observed that there was no attempt at all on the part of Members on the benches above the Gangway opposite to express any opposition to this Resolution until the Right Hon. Member for Carnarvon Boroughs [Mr. Lloyd George] indicated his opposition to the second paragraph of the Motion. When he intimated his opposition, we immediately

observed the collusion between the two sides on the benches opposite
for the purpose of embarrassing the Government. . . .

I listened to the ex-Chancellor of the Exchequer with considerable
interest, because it was the second time I have heard him. The first
time he was in the role of the bogy man of the country, over the
wireless, and on the second occasion he was the entertainer of the
House of Commons. I arrived at the conclusion that his chameleon-
like character in politics is founded upon a temperamental disability.
He fills all the rôles with such exceeding facility that his lack of
political stability is at once explained. . . .

In the beginning, we were informed that the first time we
attempted any application of Socialist principles, our day would end.
The same warning was uttered from the Liberal benches, so that we
on this side are constrained to do what we can to solve unemployment within the limitations imposed by a Parliamentary minority.
The late Chancellor of the Exchequer says that we are bound to fail,
and that the schemes submitted are inadequate. All he can say is
that he hopes that they will succeed, because if they are not adequate
to solve unemployment, we shall, of course, have to go before the
country and say that it is impossible to solve any of these problems
within the ambit of private enterprise, and that before they can be
properly tackled, the country will have to supply Parliament with
a Socialist majority to apply Socialist principles. So that the party
which the ex-Chancellor represents, and the economic interests
which he so ably represents in this House, hope that the schemes
that will be submitted will be found adequate to solve unemployment. Otherwise, all other remedies having been tried, we shall
have to ask the country for a mandate to apply Socialist principles. . . .

The speech lasted fifteen minutes. From the first few phrases
Bevan had the complete attention of the House. Once he attacked
Churchill and Churchill against all precedent interrupted a
maiden speech. Once he seemed on the verge of stuttering into
silence, recovered and pressed on. There followed a third unique
break with tradition when the following speaker failed to
congratulate Bevan and made no references to 'the pleasure of
hearing more from the Hon. Member.' It was an ominous
introduction to the House. The story that Lloyd George afterwards said: 'A future Prime Minister,' Lady Megan Lloyd George
denies.

Bevan has since described his own reactions. His first impression
was of entering a church. 'The vaulted roofs and stained glass
windows, the rows of statues of great statesmen of the past, the
echoing halls, the soft-footed attendants and the whispered

conversation, contrast depressingly with the crowded meetings, and the clang and clash of opinions he has just left behind in his election campaign. Here he is, a tribune of the people, coming to make his voice heard in the seats of power. Instead, it seems he is expected to worship; and the most conservative of all religions —ancestor worship. . . .' And after his maiden speech. . . . 'The new Member crawls out of the House with feelings of deep relief at having got it over, mingled with a paralysing sense of frustration. The stone he thought he had thrown turned out to be a sponge. . . .' [1]

He complained that the classic Parliamentary style was understatement, a style calculated to blur 'the deep antagonisms which exist in society,' but he made no attempt to follow it himself.

With his next speeches the House began to realize the audacious —even outrageous—method this newcomer from the pits proposed employing. One newspaper recorded. . . . 'The House watched with amazement the speech of Mr. Aneurin Bevan last Tuesday—I say watched for it was more a spectacle than an audition. Like some great disturbance of nature . . . a storm attacking a solitary tree. . . .' Making due allowance for journalistic hyperbole there remains more than a glint of truth in it, for the magnetic personality of Aneurin Bevan moved the House with an inexplicable uneasiness that day, and as he really swung into his stride, eyes flashing, arms pumping up and down, he swept the House along with him until he leaned right over the benches and brought both arms to bear in a trenchant attack on Neville Chamberlain which sent a wave of excitement through the whole House. The sheer vitality of the man was electric. He was so uncompromisingly alive. For a moment the House had a glimpse of the spell-binder later to hold a horrible fascination for the Conservative benches as something dangerous but irresistible.

It was consistent that his third speech—the most important yet made—should not merely deal with one of the biggest questions of the day, but should single out for attack no less a person than the Attorney-General himself, a considerable forensic presence and a man more than difficult to handle in debate. The House still did not fully appreciate that this was part of a technique which Lloyd George had inherited from Randolph Churchill, nor did it yet know how formidable a champion of Socialism had come amongst them.

[1] *In Place of Fear*—Aneurin Bevan.

There were old hands who detected a tremor under the façade that day, and sometimes the stutter broke in, but the opening preambles of the speech were impressive.

I think [Bevan began], all Members of the Committee will hope that the statement which we have had from the Attorney-General is not to be the last statement on Sub-section (2) of Clause 4 [of the Unemployment Insurance Bill] from the Government this evening. I agree that, listening to the Attorney-General, anyone who did not keep his mind glued to the language of the Clause would almost have been persuaded that the Clause meant what he said it did. Unfortunately for the Attorney-General, many Members on this side and on the opposite side of the House have had a good deal of experience of the interpretation placed upon these Clauses, and I am afraid that we are not able to agree with him as to what is actually meant . . . it says that the employment shall be of an extent that the individual could reasonably have been expected to obtain. What does that mean? Supposing the individual is informed by the Exchange official that 10 men had employment in the colliery the day before. All those jobs have been obtained. It is retrospective. You are not urging an individual to go for a job that he might have if he had tried to go. You are simply punishing the individual for not knowing about the job afterwards. In other words, it is merely retributive justice. All the time that the individual is told that 10 men have got work, there are 500 on the Exchange. . . . If you really desire that the onus of proof shall be placed on the Exchange official, why not delete the Clause? If you say that the onus is placed, under the Clause, on the official, and there is any doubt at all about it, why not confirm your own intention by deleting the Clause? Because you know that this Sub-section is intended to do something else, and the Attorney-General let the thing out in all its naked horror at the beginning of his speech. He let the Committee understand that what he desired to do was to devise a Sub-section which would leave the applicant for benefit to understand that he was expected to seek out the employer. I never expected to listen in the House of Commons to a spokesman of a Labour Government making such a statement as that. In my district, this is, for me, not a matter for further juggling; it is for me a matter of the greatest possible importance, because I have attended Courts of Referees every day for the last two years, and I know what happens. I saw men in the middle of last winter having to walk 10 and 15 miles in the worst possible weather in order to convince the Courts of Referees that they were properly seeking out employers.

I want to know exactly where we stand in the matter. Do we believe that as things are now in the distressed areas a single extra man will have employment if you put the onus of proof still on the applicant to seek out the employer? If a single man more will have employment under these conditions, then it must be assumed that there is an employer who could employ a man but is not doing so. But if this society allows an employer who can employ a man not to do so, it ought to keep the idle man who has not been able to get employment. . . .

Bevan took the simple elements of the case and wove a subtle logical pattern about them. Imaginatively he followed the implications of Clause 4, Sub-section (2) into fields which destroyed half the Attorney-General's case. Some saw his attack as hopelessly machiavellian. With immense ingenuity Bevan was undermining Sub-section (2), but there was a debating adroitness in parts of his analysis. Then came this:

I hope the Committee will realise that you are not under these provisions actually finding out the man who ought to be found out at all. You are not relieving the burden upon industry. All that you are doing is trying to thrust this burden upon the shoulders of local authorities which cannot bear it. It does not matter very much about some parts of the country, where the local authorities are able to come to the assistance of the unemployed man, but it is tragic in all seriousness in the South Wales coalfield, in Durham, and in Lanarkshire. It means in those coalfields that the local authorities are not able to come to the help of the unemployed man, and it means that by depriving him of his unemployment benefit, you are literally starving him and his wife and children. While I have tried not to be sentimental, I hope that Hon. and Right Hon. Members will realize that we are again in the middle of a dreadful winter, and that the South Wales coalfield is being attacked by floods and famine. We ought to take every step in our power to ease the burdens upon these poor people and not to allow any engines of legal intricacy to try and thrust more and more burdens on the shoulders of those who are unable to bear them. I submit that this Clause does not meet the point, and I hope the Government will not ask us to go into the Lobby and support it. . . .

There was considerable applause. A thirty-two-year-old fledgling fresh from the mines had broken open the case of the Attorney-General of England. Later in the debate Mr. Ernest Winterton said, 'The speech of the Hon. Member for Ebbw Vale was devastating, and it has not been answered and, in fact, I suggest that it cannot be answered.' Mr. Winterton was right. In the end the Attorney-General had no choice in the matter. He had

76

to withdraw Sub-section (2) of Clause 4 of the Unemployment Insurance Bill, though it was later reinserted by a recalcitrant House of Lords.

Bevan had shocked the clergymen first of all, then the mine owners, and next his own people in the trade unions. The same audacity quickly led him to the leadership of a special group in the House of Commons. Men from minefields all over the country had now broken through the restraints of education and class and come to the House of Commons to represent their kind. Will Lawther, veteran of five unsuccessful Parliamentary elections, had arrived from Barnard Castle, Ebby Edwards after two abortive attempts had brought off the third and now come to represent Morpeth. They joined forces with men like Vernon Hartshorn, George Hall, Charles Edwards and Will Jenkins—all mining M.P.s—to form the miners' group in the House, a group destined to become as vociferous and truculent as the miners were in the unions. At another level, Jim Griffiths progressed towards the presidency of the South Wales Miners' Federation, Morgan Phillips had thrown tremendous energies into the West Fulham area as Party Agent and now emerged a member of the Borough Council, and Ness Edwards followed with a seat on the Gellygaer Urban District Council. The second big phase in the emergence of the miners was moving forward at all levels. In the House of Commons, within a few years, Bevan, by tacit agreement was the most striking figure in the miners' group.

Within six months he returned to the attack on Lloyd George. It was the occasion of the Coal Mines Bill in the later days of February 1930, and in this one speech Bevan shocked the susceptibilities of at least three distinguished members of the House before he turned his attention to Lloyd George

. . . The Right Hon. Gentleman the Member for Epping [Mr. Churchill] and the Right Hon. Gentleman the Member for Carnarvon Boroughs [Mr. Lloyd George], in a temporary re-alliance, which may be carried right through to the Division Lobby in their capacity as joint executioners, said on the Second Reading that the inefficient pits would have the efficient pits at a disadvantage and would be able to go along with their quotas in their hands and say to the efficient pits, 'If you are going to produce at 100 per cent. of capacity you will have to buy us out.' But exactly the same quota allocation as prevents the efficient pit from producing at 100 per cent. will stop the inefficient pit also, and, if the efficient pit is hurt

77

by it, how much more is the inefficient pit going to be hurt? . . . But it is suggested that the Statute which is going to be poison for the efficient pit is somehow or other going to be a sort of elixir of life for the inefficient pit, which will be able to hold the rest up to ransom.

Since the very beginning in this Debate we have not been having a dispassionate examination of the conditions of the industry. We have been subject merely to a desire on the part of the Right Hon. Gentleman the Member for Carnarvon Boroughs to use his Parliamentary position for the purpose of trying to put new life into the decaying corpse of Liberalism. On the Second Reading, because of his Celtic fervour, he went much further than he intended to go, and now it is impossible for him to support Part I of the Bill, otherwise he will have to eat all the words he said on the Second Reading. . . .

. . . We have a right to say that, if it means slightly dearer coal, it is better to have slightly dearer coal than cheaper colliers. Hon. Gentlemen here must face the issue that when they vote against this Bill, they are voting for lower wages for the colliers, and they are voting at the same time for an increase in the number of accidents in the collieries. . . . It is always characteristic of Liberal hypocrisy to pay lip service to these things and refuse to face the consequences that follow from them. We say that you cannot get from the already dry veins of the miners new blood to revivify the industry. Their veins are shrunken white, and we are asking you to be, for once, decent to the miners—not to pay lip service, not to say that you are very sorry for them, not to say that you are very sorry that these accidents occur, not to say that you are very sorry for the low level of wages and for the conditions of famine which have existed in the mining districts since the War, and then to use all your Parliamentary skill, all your rhetoric, in an act of pure demagogy to expose the mining community of this country to another few years of misery. . . .

It was a fine peroration. It left the House uneasy. He still had not subdued his natural rhetoric enough, he still tended to believe that the inspiration of the moment could be a substitute for prolonged study, he relied too much on vivid phrases and an emotional undertow capable of pulling people off their feet. His performance was still uneven, sometimes brilliant, sometimes bad, but the cat was now completely out of the bag. The Conservatives knew at last what they were dealing with. This man was not only clever, audacious, fearless; he was an 'unscrupulous debater,' he had vile notions that 'his own class were not one whit inferior to any other,' he attacked personalities as much as principles and there was an element of venom in his invective which boded ill for anyone who challenged him. Some protested that this young man was going too far. High spirits were all well and good, a natural gift for invective not to be despised, and one might even make allowances for a mercurial personality with a flair for words liable to run away with itself and produce havoc beyond its real intention; but there was something calculated about these attacks which left an unpleasant taste in the mouth. Or so they saw it.

Bevan has always believed that irreverence for traditional ideas is a first requisite in any "revolutionary social architect." 'All the great social builders have had this awareness of the potential bullying of tradition,' he says. 'Marx put it—the past "lies like an Alp on the human mind." And Lincoln "We must disenthrall ourselves." ' He speaks of iconoclasm, of intellectual courage or what he refers to as 'the courage of reason.' It appears that intellectual detachment is necessary for the new social principles to be seen clearly, and yet it may be impossible to attack an abstract idea effectively unless one strikes at the personification of the idea in the man.

Doubtful as this doctrine becomes outside the heat and dust of politics, there is no gainsaying its truth in the House of Commons where ideas are much more closely tied to personalities. So it came about that Bevan pitted himself against Lloyd George as well as the Coal Mines Bill and finding the method highly successful, repeated it at intervals over the next few years, audaciously choosing nothing short of the stars against which to launch his shafts, increasing their weight and ferocity until at last he reached his final peak and his final challenge in Winston Churchill. Here were two great universals closely personified— Socialism and Capitalism. Here was the final conflict.

*　　　*　　　*

While Bevan was busy winning a reputation as iconoclast, orator and spell-binder, while political correspondents were thanking whatever gods might be for the appearance of a man who put fire into his words, and old world M.P.s sighed for the days when Socialism was nothing more than an intellectual exercise, Jennie Lee was not idle. From the start she had put up a barrage of criticism against the Labour Government which proved much too accurate for the peace of mind of the front bench, and towards the summer of 1929 came a maiden speech which one member described as "attempted assassination." She spoke with all the eloquence of strong convictions, she put the plight of the people she represented forcefully, she looked, that day, volcanic.

> . . . I must confess that this dying House is not exactly a place of inspiration, and I look upon myself more as a chip of the next Parliament which has made a rather precipitate arrival than as one really belonging to the present House. . . .
> I do not think that anyone so far has disputed the figures that have been given already from these benches showing that, out of a national income of approximately £4,000,000,000, only some £1,600,000,000 is paid as wages to the workers of this country. That represents only two-fifths of the total income, and surely, a Chancellor of the Exchequer who was genuinely concerned to improve the life of the people of this country would have had a very substantial margin, in the remaining three-fifths, in which to readjust the burdens of taxation. I discover, however, that the working women of this country are given, not the substantial readjustment that they were entitled to expect, but, instead a copper thrown to them in the form of the remission of the Tea Duty, and, seemingly, some Hon. Gentlemen imagine that this paltry thing . . . is going in some way to restore their feeling of confidence in Hon. Gentlemen opposite. . . .

The speech ran on for ten minutes with steadily mounting scorn. Then came . . .

> We say to Hon. Members opposite that there is only one explanation of the Budget. . . . In the eyes of the Chancellor of the Exchequer, the people of this country are made up in this way—the great majority of them are fools, and the remaining minority knaves. That is the only possible explanation of such a Budget as has been put before us, and I can only describe it, and with it the whole policy for which the party at present in office has been responsible, as a mixture—let me choose my words deliberately—I can only describe it as a mixture of cant, corruption and incompetence.

Jennie Lee's early speeches matched Bevan's in their irreverence, but coming as they did from the rebel periphery of the I.L.P. they were taken more light-heartedly. Bevan, wearing a shred of the official Socialist mantle, was considered more outrageous and it was not long before his enemies on both sides of the House

*Aneurin Bevan
as a boy*

*His mother,
Phoebe Bevan*

Aneurin Bevan as a young man

accused him of bitter pride, of passionate hate, and only grudgingly admitted his power to cast a spell of words. Jennie Lee they accepted as the humanist, and even her opponents warmed to her. Winston Churchill himself was no exception. The then ex-Chancellor of the Exchequer was introduced to her the day after her maiden speech, and went to some pains to try to make his own point of view clear. He was, he said, as much concerned as anyone to take drabness out of people's lives, to get rid of unemployment, and he believed that he had at last found the solution to the whole sorry business. Had she read *The American Omen* by Garrett Garrett? She had not? Ah, then, she could hardly be expected to understand. . . .[1]

The following day he lent her a copy and there she read a story which she as a Socialist could not accept. It was a story of production continually increasing under a capitalist economy, of wages marching in step, and higher wages swelling the demand for goods until yet more production became necessary and anything resembling "depressed areas" disappeared. It did not impress Jennie Lee. But Churchill meant what he said. He did not like a sordid Britain any more than Jennie Lee or Aneurin Bevan. He had a deep regard amounting to reverence for tradition, his belief that men like Marlborough and the Duke of Wellington were great involved something approaching ancestor worship, and Britain's past shone with a glory undimmed by the industrial revolution; but he also believed that Britain must think of her future, a future which for him could not be cast in a worthy mould if large sections of the population were unemployed, and the threat of poverty haunted the lives of every other person.

*　　　*　　　*

Jennie Lee was now fighting a losing battle against a flood of letters which poured in from one constituent after another. Night after night she sat in the lobbies, trying to cope, until Jimmie Maxton found her one evening, stopped and smiled down at her, hands in pockets. 'You know,' he said, in his soft, drawling way, 'we all have to make the decision some time.'

'What decision?' asked Jennie.

'Whether you mean to be a Socialist member of Parliament or just another bloody welfare worker.'

[1] *This Great Journey*—Jennie Lee.

Jennie Lee was far too idealistic to have any truck with such cynicism and continued to plough on night after night trying to keep abreast of the tide, until one day she was introduced to Dorothy Hawkin, who gave her spare time free of charge to Socialism and now agreed to become Miss Lee's private secretary. It was quite impossible to pay her. Out of her £400 salary Jennie Lee had to provide a minute flat in Soho—once the home of Karl Marx—buy acres of postage stamps, cover her expenses and help the family still living a hand to mouth existence away in Scotland but sustained by a deep pride in the incredible doings of Jennie which crept into local and national papers alike, with oddly similar openings. . . . 'Miss Jennie Lee, the youngest woman member in the House of Commons. . . .'

She belonged of course to the I.L.P. group in the House. The Independent Labour Party founded in 1893 had maintained its detachment in the face of the growth of the Labour Party proper, and now carried the anti-Government war right on to the floor of the House in the hope of bringing to its senses that extraordinary second Labour Government which fell so quickly under the spell of the bankers and industrialists. It was a Left-wing government which, before a year ran out, performed the curious feat of bitterly denouncing criticism from the Left and accepting it from the Right.

Bevan for his part was one of a number of Labour M.P.s who remained under the aegis of the official Labour Party without losing their critical voice. Perhaps that needs qualification. There were two views of him. One said he led a bachelor Bohemian life and never rose above being an arm-chair revolutionary. Brendan Bracken indeed christened him the "Bollinger Bolshevik." Another that, in his own original fashion, he waged war against what he considered inertia and timidity, raising a hue and cry after fast-fading election promises.

There remained in his bearing a streak of enquiring innocence which could be most deceptive, and W. J. Brown wrote of him: 'He had a slight stammer which excited sympathy, but the brain behind the stammer was lightning-like in its movement, and was used on occasion with the precision of a steam-hammer. In Parliamentary performance he was very uneven, sometimes brilliant, sometimes badly missing fire. He was the only man in that Parliament whom I ever saw put Mr. Lloyd George to complete discomfiture.'

It was a thankless task opposing the Labour Cabinet of those days. Mesmerized by the extraordinary influence of MacDonald's golden voice and lofty manner, back-benchers waited on his every word and nothing could be challenged without his sanction. They were devoted disciples. To oppose him meant breaking faith. And yet some questions multiplied. Just how many people clearly understood what was meant when the directors of the Bank of England conjured up the gold standard bogy, and just how badly would it hit the economic machine if this ancient, encrusted device was allowed to lapse for a time? It had happened before without throwing the British economy into confusion, and there were even primitive, ill-informed and completely unwary countries which had never yet been on the gold standard.

MacDonald's reply was resonant. . . . 'If we go off the gold standard our money will become worthless, utterly worthless,' and to prove irrefutably the truth of what he said, he brandished a German Reichsmark note carefully preserved as a souvenir from the days when a loaf of bread cost 1,000 Reichsmarks in Germany. The speech only served to increase the number of rebels. Sir Charles Trevelyan resigned from the Cabinet, Sir Oswald Mosley threw in his hand when the Government refused to adopt his plan for unemployment, Fenner Brockway was named and suspended in the House and John Beckett, on the same day, shocked M.P.s of every shade by suddenly grabbing up the Mace and trying to carry it out of the House. Two messengers closed with him, and the Mace was replaced amidst uproar. Traditional idolatries were as strong amongst Socialist as Conservative M.P.s and everyone was scandalized.

The I.L.P. made considerable capital from it all. Live, impatient, imaginative members of the Labour Party were beginning to shoot off at tangents in all directions, with John Strachey heading fast towards a new party and, briefly, Communism; W. J. Brown into the no-man's-land of the independents and Beckett and Mosley towards Fascism. Bevan said to Jennie Lee one day, 'And you, where do you think you're heading? . . . Why don't you get yourself to a nunnery and be done with it. . . . My poor Salvation Army lassie. . . . I tell you it's the Labour Party or nothing. . . . I know all its faults and all its dangers. . . . And I am by no means convinced that something cannot yet be made of it. . . .' [1]

[1] *This Great Journey*—Jennie Lee.

There were others who tried not dissimilar tactics on Bevan himself. Oswald Mosley was one. A man without any real roots in the Socialist movement, Mosley was shrewd enough to see the hopelessness of battling against the cynicism and apathy which had overtaken highly placed members of the Government, and one Sunday, H. J. Massingham broke the news in the *Observer* that Sir Oswald had abandoned the Labour Party and formed a completely new political party to be distinguished in the end more by the colour of the shirts it wore than by its devotion to democracy.

Immediately, the Mosley Party grew out of the Mosley Ginger Group inside the Labour Party. W. J. Brown gave his explanation of its history in a letter to me:

> The Mosley Ginger Group consisted of a number of members of the Labour Party and the Independent Labour Party, and I helped it in a secretarial capacity. It was this Group which produced what was known as "the Mosley Manifesto"—a series of proposals for coping with the unemployment which at that time was a distressing feature of British life.
>
> Aneurin Bevan was associated with the Group. When we found that no pressure that we could bring to bear upon the Government —not even Mosley's own resignation from the Government—could secure from it the necessary resolute action to cope with unemployment, there emerged the project of forming "The New Party." A concerted resignation of a number of members of the Labour Party from the Labour Party in Parliament was arranged for a given date. ... A number of Members of Parliament did resign, including myself. ...
>
> The New Party came into being, although I did not myself join it, remaining for the rest of that Parliament as an Independent M.P.
>
> The course of events in the New Party you are probably familiar with. It began on the basis of the Mosley Manifesto to which I have referred, but gradually moved more and more to the Right and finally became openly Fascist. Forgan, John Strachey and one or two others went with the New Party, but one by one dropped away as the growingly Fascist character of Mosley's course became apparent.

According to Jennie Lee's book, *This Great Journey*, Bevan 'argued vociferously' against the formation of a New Party from the start. 'I tell you now where you will end up—you will end up as a Fascist Party. . . .'

And Fenner Brockway comments: 'I have never heard that Nye ever favourably endorsed the idea of a New Party. . . . He was so fundamentally against leaving the Labour Party and argued so strongly with us in the I.L.P., that I find it difficult to believe W. J. Brown's statement. . . .'

Some time in 1930 Bevan put down a resolution asking for a special National Conference of the Labour Party. Before the Parliamentary Labour Party discussed it, MacDonald sent for Bevan. The resolution was very embarrassing, he said, and since his economic advisers considered the worst of the crisis past, it would be much wiser to withdraw it. Bevan refused. The resolution was discussed and overwhelmingly defeated.

'There is one situation which is fatal for a democratic parliament,' Bevan wrote later, 'that is helplessness in face of economic difficulties. At first this may seem trite. But it is just the lesson the Labour Party in Britain did not learn in 1924, nor again in 1929, and it is by no means clear that it has even now learned it' (1952).

In 1931 there followed a political manœuvre at the highest level of the Labour Party which today reads like pure farce to anyone bred in the harsh cradle of party politics. Certainly no other interpretation would have been possible if a Conservative Government, overwrought by the responsibilities of office, had suddenly decided to invite a committee drawn from members of the Labour Party, to investigate the financial measures it proposed putting into operation. If the same Government went even further and accepted the recommendations of such a committee with the timidity of the pupil given lines by his schoolmaster, the ghosts of Marlborough and Palmerston would have risen from their graves. Yet that was just what the Labour Government now did. The May Committee composed of elements quite alien to the Labour Party, sat to consider the situation. Its final minutes were fertile ground for a Gilbert and Sullivan farce, but the more truculent minority inside the Labour Party saw it as a tragic symptom of a bigger betrayal already developing in the background. For the May Committee produced a report which Left-wing thinkers looked upon as a device designed to scare the wits out of the Labour Government. Under the chairmanship of Sir George May it estimated the coming deficit at £120,000,000. The figure rang like a knell in the ears of MacDonald and Snowden, and brought another outburst from the rebels. The Committee had its remedies. £60,000,000 could be saved from the unemployment benefit by the simple process of cutting the dole to the unemployed by 10 per cent. Mr. MacDonald was prepared to suffer Right-wing enlightenment about his policy and even to accept a little intimidation lightly disguised as guidance, but Arthur Henderson stuck at denuding the group least able to sustain it, of the means of subsistence. His was one of the few firm stands in a morass of uncertainty but it could not satisfy Labour Party rebels. Why not, they asked, hand the Labour Party over lock, stock and barrel to the May Committee? Why not doff the lowly Socialist coat and try on something more lordly?

Heavy-handed ironies were unwittingly prophetic. Within a few weeks the veils, if not the coats, were off. On Sunday, 23 August 1931, the Cabinet split and Ramsay MacDonald, Snowden, Sankey and Thomas moved across to form a Coalition with the Conservatives. According to Hugh Dalton a 'weak majority' of the Cabinet agreed to 'MacDonald's proposal to cut unemployment benefit,' and the Government only broke up because a 'strong minority,' amongst them Herbert Morrison, 'were prepared to resign rather than agree.' The shock to the rank and file of the Labour Party might have broken the back of the whole movement. Their spiritual leaders had deserted them in the moment of greatest crisis. But instead of moral collapse, a howl of execration went up and the Party demanded the heads of MacDonald and Snowden as though by some such titular sacrifice they could salvage something from the wreck, without stopping to ask whether these men were merely the symptoms of a far deeper disease.

Bevan looked upon MacDonald and Snowden as representatives of a brand of Socialism which expected the Conservatives to stand by and watch themselves legislated out of existence. It was Socialism by Conservative consent. It kept an even course in fair weather. In foul it ran before whichever wind threatened most. Then, as later in the history of the Labour Party, it had no policy forceful enough to meet unexpected crisis or flexible enough to change with violently changing circumstances.

So, abruptly in 1931, after a score or so of disastrous months in office, came another General Election which played havoc with the safest Labour seats, swelled the Conservative vote to 11,900,000 and reduced Labour to 6,648,000. How else could it be when the Labour candidates were still tarred with a policy which had "brought the country to the brink of disaster," and Snowden sweepingly recanted his old creed to the point of accusing the

Labour Party of preparing to rob the British Post Office Savings Bank.

In 1926 a gigantic national strike had been converted into an ignominious rout. Now, five years later, a Labour Government had been converted into a coalition. Yet the Labour Government's record was not, on the face of it, as bad as all that. Before the peak of the crisis arrived, they did succeed in reducing the hardships of unemployment insurance, some members refused to accept the May Committee's suggestion of a £60,000,000 cut in unemployment relief, others carried through the Coal Mines Act of 1930, largely emasculated though that was, others again set big slum clearance schemes moving under the Housing Act, and negotiated a Land Utilization Act, seriously curtailed by the House of Lords, but lit with some small spark of imagination.

In all this, there was one big thing lacking. It had no breadth and vision. It was bogged down by caution and the fear of men given huge responsibilities for the first time and vaguely uneasy in case they could not rise to them.

7

Aneurin Bevan was now thirty-five. The world about him, deeply disrupted, sought some panacea which did not intrude too far on the old traditions or demand too big a personal effort from anyone. Ramsay MacDonald had performed the curious feat of leaving his own sinking ship to captain the ship which had sunk it, only to find the shadow of Baldwin immediately across his path and growing steadily more obtrusive. The National Government elected in a panic to save the pound immediately ate its own words by going off the gold standard. The national income had declined catastrophically, overall production and wholesale prices had fallen, hundreds of farmers were on the verge of ruin, the bankrupt rate rising, and even big industrialists facing crippling losses. Counsels were tragically divided. . . . 'Some' suggest 'economy,' Bevan said, 'others toy with inflation, some advocate general free trade; others Imperial Preference. In the meantime Mr. MacDonald treads his resolutionary path from Conference to Conference, while Lord —— calls for Bacchanals in the West End. . . .' Amongst it all unemployment flourished.

Some intellectuals in the Labour Party put the blame for three-quarters of the current troubles on the shoulders of the Bankers. They continually pointed out that at root the crisis was the result of under-consumption and over-production, of too many goods in the shops and too little money in people's pockets; nobody listened. The I.L.P. had pressed its constitutional right to vote against the Government and was now on the verge of breaking away from the Labour Party by reason of this comparatively minor issue. A third group of Socialists, devoted to Socialism in the raw, conceived the broad outlines of the Socialist League which, when it finally took shape and form, included some of the best brains in the Left-wing movement—Stafford Cripps, Professor G. D. H. Cole, Sir Charles Trevelyan, William Mellor, E. F. Wise and H. N. Brailsford. The heritage of British Socialism was eclectic. Chartist Radicalism, Owenite optimism and Christian Socialism combined with Fabianism, William Morris and Marxist materialism to produce a highly complex pattern of thinking. Marxism had been of little significance until 1931. Now, in *theory*, it gained considerable ground amongst the intellectuals.

The whole teaching of Laski and Cripps was now based on the assumption that Socialism was not susceptible of Parliamentary realization without constitutional upheaval. Any Socialist Government with a solid majority would strain Parliament beyond its intent. This conclusion had been forced on them by the fiascos of 1924 and 1929–31. The year 1934 was the beginning of the hey-day of the Left Book Club. Tawney, Laski, the Webbs and Strachey came to dominate the thought of young Socialists in the 1930s and 'deeply influenced many practical politicians in the Shadow Cabinet. The Left Book Club replaced the Fabian Society as the home of the intellectual *avant garde*. . . . But this victory of Marxist theory was to be short lived,' [1] a return to gradualism soon overwhelming it. For the moment clenched fists were the order of the day.

In the international scene the French were busy electing another stop-gap government and prices threatened to defeat those Americans who annually imbibed their culture from the ineffable graces of Paris. Mussolini, attempting to imitate his imperial predecessor, achieved the one resemblance that they both lived in Rome. The talk in Spain ran furtively on revolution. German women performed tremendous feats at the Olympic Games and a person with the odd name of Hitler was talking a lot in a loud way. The newspapers of Britain occasionally admitted these facts in their columns, but by their very nature they could do little more. There were far bigger things happening at home and far more important people. Aneurin Bevan for instance. Here was a man who should be watched if the fine old traditions of Britain's heritage were not to be wrecked out of hand. The *Sunday Express* put it more bluntly:

> Mr. Bevan is an extremist. . . . Let me deal frankly with him . . . brilliant, bitter, proud, class conscious, boastful of his ancestry and his family. But do not let it be supposed that his boastfulness takes the form of saying: 'I am the descendant of Brian Boru or of Robert the Bruce.' Not at all. His boastfulness makes him claim that he is the descendant of the commonest and the lowest, the friend of the poor and the downtrodden. He carries this attitude so far

[1] *New Fabian Essays, 1952*—R. H. S. Crossman.

that it becomes a form of class consciousness which is quite as objectionable as it is in the man who boasts of Norman blood.

Bevan has been in gaol. Most men who have been in gaol try to conceal it. Many of them go to great pains to hide the fact from the public. Not he. At a moment of silence when he is dining in company more or less distinguished, suddenly his voice rings out: 'When I was in gaol. . . .'

He was asked: 'Does your mother read much?' The reply was: 'My mother can neither read nor write.' Another man saying this would have added some word of explanation or apology. Not Bevan. It was a boast on this man's lips concerning the class which he believes is going to occupy the seats of the mighty. It is from this mother who can neither read nor write that Bevan inherits his abilities. But Bevan cannot only read and write; he can talk—far too much.

This is the man of whom ordered society and established institutions should take note. He is the dangerous fellow who looks quite dispassionately on all that goes on about him, but with every intention of tearing down the pillars of society, as he knows it, if he can. . . .

So one Right-wing newspaper saw him at thirty-five. Bevan replied to the article. Beaverbrook rarely made the mistake of denying heretics a hearing in his paper and now gave him the freedom of the *Daily Express*. Someone chose a flawless title— 'Down with Beaverbrook and Company.'

'I have been made the subject of attack by the *Sunday Express*,' wrote Bevan.

In the course of that attack I was described as bitter, boastful of my working-class ancestry, and a menace to the capitalist system. To the first two charges I plead guilty. As to the third, it is my ambition to prove it true. Up to the present, the owner of the *Sunday Express*, Lord Beaverbrook, and his political associates have proved more dangerous in the established order than I can ever hope to be. The management of industry, commerce and finance is in their hands.

Look around the world today and see what they have made of it! In the capitalist countries of the world three hundred millions of men stand staring in helpless bewilderment at the idle machines to which they must have access in order to live. If it be dangerous to ask men to note these things and to call on them to sweep away those who sit in the places of power then indeed I am dangerous—to Lord Beaverbrook and his friends. . . .

As to his boastfulness about his origins, there he was at a disadvantage with Lord ——, who was ' able to change the occupation followed by his grandfather to suit the character of his audience.' The full realization of his own parental good fortune only dawned on him when he came into contact with the children of the rich. It reinforced his view that modern civilization would have to be rescued from its plight by men and women of the working classes.

If this was the same Bevan who accepted invitations to week-ends with Lord Beaverbrook, and there were those in the Labour Party prepared to swear that the fleshpots were overpowering the Socialist, wherever he moved in high society he continued to speak his mind bluntly, outrageously. Remember, he told one distinguished gentleman, at a lavish party in Beaverbrook's salon, when I get into power I may have to dispense with you. And of Beaverbrook . . . You know, one day we will have to hang that likeable rascal Max. Delivering himself of a brilliant aphorism he would sweep his arm around the assembled company and destroy its most distinguished members in revolutionary terms, enjoying the fact that they did not quite know how to take him. But Francis Williams wrote of this period: 'He allowed himself to be taken up by society of a sort . . . for a serious politician of the Left, he seemed oddly attracted by the dubious laurels to be won as a licensed jester at Lord Beaverbrook's dinner table. . . .' (*Public Opinion*, 1951.)

One week-end guest told this story. Busy writing a speech upstairs, the guest heard Lord Beaverbrook shouting somewhere below. He turned to his secretary. 'Your employer,' he said, solemnly, 'appears to be agitated.' He went on dictating as the sounds below increased in volume and at one moment seemed indistinguishable from cries for help. The speech concerned coal. 'I didn't know it was so inflammable,' the guest murmured and continued dictating. The cries now redoubled. At last the guest stirred himself enough to reach the head of the stairs. 'Where is everyone?' Lord Beaverbrook was shouting. 'The house is on fire!'

Smoke and flames were indeed coming from outside, and there, at the top of a ladder, already at action station, was Aneurin Bevan. He carried a somewhat inadequate bucket which appeared to contain water, and was about to precipitate this on the flames when Lord Beaverbrook restrained him. 'I won't be responsible for what happens to you, Nye!'

Bevan turned a pained look downwards. 'And no compensation!' shouted His Lordship. Wearily, Bevan balanced his bucket afresh and began to descend the ladder. 'There's no gratitude in the bloody capitalist world,' he muttered as he confronted Lord Beaverbrook. The fire brigade then proceeded to extinguish the fire. A far less romantic version of the story, told me by Lord Beaverbrook himself, simply said that Bevan helped to remove some curtains when fire broke out. Probably the first version is apocryphal. Beaverbrook says that whenever Bevan argued his case, he remained imperturbably dignified. Sitting over the fire with Churchill they had sustained exchanges. Churchill referred to him as Bevan and was himself addressed as Churchill. It all bore some resemblance to a dress rehearsal for what waited ten years away. Bevan undoubtedly carried his Socialistic dialectics right into the heart of the enemy's camp.

Some said Bevan revelled in these week-ends the better to understand the people he had to undermine. There was much talk far into the night, but the swimming pool where many a famous actress swam, had few attractions for him. "Society," sometimes numbered amongst the company, loved him. In their bored, blasé way they looked upon Bevan as the revolutionary bear who performed so well he almost made one think he meant it, and then, unexpectedly, a growl came out of the depths and set them wondering whether this attitude was altogether wise.

Revolutionary? In one sense. But privately a man who still read poetry and took a deep interest in ballet. Next to politics, words remained a first love and with his memory he would stream back quotations from many poets and writers. Eliot might almost have written for him. . . . (*The Rock*)

> No man has hired us.
> With pocketed hands
> And lowered faces
> We stand about in open places
> And shiver in unlit rooms.
> Only the wind moves
> Over empty fields, untilled
> Where the plough rests, at an angle
> To the furrow. In this land
> There shall be one cigarette to two men,
> To two women one half pint of bitter
> Ale. In this land
> No man has hired us.
> Our life is unwelcome, our death
> Unmentioned in the Times. . . .

There was and is a streak of Rabelais. It enjoyed the far more full-blooded moments of Donne and Sheridan and Shakespeare, it quoted with relish Colonel Rainbro', 'The poorest he that is in England has a life to live as the richest he.' His metaphor had a tendency towards the biological. But, given his own choice, Bevan still appeared to prefer philosophy. It is commonly supposed amongst classical philosophers of the old tradition that the dialectical materialism of Karl Marx cannot be considered in the same breath with the great systems of thought elaborated by men like Kant and Hegel, and it was part of the constitutional irreverence which Bevan entertained for venerable ideologies that he inverted this attitude. He was by now a very considerable Marxian scholar, but quoting long passages from the Master did not make him an unquestioning disciple, if that rôle could ever successfully be played by Bevan. Amongst other things Marx, he said, did not make sufficient allowance for the intervention of political democracy.

He lived now in a London flat with Frank Owen, a tough Welsh compatriot, bred in the harsh ways of journalism with a voice capable of filling the Albert Hall, and a craggy manner which matched the political intransigence of Bevan. They were a mighty pair on any platform or in any company. They lived to the full. They were liable to stay up half the night and next day arguing, and their intellectual bohemianism included an occasional delay in paying the rent. The first of the two flats they shared off Gloucester Road, Kensington, cost £2 a week. Their landlord was a considerable member of the plutocracy and it became fairly customary for one to say to the other when the rent was overdue, 'Have you paid that rent yet—(Owen?) (Bevan?)'

The flat was small. Each had a separate room. Whenever one or the other was not to be disturbed he hung his hat on the right or left of the hat stand. One of them joked: 'The hat stand had tall antler-like arms. They were worn down to little pegs by the time we left!'

Somehow the rent got paid, somehow the woman who charred for them failed to resign: 'She was making breakfast any time between 8.30 a.m. and 2 p.m.,' said Owen. 'Long after the arguments ended Bevan lay in bed and read and read—sometimes till dawn I think. There were mornings when he still slept at noon. Why not? There are all-night shifts in other places than factories.' It increased rather than damaged his devotion to Socialism. Frank

Owen found Bevan completely sincere in his beliefs, and if there were times when he did not hurry unduly to the House of Commons, his convictions were ferociously reflected in his utterances when he did arrive, utterances which filled many columns of Hansard.

* * *

With the Labour Government of 1929–31 replaced by a National Government, the old restraints were removed for Bevan. He might snipe at a Labour Government fallen into apathy, he might challenge its precepts and actions, but he did not, at this stage, release the full force of his armoury against his own kind. With the National Government it was different.

He began his attacks in December 1931. The questions of unemployment and living standards were under debate. . . . The National Government, he said, consisted of all the failures of the last ten years, including second-rate Tories and Liberals led by a second-hand Socialist. It followed from the constitution of the Government that nothing would emerge which could solve the economic problems of the country or satisfy the demands of the people, and the Tories had better make an end of it as quickly as possible. . . . 'I would prefer to see in power a strong party Government with a party programme, clearly thought out and boldly executed, than this stalemate; this miserable conspiracy. . . .' The House of Commons had become a squalid struggle among the bandits of industry to get a share of the swag, and the Government was a collection of political gangsters busily engaged in the "racket" of protecting profits. His opinion was that such a Government would never be able to persuade individual captains of industry to put new industries into the South Wales valleys. There was only one way to get them there—by legislation.

He followed this up with a full-scale attack on the Means Test.

. . . The Members upon these benches and my Hon. Friends on the bench below the gangway have been accused of inconsistency here and demagoguery there. I propose to accuse both the Conservative and Liberal Members of the House of Commons of hypocrisy and humbug. . . . I propose further to offend them by proving it. . . .

MR. KNIGHT, Hon. Member for South Nottingham: 'I hope that the Hon. Gentleman will exclude me from that criticism. While I have accepted the means test, I believe that the provisions of the Bill are just a temporary step towards the revision of the whole matter.'

MR. BEVAN: 'Of course, I will exclude the Hon. and learned Member because I was not going to do him the disservice of examining the speech which he has made. It was so extraordinary that I thought that I had better let it pass in silence. The Liberal and Conservative Members of the House who have favoured us with their speeches hitherto have been having the best of both worlds. They are led to express their indignation against this particular means test and still give lip service to a means test in the abstract. I regard that as cant and humbug. If you want to have a means test, stand or fall by your definition of it, and do not try to swell the chorus of indignation against the means test of the Government. . . . By passing this Bill the House has by no means finished with the matter. Before the end of the winter resentment will have increased in volume. The National Government came in to save the savings of the poor. We are now informed what they consider to be the bulwark, the savings of the poor, which they must protect. It amounts to £49 19s. 11d. That is their idea of the shelter that a working class family ought to put up between itself and the hazards of life. Those are the savings which the Government propose to protect. . . . This National Government which came in on no demagogic principles has become so demagogic that we on this side have not even learned the A.B.C. of demagogy. . . .'

There was much more in a similar vein. If the Conservatives had not by then firmly established their ascendancy in the House, the speech might have taken greater effect, but it was clear that the National Government was little less than a Conservative Government masquerading under a multiple flag. The country had gone off the gold standard without being swallowed up in the black pit foreseen by the soothsayers, but nobody was able to bring home the significance of this survival to the ordinary people of Britain. Unemployment had mounted to alarming proportions, but the Labour Party, still recovering from the shock of betrayal by its leaders, was in no condition to do very much about it. There was diffusion of energy and ideas inside the Party which left it weakened and divided. In one breath at the Leicester Conference of 1932 it swung further to the left and declared that the next Labour Government must nationalize the joint stock banks as well as the Bank of England, and in another it failed to make its voice effectively heard in the House of Commons. In one breath it opposed the armaments necessary to back the policy of the League of Nations and in the next vigorously condemned Japan's action in seizing Manchuria. At least it saw the League's failure to challenge Japan as a major disaster. Unable to contain itself against these contradictions, in 1932 the I.L.P. broke off all organizational contact with the Labour Party.

Presently, unemployment reached almost three million. Jarrow was rapidly becoming a desert of unemployment, and the National Shipbuilding Security, Ltd., had begun its curious policy of dismantling shipbuilding plant on a pretext of greater efficiency which was said by some to be a matter of financial expediency.

Something far more sinister was happening in the wider scene to the confusion of power politics. In January 1933 Hitler came to power. The newspaper files for the following few weeks show that people did not take him very seriously and on the very day he was elected a daily paper came out with the bewildering headline 'Hitler Baulked of Power.' But if Hitler and his satellites escaped close attention from the newspapers, they sent a wave of dissension through the ranks of the Labour Party.

Fascism in Italy had been regarded as slightly farcical in the beginning, but when it overwhelmed the great Social Democratic and trade union movements of Germany and the far more militant Communists collapsed before it without any serious gesture of defiance, it seemed urgently necessary to take fresh stock; time in fact to review the whole position of world Socialism. The Labour Party drew some interesting conclusions. Fascism, it argued, was the antithesis of Communism and one gave life to the other. Wherever the workers adopted the militant methods of the Communists it would drive the Conservatives to the extremes of Fascism, with the results witnessed in Germany. It was far better for the Labour Party to repudiate Communism and maintain its conventional gradualist programme, than to court disaster by quick and violent action, if indeed violent action belonged to the Labour Party at all.

These were the days of mass demonstrations in Hyde Park, when Mosley attempted to march his blackshirts through the East End of London, and the East Enders, with no co-ordination and little leadership but with an almost complete spontaneity, swarmed to their main approaches and blocked them, hundreds deep, until nothing—not even the mounted police—could pass. These were the days when thousands of unemployed workers organized marches from the far north and South Wales and converged on London and the House of Commons, only to be

Aneurin Bevan and Jennie Lee on their wedding day in 1934

Aneurin Bevan, M.P. and his wife, Jennie Lee, M.P. on their way to the Houses of Parliament for a crucial meeting of the Parliamentary Labour Party in 1952

met, inexplicably, with impassable barriers at the door of the House of Commons. These were the days which stirred the fire in Bevan's belly. It was cold, bitter weather, thousands of the marchers had come hundreds of miles, the newspapers relayed their story dramatically step by step, and there was something disturbing to the conscience of England in the spectacle of a hunger march which led to barred doors.

A scene followed in the House with Bevan, McGovern and Buchanan as ringleaders. They complained of the intolerable situation where 'everyone who is deemed even to look like an unemployed person is put in a queue which is standing outside in the rain and sleet. . . .' The complaint was received solemnly enough by Cabinet Ministers who said that they fully 'understood the plight and the problems of the unemployed, and were giving them every attention.' Anxious to avoid contact with the raw material of a situation which they had completely failed to solve, they fell back on rolling periods, and Labour M.P.s, torn between sympathy for the marchers and the possible stigma of Communism, produced between them some equally fine phrases and no material effect on the waiting queue of unemployed.

Late one afternoon it fell to Bevan to bring matters to a head. 'In the course of the last Budget debate the Co-operative Society sent very large numbers of persons to this House, and they were all admitted to the outer lobby without any difficulty. Today, although there is plenty of room . . . all these men, who are poorly dressed and underfed, are being kept in a long queue in the open air and snow. . . . Are we not entitled to ask why the rules are different for poorly dressed people as against well-dressed people?'

He gave notice that he would put a motion on the Order Paper to 'call attention to the alleged discrimination between marchers and other persons desiring to visit the House.' McGovern lost his temper and described the situation as a 'damnable outrage.' There were cries of 'Order! Order!' McGovern shouted 'To hell with you and your order. . . . If these people are not fit to be admitted to the House I may as well leave the House. . . .'

All over again the biggest issue of the political day was unemployment, and Bevan was in the thick of some of the House of Commons battles. It was to recur constantly over the next few years, and his name came and went in the newspaper headlines, the most violent advocate the unemployed had known in many

H

a year. In 1932, he launched a searing attack on the Unemployment Bill—and in particular the Unemployment Assistance Board—which led in the end to a widespread skirmish with half the House. Under this Bill an unemployed person was expected to appeal to a new engine of bureaucracy called the Unemployment Assistance Board and not to the local body responsible to elected representatives, whenever he found himself facing extreme hardship or destitution.

The Unemployment Assistance Board, said Bevan, had been defended by Lord Percy 'on the ground that it was necessary . . . because there had crept into public life what he described as the patronage of the elected person.' Apparently the noble Lord and the Government thought it undesirable that a man who received public assistance should be allowed to persuade members of his local council to increase the amount of that assistance. But, Bevan pointed out, if income-tax payers at election time said to their Member of Parliament 'Unless you vote for a reduction of income-tax, I will not vote for you' that was not corruption but high ethics. 'The proposition now before the Committee is that a poor person cannot be permitted to exercise his political liberty in such a way as to redress his poverty. . . . Unemployment assistance should not be regarded merely as an obligation undertaken by the State, but as a right to be claimed by the citizen. This part of the Bill deprives the citizen of that right. . . .'

'. . . I am alarmed,' he went on, 'by the prospect of what will happen in South Wales when unemployment assistance allowance officers set to work. If Durham is to be taken as a pattern the situation in South Wales will be desperate and I suggest to Hon. Members that there is a limit to what men will put up with. . . . You can never trust a permanent official to treat the poor decently. . . .' Here the House rose in vigorous protest. Mr. Boothby, making himself heard above the din, wanted to know whether Mr. Bevan would apply this doctrine to officials 'appointed under nationalization schemes.' Bevan replied, 'Under nationalization the veto will remain with Parliament. Under this Bill it is taken from Parliament.'

MR. HANNON broke in . . . 'Does the Hon. Member seriously suggest that the public officials of this country, charged with the administration of the laws of this country on behalf of the poor, have not done their best in every single circumstance to help the poor?'

Bevan said the answer was to be found in our system of local government, under which every citizen had the right of appeal to his elected representative.

MR. HANNON: 'Which he has always had.'

BEVAN: 'And which is now being taken away from him. . . . There will be nothing left for unemployed persons between elections if this goes through, except organized rebellion against the State. If you close the avenues of appeal between the citizen and the State in between elections, then you must realize that human beings are not going to have the patience to sit down in resignation for five years until they have another chance at the ballot.'

MR. ORMSBY-GORE, First Commissioner of Works: 'I understood that a large number of the Opposition wished to make it seven years, or longer.'

BEVAN: 'If the Opposition were the Government, they would be so successful that the people would not want an election.' (Ministerial laughter and Opposition cheers.)

MR. ORMSBY-GORE: 'Then do I understand that if the Labour Government ever come into power again, they will suspend Parliament and carry on?'

BEVAN: 'What the Labour Party would do if it came into power would be to maintain the reality of democracy and not to sacrifice the reality of democracy to the form.'

It was difficult in these debates to outwit Aneurin Bevan. He could still use the mental slapstick of the public meeting with a skill which was rare in the House, but his parliamentary range had developed and in sheer debating brilliance he showed signs of out-matching men who had given their lives to it. There were some who complained of that. He constantly won the debate and obscured the principle, they said, and were immediately answered by his devotees who believed that it was nothing less than principles which he illumined in a mass of superficialities.

Professor Harold Laski now said of Bevan:

He has plenty of brains; he is really getting hold of the difficult art of subduing his natural rhetoric to the material which Parliamentary discussion requires; and the horizon of his interests has widened continuously in these last years. He has indeed his faults. Like most natural orators he is tempted to think that the inspiration of the moment is enough. . . . He yields a little, too, to a certain instability of temper; but he has shown, in the debates on the Unemployment Bill, a devotion and a persistency which will, I hope, convince him that incessant study of the documents is not less important than the

99

reputation of being a thoroughly good fellow. He has got to learn to think of himself as a member of a future Socialist Government and recognize that the hard labour of thought is involved in that responsibility.

Many more unemployment battles followed, and then, at the Labour Party Conference of 1934, what was to become the second big issue of the day, the United Front, suddenly arose with renewed force. Already in high disfavour for his avowed sympathies with the cause, Bevan shocked the Annual Conference with a display of dialectics which left the Executive disgruntled and the rank and file divided between rage, laughter and delight. His speech came after some fiery exchanges between the platform and the delegates, but it stood out sharply. '. . . In the past the Party has limited itself to saying what a man shall *not* do,' Bevan began.

In the future the Party is going to decide what he *shall* do. You have, not merely a negative limitation of certain activities, but you have a positive statement that men shall not undertake any propaganda on their own initiative without first of all getting the permission of the Party Executive. Now that is an intolerable situation for any member of any political party. We are informed that in the future it is not membership of an organization which is wrong, but *association* with members of proscribed organizations. I am not a member of any of the proscribed organizations, but I have associated myself in ad hoc activities from time to time. . . . Where an organization has invited me to go on the platform for a special job in which I have believed, I have felt it my duty to co-operate with them. In future, however, if I speak on the platform with a member of the Communist Party then I am immediately associating with a proscribed organization; but if I speak on a platform with a Tory I am not.

There is no mention in this document of the League of Nations. The members of the Executive, the leaders of the Party, can—to use Mr. Morrison's words—confuse the minds of the rank and file by appearing on the platform with leading members of the Conservative Party, and nothing is done. But if we appear on the platform with members of the Communist Party in the carrying out of Labour propaganda, we are to be subject to expulsion without even a Party Conference considering the matter at all. Where is the Executive going to stop? Are they going to expel Mr. Lansbury and Major Attlee and Mr. Wall for associating with Communist members on the Council for Civil Liberties? Are they going to expel themselves from the Second International for associating with the French Party which has formed a united front with the Communist Party?

I beg the Conference not to give these formidable powers to the Executive; they are too vague and ambiguous. If you are going to expel a man from this Party merely because he meets Gibarti, or Muenzenberg, or talks to Harry Pollitt, as Mr. Morrison said this morning—if you do that then this Party will get itself laughed out of court.

Bevan was challenging his own Party at the Executive level and a powerful group set up a hue and cry after his blood. In moments of extremity there might be none so able to dismay and disrupt the Tory Opposition, but that could not outweigh his appalling heresies, and suddenly they wanted the turbulent Welshman shown his place. They asked, in the end, for his expulsion, as the preacher had asked for his expulsion. But that was not yet.

8

ONE day, in the middle months of 1934, Bevan made this formal pronouncement: 'We became engaged on Sunday. I had just returned from America. Miss Lee and I had a discussion at her chambers in the Middle Temple. We agreed to get married and became engaged on the spot. . . .'

In October the announcement was followed by an obscure wedding in one of the backwaters of Holborn. Jennie Lee was twenty-nine and Aneurin thirty-six. Miss Lee walked to the registry office, hatless and gloveless, with Will Bevan, brother of Aneurin Bevan, Archie Lush and Mrs. Balderston, wife of the playwright. According to press reports, when it came to the actual ceremony Miss Haldane the registrar said: 'I understand you don't intend to use a ring?'

'After all this fuss,' Jennie told me, 'we decided to go to Spain to get over it.'

Events now crowded in upon them. Immense things, personal and public, were compressed into the next few months, one rapidly overtaking the other, until they ended explosively in expulsion from the House. Spain, where it all began, was by no means their first excursion abroad. In 1930 Bevan had visited Russia and was reported as saying: 'In the vast unified effort of Russia today, mistakes have undoubtedly been made. Russia has always been poorer than Great Britain. Equally indisputable it is that the workers' share in the available wealth is much higher in Russia. . . .' Another phrase was quoted at the time which I have been unable to check. 'They are accepting privation which undoubtedly exists in the confident belief that the future will bring a rich reward. . . .' In 1932 Jennie had penetrated into the famine-stricken areas of the Ukraine, which few foreigners ever reached, and seen hunger and death abroad amongst thousands of people who killed their livestock and refused to cultivate the land rather than conform to Soviet methods of farming. Miss Lee experienced hunger herself before the trip was out until—the whole meaning of life seemed to consist in reaching some place where one could get white rolls and butter. She left Russia to some extent inspired by what she had seen.

Then came America, with Miss Lee built up by lecture agents into a young goddess with a gift of eloquence, who had enthralled multitudes from the day she left the cradle; America and the deep South where she loved the names like Memphis and New Orleans and the husky voices and the quick warmth of people living in a flame and scarlet world of flowers and sunshine. . . . 'My idea of wealth is to have masses of flowers.' America of the tumble-down wooden shacks and luxury sky-scrapers, of the great mining areas of Illinois, of the sentimental and hard-boiled, John L. Lewis and Roosevelt, and the tragically divided unions.

Yes, Aneurin Bevan and Jennie Lee had seen a great deal of the world before they married and decided to take their honeymoon in Spain. There followed one of the most exciting periods, hardly more than a snapshot, when for a brief space of time they lived the vivid life of Andalusia, with its orange groves and mountains, its dark, passionate people, sombreros and glorious disregard for city ways. Bevan was at home amongst it all.

Set down amidst the rather staid English, Jennie Lee had always found something alien about Bevan. He was so uncompromisingly alive. And now, one morning in the orange groves of Andalusia, the conviction overtook her that he belonged far more to these proud spirited people than to dull, Anglo-Saxon England. They breakfasted in the open air, with a soft green sea below and the great sweep of the Sierra Nevada away on the skyline. Bevan donned Spanish cloak and *facha* and they entered into the life of the village until many villagers, 'once they knew we were on their side . . . smiled and were friendly,' despite certain complications with the language. For once the men of Torre Molinos realized who the two visitors were and what they stood for, they took them to their hearts, and presently, when Bevan with a vast hat on his head and the rolling gait of a pirate, paraded down the village street, it was the signal for a burst of merry-making. They became close friends with some of the villagers. They learnt at first hand just how the Spanish peasant lived, and that was to have repercussions. But the days slipped away so quickly and a holiday which was to remain vividly in their memories was over, and abruptly they were back again in England, London and the House of Commons, listening once more to the somnambulistic utterances of Mr. Baldwin, awake in another generation and asleep

103

in this. Mr. Churchill was giving his opinion of Baldwin in his usual colourful way. . . . 'Decided only to be undecided, resolved to be irresolute, adamant for drift, solid for fluidity, all-powerful to be impotent. . . .' Bevan, like Churchill, was now haunted by a vision of 'the great wheels revolving and the great hammers descending day and night in Germany. . . .'

Other events were toward at home which quickly swept aside memories of Spain, overshadowed Germany and international affairs. The biggest piece of pomp and pageantry which Britain had witnessed since the coronation of King George V, was now beginning to grip the imagination of the ordinary working man as preparations went forward on a vast scale for the celebration of King George V's Jubilee. It was said that the Jubilee caused the King himself some misgivings. A nation still haunted by unemployment, poverty and hardship was not the best material to respond to royal celebrations, but the Labour Party decided to co-operate, and the East End districts of London put their feelings in the slogan "Lousy but loyal." May 6th, the key day, was a flawless summer day of blue skies and brilliant sunshine, and the great processions and marches mounted to the climax of the Royal Family driving in state to St. Paul's, rapturously received by milling crowds. Some deeper consciousness, some fusion in prayers, worship, even gaiety, stirred people inexplicably and hardship momentarily sank into the background.

Simultaneously Ramsay MacDonald soared into the empyrean with one speech after another. His words came echoing back from outer space touched with lofty confusions. . . . 'Society goes on and on. It is the same with ideas. . . .' Society must . . . 'keep in touch not only with progressive, but also with retrograding movements in our advance. . . .'

Those machiavellian spirits who read the worst interpretation into every event of a political character said that the National Government pricked up its ears at all this. Never at a loss to seize the right psychological moment, it decided that such an outburst of loyalty and such a Prime Minister was just what it needed.

Certainly the General Election, not due until 1936, was "put forward" to November 1935, and if the Conservatives did in fact hope that the flood of national fervour would overrun and swamp any partisan feelings, they were not altogether mistaken; but the election had its awkward moments. Ramsay MacDonald almost failed to get a hearing at his Seaham constituency, a stone was thrown through the glass roof of the hall in which Neville Chamberlain was speaking in Birmingham, Walter Elliot had to fight his way to the platform at Glasgow, and Leslie Thomas, son of J. H. Thomas, candidate for Leek, was tripped up and pinned to the ground at one of his meetings. The most plaintive note came from Sir John Simon, the National Liberal leader, who pleaded . . . 'I am facing the music, but you will not give me a chance. . . .'

In the end, the Conservatives polled some ten million votes and the Socialists eight million, yet the Socialists held only 151 seats against the Conservatives' 438. Ramsay MacDonald lost his seat at Seaham by 20,000 votes, and was immediately smuggled back to the House again from the backwaters of the Scottish Universities. Bevan easily held his Ebbw Vale seat. Mrs. Bevan faced another three-cornered fight between the Conservatives, the I.L.P. and the Labour Party, which shocked the minds of the North Lanark folk who cried out against such fratricidal strife. It led to disaster. The Conservatives polled 22,301, the I.L.P. 17,267 and the Labour Party just 6,763. Mrs. Bevan was out.

The abdication crisis followed. If King Edward's desire to enter into a morganatic marriage with Mrs. Simpson shocked the majority of people in this country, it horrified the far finer susceptibilities of Mr. Baldwin, reared in an age when royalty was emotionally infallible, and brought him post haste to deal with the King in a manner far more abrupt than any he had brought to bear on the "King's enemies." Churchill pleaded for "time and patience," and asked whether it was the essence of sagacity to contemplate German rearmament without stirring a finger for years, and not to give the same number of months to the King's predicament, but Baldwin brushed him aside, dealt with the situation in five brief days and King Edward's abdication was confirmed.

One of the biggest upheavals in the constitutional life of Britain, the abdication momentarily pushed into the background something with much deeper implications for the peace of the world, which was rapidly getting out of hand in Spain but was still looked upon as a minor tantrum in international affairs. A handful of heretics, with Bevan amongst them, talked forcibly about Spain and its significance, to the irritation of Mr. Baldwin and his Government, but nobody of consequence appeared to listen. Bevan did not believe that the civil war in Spain between

Franco and the Republicans—now running wild—would remain confined to the Iberian Peninsula. He believed it involved the very fundamentals of the historical process which would never stop short at Spain or Germany or Italy, but might overrun half the earth before its force was spent, and he did his best to press this view against a wall of indifference. The world had recovered reasonably well from Manchukuo and Abyssinia, France had survived the Stavisky scandals and Hitler in the German Rhineland, but the 'emasculated diplomacy known as non-intervention in Spain' left Blum visibly weeping and shocked the Left-wing movement throughout the world. Bevan felt that Spain and its elected Government were about to be sacrificed to a mediæval Catholic hierarchy, aided and abetted by Fascist governments ready to try out their armies and equipment. In the background ghost armies were rising in Germany and Italy, a vast war potential was steadily absorbing more men and more materials and the "fever of Fascism" beginning to run high. In 1936, night was coming down on Europe but few people noticed.

Spain proved to be the big issue at the Labour Party Conference in that year. Bevan went as a delegate and Jennie Lee sat in the Press box reporting the proceedings for the *New Leader*. The crisis arrived when non-intervention came under analysis and it was quickly evident that opinions were savagely divided. What did the situation amount to, the Executive asked? Here was the Spanish Government clamouring for arms to suppress the insurgents and the British Government quite unable to take sides in a battle outside its own frontiers and jurisdiction. It refused to supply arms either to the Spanish Government or the insurgents. It was that form of equilibrium best described as non-intervention.

There were those amongst the rank and file of the Labour Party who listened sceptically. The Spanish Government had produced evidence, convincing enough in their eyes, to show that the insurgents were not only receiving arms from other Fascist countries, but men as well, and they believed that this easy talk of non-intervention did not bear examination. They wanted arms supplied to Spain at once, but that would have meant developing whatever subterranean supplies were arriving from Germany and Italy into an open traffic, with the inevitable diplomatic clash between the Western powers and the not inconsiderable danger of a "local" war immediately becoming a world war. Yet it was better, they believed, to challenge Spain instead of waiting for the world war to which the gathering forces of Fascism must inevitably in the long run lead. Challenged at once it might hesitate to threaten war in future. Unchallenged it was encouraged to run amok.

Bevan put the case forcibly:

> We have been told by Mr. Bevin and we were told by Mr. Greenwood that those of us who were critical of the official policy of the Party were being governed by our sentiments and not by our heads. . . . I listened to Mr. Dukes with great care, and if Mr. Dukes is representative of the cool, cold, calculated and well-informed manner in which the official policy of the Party is being decided, then I am all for sentiment and emotion. He told us there was no evidence before the National Council of Labour as to the supply of arms to the rebels in Spain. Every reputable visitor from Spain informs us that the Government of Spain is without arms from outside and the rebels are getting all they need to support them. Every newspaper office in London is full of information about arms pouring in through Lisbon. Del Vayo has made statements at Geneva and laid a document before the League to the effect that arms are pouring in to the rebels and that now the rebels are superior in the air. Everybody in the world knows about the rebels getting arms—except the National Council of Labour. . . . Has Mr. Bevin and the National Council considered the fate of the Blum Government if a Fascist Government is established in Spain? How long will French democracy stand against Fascism in Germany, Fascism in Italy, Fascism in Spain and Fascism in Portugal? How long will French democracy stand if the French Fascists attempt a *coup d'état* against the French Popular Front Government, and are supplied with arms by friends in Spain?
>
> We have the suggestion that for the sake of avoiding a European war we must maintain a neutral attitude. If the Popular Front French Government is destroyed and democracy in France is destroyed, then the Franco-Soviet Pact will soon be denounced, and democracy in Europe will soon be in ruins. That is the consequence of this policy. . . .

A roar of applause came up from the delegates as Bevan left the stand and everyone turned, eager to hear the case of the Spanish Government's own representative, Isabel de Palencia. Alas, it needed much off-stage diplomacy. Solidly, the Conference ploughed on and nobody seemed to know whether the order of the speakers had been rigged to keep de Palencia off the platform for the moment, or whether she had missed her cue. The vote came next and it was a curious vote. Scores of local Labour Party representatives backed the "arms for Spain" cry, although there were a number of abstainers, but when it came to the big block votes of the unions, many were solidly behind non-intervention, and non-intervention carried the day.

Yet Isabel de Palencia had still to speak and when she did appear she made an appeal which moved everyone and the delegates rose to her. Once more feeling against non-intervention ran high. Anxiously the Party leaders pleaded for objective consideration of the facts and promised to insist on the religious recognition of non-intervention by Italy and Germany, but the Conference broke up uncertainly, and the singing of the Labour Party anthem had a hollow ring.

Depressed, Jennie Lee walked out of the Press box and collided with Bevan, a very melancholy, almost haggard Bevan who had been unwell for some time. They walked away gloomily and the gloom was to persist for many weeks. For them a vital spark had gone out of the Left-wing movement in Britain. The old crusading zest which took in half the world had dwindled to a series of polite gestures at a number of conferences where men met together in far greater numbers and greater power than ever before, but produced at the end a dowdy and highly diplomatic mouse.

Nine months later, on the Aragon front in Spain, Jennie Lee sat in an ancient mill-house two miles from Huesca and listened to the thunder of Franco's guns trying to obliterate a gnat in their path defended by a few score youngsters armed with antiquated rifles and a great enthusiasm. She had come to Spain again, this time to see for herself how the war was shaping, and now she heard a Spanish officer telling his Catalan troops: 'There are not enough arms to meet the needs on all the fronts. . . . They have to be concentrated on the Madrid sector. . . .' When the firing became too hot she was ordered down into the basement of the mill-house and watched two telephone operators desperately trying to establish contact with various parts of the line which, in some sectors, they could only do after endless effort and in others not at all.

She saw many other sides of the Spanish scene: '. . . a child could have told that these youngsters with their antiquated guns, their improvised quarters and their eager air, had not yet seen any real fighting and would go down like chaff before efficiently trained and armed soldiery . . .' she wrote in her excellent book *Tomorrow is a New Day*.[1] It happened some weeks later when the fighting flared into a mass attack on the Aragon front.

Back in England thousands of men from the Clyde and the Tyne, from South Wales and Lancashire were preoccupied with other matters. They were converging on London in mass protest against a device which they said made the lives of the unemployed intolerable—The Means Test—but what was directed at this highly domestic issue eventually involved the Spanish question once again. The marchers came together in Hyde Park on Sunday, 8 November. They were joined by processions of local Labour Parties, trade unions, Communists and Co-operative Guilds, all forgetting Party differences to subscribe to a cause they held in common. It was an occasion of magnificent contradictions. Communists stood cheek by jowl with hated trade union leaders, liberal minded Co-operatives joined lustily in singing the "Red Flag," and Aneurin Bevan, hatless, vigorous and once again in fine fettle, said '. . . the Hunger Marchers have achieved one thing. They have, for the first time in the history of the national Labour movement, achieved a united platform.'

It was, of course, never to get "united" leadership, but the long story of the struggle for a united front had by no means spent itself yet, and although once again Labour Party leaders came out strongly and convincingly against it, there were others who now went on to link the issue with Spain. Inevitably the tireless Bevan had his say: 'Responsibility for the slaughter of democracy in Spain lies as much with Britain as it does with Germany and Italy. The people of this country will soon pay a terrible price if they allow the forces of Fascism to triumph. In spite of all the evidence of Fascist intervention, which the Labour leaders had long before the Spanish delegates spoke at the Edinburgh Conference, their policy is still neutrality.[2] We have to move quickly. This is a matter of life and death. Every worker must play his part. We must demand that the British Labour movement insists on arms for Spain. . . .'

It was a firebrand effort likely to inflame exacerbated feelings. The speech angered Labour Party headquarters. Already suspect,

[1] Entitled, in other editions, *This Great Journey*.
[2] Later, the Labour Party's policy was reversed. Herbert Morrison had never subscribed to a policy of non-intervention, although as a member of the National Executive Committee, he had to accept collective responsibility for its policy.

already notorious for his United Front agitation, this new attempt to revive "old issues" brought fresh fire down on Bevan's head. There was a difference, said certain Labour Party leaders, between a man of principle who kept his criticisms within reasonable bounds, and this political free-booter who was liable to attack their most cherished shibboleths with a scandalous lack of propriety. How much longer were they going to tolerate such behaviour? 'Why, anyone would imagine,' one highly placed member put it, 'that he was the only Socialist amongst us. . . . He's such a bloody paragon—and paragons are hopeless to live with.

'The object of the United Front,' Fenner Brockway wrote to me, 'was to bring the I.L.P. and the Communist Party into the Labour Party. The C.P. wanted to get in. The I.L.P. was hesitant, but Maxton said that if the Labour Party Conference declared in favour of the two Parties joining the Labour Party, he would regard that as a sufficient indication of a change of mind to justify the I.L.P. entering. This main purpose of the campaign was accompanied by a programme of demands. The I.L.P. wasn't prepared to endorse Soviet Russia's foreign policy and it stood for the Union of Socialist Governments rather than the Popular Front idea of a union of all Governments, parties and peoples who were anti-Fascist. . . .'

The official Labour Party case against the United Front had remained unchanged for years. It had two sides. First, the fear that any blood relationship with the Communists would merely provoke premature and unnecessary Fascism from the extreme Right, and second, that the Communists once firmly established inside the Labour Party would undermine its leadership, vitiate policy and eventually overwhelm it. But all was not honeyed accord inside the United Front movement itself. It remained quite common to find members of the three parties selling literature at their joint meetings bitterly denouncing one another, and Sir Stafford Cripps shrank from such internecine strife. It was the outward symbol of private squabbling which had developed at the secret meetings in Cripps' chambers in the Middle Temple. Cripps as Chairman desperately tried to reconcile the differences of the Communists (Palme Dutt, Harry Pollitt and W. Rust) the Socialist League (Cripps himself, Aneurin Bevan and Will Mellor) and the I.L.P. (Jennie Lee, Fenner Brockway, James Maxton). Palme Dutt wanted total support for the Soviet foreign policy before he would back the Unity campaign and Fenner Brockway opposed the demand vigorously. Negotiations were continually on the verge of breaking down. At each new crisis they would leave the polished mahogany table in Cripps' study while Sir Stafford talked to the delegates separately. The air was continually charged with suspicion. It remained so even when they reached uneasy compromise and the campaign swung into its stride again.

Time and again in the past, when tides were running strongly against the Labour Party, Bevan, inspired by some new "outrage of the Conservatives," had called up all the dark passion in his soul, and turned the full weight of his invective against the enemy, releasing a flood of devastation which left Labour leaders —in spite of themselves—aghast with admiration and willing to forget and forgive, but what they looked upon as recurring acts of redemption lost their value in proportion as his attacks upon officially endorsed policy became more virulent. And now with the United Front, 'he had developed such supreme confidence in his intellectual superiority over us, his political vision was so flawless—there was no holding him.' Yet even in full cry after him again, they still admitted a brand of ultimate courage, an ability to risk personal disaster, sometimes, they suspected, as a political manœuvre, and sometimes with a fire in his belly. It had happened several times before. It was destined to happen again and again, and since by now he had grown in political and mental stature, he had much more to lose.

It led first to his losing his place in the House of Commons. It was the occasion—phenomenal then, but later commonplace— when the House began debating the Special Areas Bill one after-noon, and continued without pause right through the night and on into the next morning. Ernest Brown, Minister of Labour, steadily resisted every form of amendment and exasperated one opponent after another by his unimaginative stone-walling. The atmosphere became sultry around midnight. By the early hours of the morning tempers were badly frayed, and everyone wondered whether the latest amendment from Miss Ward would keep the House at full stretch till breakfast time. The amendment centred around the notorious Financial Resolution on which the Bill was founded. By breaking into this, the critics hoped to bring some humanity into a document which approached the problem of the depressed areas as though it were an exercise in logistics.

And then, suddenly and unexpectedly, Captain Margesson moved the closure. The Labour Opposition benches broke into shouts of 'Gag!' and 'No!' Whereupon Miss Ward borrowed a handkerchief to cover her head, sat down and asked leave to withdraw the amendment. It was refused. The closure was then carried and Miss Ward's amendment negatived without division.

Mr. Shinwell now arose in all his blunt fury. Amid considerable excitement he suggested "reporting progress," and said that Captain Margesson had moved the closure in an unwarrantable manner. The Chairman replied that it was not within Mr. Shinwell's power to discuss the closure, after which Shinwell moved 'that the Chairman do now leave the Chair,' and that released another outburst which ended in uproar. One voice heard clearly above the rest was Aneurin Bevan's. It said 'Leave the Chair, your conduct has been abominable.' The Chairman asked for immediate withdrawal of this remark. Bevan answered : 'I say I have been in this House for seven years and your conduct has been abominable. I have never seen anything as bad.' The Chairman repeated his request for withdrawal and Bevan stonily reiterated: 'I say your conduct has been abominable in the Committee tonight and I refuse to withdraw.' The Chairman thereupon named Mr. Bevan for disregarding the authority of the chair.

By now the Speaker had been sent for and came in at four o'clock to find an electric silence. The House was still well filled. The solemn ritual of suspension began, Members coughed and shuffled uneasily, the Speaker's voice reached the crucial words and Bevan rose from his place, bowed low and withdrew to cheers from Labour benches. For the next five days he was a political outcast, but the effect of his suspension was at least as profound as anything he could have said or done in the House in that time.

It was almost inevitable at some period in his career that this should have happened. Nobody with his invective, his fearlessness, could hope to escape Parliamentary censure at some point, but where other men had suffered at the hands of procedure and a handful reached the high notoriety of suspension, this was only the first of a series of upheavals with Bevan which led in the end to expulsion from his own Party.

9

1939 took Bevan and his wife out of their small London flat where they had been living an unsettled, suitcase life, into the country for a brief spell away from the impossible pressures of politics. Illness had forced Bevan to retire to bed (Churchill was said to have murmured 'Nothing trivial I trust') and when he got up again he was told he must take things easily. He had in fact suffered a number of illnesses beginning in 1936, with the doctors insisting that he rest, and developing into appendix trouble. There were a number of unpleasant operations.

In 1939 he and his wife went in search of a country haven, and fell in love with an old thatched cottage fifty miles from London, which had all the charm of the conventional cottage and little of its constricting gloom. Here, they expected to find new roots, here they would give up the nomadic life which had become so exhausting with the flat as a mere *pied-à-terre*. Romantically they plunged into furnishing and gardening and cleaning, both highly energetic in their different ways, Jennie wanting an 'extravagantly large flower garden,' and Aneurin all for fruit trees and cabbages; Bevan quickly rigging up the gramophone and Jennie remaining unmusical; Bevan discovering that the fireplace could be restored to its old Elizabethan proportions and that giving him rather more satisfaction than anyone else. They both threw themselves with zest into this experiment, but they had overlooked the multiple ties which a garden and cottage of this kind involve, and in no time their attacks on garden and household led to complications. Ruefully they had to admit that they would need 'to dedicate' their 'entire lives and energies to the cottage and garden' if they 'were really to cope with this business of living in the country,'[1] but the sun was shining, the fullness of a lovely English summer unfolded new wonders every week, and if the machinery now threatened to overwhelm them, they still enjoyed the country life; yet something had to be done about the sheer mechanics of the cottage. In the end it took the form of an S.O.S. to Mrs. Bevan's parents in Scotland. Would they abandon their own

[1] *Tomorrow is a New Day*—Jennie Lee.

house and take charge of Aneurin Bevan's? It was a big question
to spring on people whose roots were sunk deep in Scotland's
soil, but they accepted. At first they came for a lengthy holiday,
then a small cottage of their own was built at one end of the
garden, and at last the whole domestic machine began to run
smoothly and efficiently. Friends came every week-end, there was
a great deal of gardening, Bevan wielded an axe heroically in
search of firewood for their log fire, and bustled erratically about
the countryside in his Rover Fourteen. Somehow between the
sun and the flowers and the flow of good talk with distinguished
visitors adding their stimulus, they still contrived to find stretches
of idleness when they did nothing but lie in the garden and turn
back the past, or sit in the evening before the Elizabethan fireplace
with politics barred and literature and music the order of the
day.[1]

Bevan had read Mumford's *Culture of Cities*. The book stirred
him. That cities should have an optimum size, that they should
be full of light and grace, that they should express a way of life
unscarred by slums and the ugliness of poverty, had long been one
of his favourite themes. He now embroidered it. As I remember
it, Bevan saw Mumford as a modern Encyclopædist, and found
him immensely satisfying, but he knew the weakness of these lofty
appraisals. He put it to me one day something like this: The more
universal an idea, the more satisfying it becomes to the human
spirit, and the less exact are its possibilities of action.

Life in Lane End Cottage ran on pleasantly enough. It was all
quiet and easy and full of soft excitements, it made no exacting
demands upon anyone, and perhaps for that very reason it could
not last. Two people like Bevan and Jennie Lee torn out of their
political context and granted an eternity of rustic seclusion,
would never have found serenity. They were too energetic, they
had too many outside ties, they were too much part of events
which went on shaping themselves, and they were quickly
overwhelmed with the feeling that they were neglecting something. With every small piece of news which penetrated their
retreat the conviction grew. Even so, as it had taken one crisis to
bring them into the backwaters of Berkshire—the crisis of illness
—it now took another to carry them away again.

The air inside the Labour Party was thunderous in the closing
days of 1938. Bevan and his wife had campaigned together for

[1] *Tomorrow is a New Day*—Jennie Lee.

the Austrian Socialists, for the Spanish Republicans,[1] for anti-Fascists from every country, and nearly always they were on the losing side. Then a handful of rebellious spirits formed a coterie which began to launch devastating broadsides against Party policy from the radical decks of the *Tribune*. It was a very different paper in those days from the *Tribune* of the late 1940s. It indulged the splash headline, it used straight, vigorous journalese and if it had none of the literary pretensions of its post-war counterpart and came close, on occasion, to naïveté, it was a fearlessly outspoken product which caused a considerable stir in political circles. Bevan was one of the moving forces behind this paper which carried on guerilla warfare not only against the National Government and all the stock evils of the day, but against the sacred Druid's circle of its own kind—the Parliamentary Labour Party—and it was usually Bevan who added that final dash of audacity which set the National Executive roaring to issue another Papal Bull against this fanatical rebel who still had not learnt that elders, in the political world, were without question betters.

He deftly anticipated trouble. The very titles of his articles asked for it. 'You Will Want To Attack Me For This' said the issue dated Friday, 25 November 1938. The article committed at least three unforgivable sins. It said the Parliamentary Labour Party lacked punch, it accused the *Daily Herald* of something close to delusions, and it bluntly called on no less a person than the Labour Party's Chief Whip to resign.'... I am going to be very frank,' Bevan wrote with that disarming openness which never quite prepared the faithful for the extent of the shocks to follow.

> It is certain that what I am going to say will arouse controversy and probably bitter recrimination. Nevertheless, it must be said. It is probable, more, it is certain, that I shall be attacked for saying it. ...
> ... What is our common purpose in the immediate issue before us? It is to make the Parliamentary Labour Party an efficient instrument of opposition to the National Government and an effective expression of the rank and file of the Party outside the House. It cannot honestly be claimed that it is so at present. There is something wrong with it that cannot easily be defined, and as we have just started a new Parliamentary Session it is just as well that we should try to understand what is wrong. The Parliamentary Labour Party is not getting

[1] Bevan was one of a party of nine M.P.s who visited the Spanish front in January 1938.

across to the country as it should. . . . It presents the appearance of a second-class exponent of a first-class case. . . .

The Parliamentary Labour Party was not guilty alone. The *Daily Herald* appeared to proceed on the assumption that it was 'eager to put any case except the one put by the Parliamentary Party,' and that Mr. Churchill's words were of greater interest.

Then came the attack on the Chief Whip.

> . . . If [the Chief Labour Party Whip] cannot do better . . . he should resign. . . . There is a softness in the Labour Party which is frightening in its portents for the future. The same can be said for a number of others who sit on the Front Bench.

Controversy, recrimination. . . . How right Bevan was. The machinery of the Labour Party covered up flawlessly but there was much coming and going behind many scenes, and while the *Tribune* sold out overnight, several august heads came together to consider the latest aberration of what they were now coming to regard as this political pirate.

One ex-Cabinet Minister personally rebuked Bevan, or so the story ran. The Chief Whip attacked him for his division record, and Bevan—if internal evidence from the Parliamentary Labour Party means anything—quietly explained that he had charged the Chief Whip with old age for which he was not responsible, and had also charged him with incompetence and there the Whip must bear the whole burden of his shortcomings.

Bigger shocks portended. The campaign for a Popular Front was now renewing itself with tremendous vitality and in the early days of 1939 the *Tribune* released one broadside after another at the Labour Party and the National Executive, demanding unity of all progressives against Chamberlain and Fascism.

Friday, 20 January, brought this dramatic opening on the front page of *Tribune*, written by Cripps. 'Last May when a memorandum was submitted to the Executive . . . the signatories did not circulate it to the Party, with the result that the membership of the Party heard only one side of the argument, namely the majority views. It was in the light of that experience that I decided on the present occasion to assert my right as a member of the Executive to circulate strictly within the Party a copy of my memorandum. . . .'

In a word Cripps had quietly turned the tables and made certain that the whole movement knew his precise case for the Popular

Front. Events raced away after that. Cripps was expelled from the Party. They could hardly have a member of the Executive helping the Party to commit what they considered suicide, nor indeed could heresy of this kind and membership of the Executive go hand in hand. A mass meeting followed at the Queen's Hall, and the crowd rose and cheered as Cripps took the platform.

'This is the first time in my life,' he said, 'I have ever addressed a large audience otherwise than as a member of the Labour Party. . . . I am convinced that if tonight we could take a plebiscite of all the common people of our land on the simple question "Is the Spanish Government to be allowed arms with which to defend its liberties?" the answer would be an overwhelming "Yes." We have a Government that gives the answer "No." . . . It was for answering that question and for circulating the answer that I was deprived of my membership of the Labour Party. . . .'

Bevan then took over and delivered a speech all fire and brimstone. 'If Sir Stafford Cripps is expelled for wanting to unite the forces of freedom and democracy,' he said, 'they can go on expelling others. They can expel me. His crime is my crime. . . .'

The fat was now fully in the fire. At least half a dozen well-known Labour M.P.s backed the Popular Front movement, the miners added their considerable weight, and hundreds of local Labour Parties showed restive signs of moving with the rebels. Next came a letter from seven M.P.s—Bevan, S. O. Davies, John Parker, G. C. Poole, Phillips Price, G. R. Strauss and Ben Riley—protesting vigorously against the expulsion of Cripps. The letter said that the expulsion was 'both irresponsible and unrepresentative. . . . We regard it as in keeping with the failure of the Executive to mobilize effectively the opposition to the National Government which exists in the country amongst members of all parties and amongst those who belong to no party. There is grave danger that this failure, if continued, will reduce the Labour Party to political impotence.' Twenty-nine Labour candidates added their signatures, and now the National Executive saw that something had to be done quickly before the next Party Conference. A series of consultations began. Confronted with growing rebellion inside the Party the National Executive had already taken the drastic step of expelling Cripps, and now an abrupt letter emerged addressed to G. R. Strauss, Aneurin Bevan and three others. It said in effect—sever all connections with Sir Stafford Cripps or get out.

Publicly, Bevan instantly hit back. '... the Executive has insisted that only its side of the case shall be heard. If we state our side we shall be expelled from the Party and thus prevented from appearing at Conference....' Officially he and G. R. Strauss wrote this adroit reply:

We have received your yesterday's letter and at the moment desire only to reply to that part of it which refers us to the Party Constitution.

We have examined the Constitution and can find no part of it which is relevant to our request to you except No. 3 of the Standing Orders of the Parliamentary Labour Party, which states: 'Members should take the fullest advantages of the opportunity at Party Meetings of raising questions of Party Policy concerning which they may have doubts.'

We have therefore applied to the Leader of the Parliamentary Labour Party to have this matter raised at the earliest opportunity. Until this has occurred, we are in no position to reply to the remainder of your letter.

The National Agent replied:

I beg to acknowledge receipt of your letter of March 24 and to say that your proposal to approach the Parliamentary Labour Party cannot delay action under the decision of the National Executive Committee which gave you a period of seven days within which to withdraw from the "Popular Front" agitation and to re-affirm your adherence to the Party's Constitution, Programme, Principles, and Policy....

Next came this from Strauss and Bevan:

In reply to your last letter ... you will understand that we must claim the right to try to persuade the Party that the resolutions which appear on the Agenda of the Conference in the names of many affiliated organizations in support of the Popular Front should be carried, and to this end we shall speak in support of them. Further, we must not be understood to accept the accusations made against us in your letter.

We are, however, prepared to refrain from addressing any public meeting in support of the resolutions on the Conference Agenda, to which we have already referred, except at meetings held under the auspices of an affiliated organization of the Party. It is understood that no objections will be taken to local Labour, Trade Union or other affiliated organizations of the Party holding such meetings.

The letter continued that talk of splits or expulsions seemed unnecessary in resolving differences within the Party. They were convinced that a unified Labour Party was imperative to face 'the perils from Fascism at home and abroad. We feel sure that the common sense of our Movement will enable our differences to be resolved within the Movement itself.'

The National Agent replied on 30 March 1939:

I beg to acknowledge receipt of your letter of March 29th in reply to the National Executive Committee's letter of March 23rd and in particular to the following paragraph: 'The National Executive Committee finds it difficult to avoid the conclusion that your letter is an attempt to prevent further Executive Committee action before the Annual Party Conference. Such delay cannot be agreed to and unless a communication is received from you indicating your withdrawal from the "Popular Front" Campaign and re-affirming your loyal adherence to the Constitution, Programme, Principles and Policy of the Labour Party within seven days, exclusion from the Party will automatically follow. . . .'

Your letter does not fulfil the requirements set out in the paragraph quoted above. You neither withdraw from the "Popular Front" Campaign nor re-affirm your adherence to the Constitution, Programme, Principles and Policy of the Labour Party. . . .

Still Bevan did not sever his connections with Cripps, still he continued vociferously to protest, and at last on 1 April he, with four others, was expelled from the Party. Even then they did not admit defeat. On 21 April the final letter went to the National Agent saying that they could not accept the expulsion as in the spirit of the Constitution of the Party, or as representative of majority opinion.

The refusal of the Executive to allow us to appear before it so that we might defend ourselves; its failure to give us clear guidance as to the manner in which we could advocate our views without coming into collision with the Constitution; its rejection of the reasonable assurances which we were prepared to give in our last letter; the fact that it listened to letters read containing charges against us without giving us the elementary right of even being told of them, much less the chance of defending ourselves against them; all these force us to the conclusion that the Executive has allowed itself to become party to a controversy rather than to remain the administrative head of a great political organization.

In these circumstances, the letter continued, they wished to say that it was impossible for them to accept the decision to expel them. Moreover they felt justified in asking for facilities to put their own case to the Whitsun Conference.

It was of no avail. At the Labour Party Annual Conference, the cause of unity was defeated more heavily than ever before and it was something entirely extraneous to Britain and unforeseen by Bevan, which had delivered the final blow. Reports of the great Moscow trials with their savage sentences and somnambulistic confessions were then coming through, and they left a deep revulsion in the minds of many British workmen, who began to wonder, if this was any example of Communist behaviour, just what Communism really meant.

Suddenly Bevan fell ill. Some said expulsion was too much for an ambitious man. Some said the enormous strains of the past few years, the flood of energy expended on the Popular Front campaign and the great battle of expulsion, had exhausted even his reserves of strength. Whatever the cause, he was taken to hospital, and the doctors warned his wife that he must take things easily. As a result, they went off together to the cottage in Berkshire.

*   *   *

The restlessness which showed itself in the first few months of their country life grew steadily worse. They were not completely isolated. There were many trips to London, but London lay fifty miles away. Bevan continued to wield his woodsman's axe with tremendous vigour, roved the countryside in his car, entertained, talked, gardened and read, but nothing could give him quite the same satisfactions as the hurly-burly of the political market-place. Even the long evenings when he read to Jennie from A. E. Housman, from Hazlitt and Junius, were now apt to end uneasily with a sudden turn of phrase, a glancing implication which took them abruptly into the outside world again. It happened with passages like:

> Be still, be still my soul; it is but for a season;
> Let us endure an hour and see injustice done. . . .

They could not shut out the world. They were aware of a constantly widening gap. Housman, Hazlitt and Junius sounded and were remote from the physical outrage of war in Spain, the rampagings of Hitler and the attempts of the Chamberlain Government to appease the paranoiacs. Away from it all—even by fifty miles—they were not completely alive. And then abruptly, that fateful Sunday in September 1939, Bevan switched on the one o'clock news in the cottage to hear that Britain was at war with Germany, and the second crisis was upon them.

The excitement of the moment left him, for once, almost speechless. He paced up and down the long, low sitting-room with his wife watching from a chair. This climax had even more significance for them than for the ordinary people of Britain. It spelt Spain and the long crusade for the Spanish Government, it was linked with a dozen situations where the forces of "Fascism" had shed, or were beginning to shed, all pretence of compromise, and where brutal authoritarianism was breaking through. Now at last Britain could come into the open, and 'all sides of the Left-wing movement unite to challenge totalitarianism wherever they found it.' Bevan suddenly dived to one corner of the room and began rummaging amongst a heap of gramophone records. A moment later the Berkshire cottage rang to the alien strains of Spanish marching songs and his wife was back once again at the Spanish front, and the old farmhouse, and young Bob Smillie talking between the thunder of guns. The Spanish front might have crumbled to dust and the workers abandoned hope of outside help long ago, but retribution would now come riding in with all the power of the British Navy, Army and Air Force. It rang true then. It seemed the inevitable conclusion to those who were intransigently opposed to Fascism wherever they encountered it. But eight years later it still had not happened.

For the moment, with strange rumours coming from London of bombs dropping in the East End, Bevan could not contain himself, and rushed off in his Rover taking the hills and corners like a knight at arms fully stretched to find the enemy. In the rush of the moment he was concerned only to get to grips with the new situation, in any way open to him.

London he found in a curious state. People talked in pubs and restaurants about Chamberlain's proclamation of war, and there were those who drank toasts to King and Country, but the fire and enthusiasm refused to come alive, and it was difficult to believe that such a slow, considered reaction to a world upheaval could ever rouse itself to the ultimate sacrifice which war demanded. Something had happened which would break into the lives of the least amongst the people, but they showed no signs of panic, of passion or even elementary alarm. Perhaps the English never quite understood what had struck at their very roots until they survived the blow? Perhaps what was called fortitude sometimes turned out to be lack of imagination, and the unshakable balance of the British a more pleasant way of saying that they were stolid? There was a dash of such cynicism abroad now, but it could not reduce the stature of a people who refused to be stampeded into demonstrations and committed themselves in a complete, measured, silent way to what many had gradually come to consider the inevitability of war. People were going to war under the compulsion of believing in peace. The mass hysteria of 1914 was dead and done with; the British people were growing up.

When Bevan left for London, his wife, alone in the cottage, tried to cope with the mass of contradictions crowding her mind. War against Fascism was all well and good but was that a clear enough definition of something which once closely examined became horribly complex? Wasn't it too negative? Where would Imperialist war lead the country? Could she wholeheartedly back a war under Chamberlain's leadership, knowing that his war aims and hers were two very different things? Did it mean that at bottom the whole situation was just another plot engineered by power politics quite unconcerned for the ordinary men and women who must carry it out? And weren't Aneurin's words the words of a fervid Welshman overtaken by the first rush of events which would look very different a few weeks hence? In the hours before Bevan returned home, his wife shook a great deal of confusion out of her mind. She was seeing things much more clearly when he burst in full of "news and views."

The situation now became quite unreal. The British people might have performed some macabre mime with the certain knowledge that war did not exist, so comic, so utterly casual were the efforts made to meet it. Parliament quarrelled over the payment of air raid wardens, industry made petulant plans to accommodate the nuisance, talk of gas masks and conscription, of black-out and bombs, intensified, and massive plans were made for evacuating whole towns and creating walls against invasion; but everything continued to run in its accustomed grooves, as though the nation refused to believe that anyone would be quite so mad as to ride the whirlwind now released. This pleased the German High Command. It was part of Hitler's plan to leave Britain alone. One never quite knew what would happen when one challenged that incalculable handful of mist-enshrouded islanders and they could better be dealt with when isolated from a Nazi-dominated Europe. For its part, Britain complacently considered the great Expeditionary Force sent to France with tanks, guns, planes and all the mechanical paraphernalia of modern war, a certain bulwark against any threat to the Channel, unaware of the ironic inadequacy of this highly romanticized band. The Expeditionary Force which stood between Britain and Hitler might have been bowmen from sixteenth-century England, for all the use their weapons were against the brutally mechanized German Army.

In the House, Bevan now stressed our failure to mobilize national resources. His spectacular expulsion from the Party had been followed in December 1939 by reconciliation. Bevan had been advised by the Executive of the Miners' Federation to accept the conditions laid down by the Labour Party Executive and seek re-admission. In politics it is possible to fall on one's sword and find the blade wooden, and Bevan now rose violently from his own deathbed and re-entered the House of Commons with all his old gusto and fire. He belonged to a group of back-benchers on the Left fringe of the Labour Party who created, if they could not find, opportunity to vilify appeasement and its apotheosis, Mr. Chamberlain, and clamoured for the old gentleman from Brummagem to go. In the end Mr. Churchill was grudgingly admitted to the War Cabinet and immediately denounced 'Herr Hitler and his group of wicked men whose hands are stained with blood and soiled with corruption.' Something was stirring the aged frame of England.

It stirred more vigorously when an Allied military force was landed in Norway and taken off again with nothing accomplished in the interval. Parliament now showed signs of anger. Conservatives re-echoed the cries of the Opposition for some sign of leadership amongst this steady accumulation of incompetence, and Churchill sounded the first notes of that aggressive diapason which was to echo through the country and unify the spirit of England against the 'satanic forces of Nahzee Germany.' But Churchill tended to simplify the spectacle of a besieged and slightly bewildered Britain as springing from '. . . our failure in the

last five years to maintain or regain air parity with Germany. . . .'
It was much more complicated.

A vote revealed that the Government's majority had fallen catastrophically from 200 to 81. In the ninth month of war, Mr. Churchill became Prime Minister. He quickly formed a Coalition Government with Labour and Liberal leaders in the Cabinet, but unaware of the dramatic challenge Bevan was about to issue he paid little attention to the truculent Welshman on the rebel fringe of the Labour Party.

The collapse of France followed with the shock of an amputation. Then came Dunkirk and the epic story of the little ships crammed to sinking point, bringing a whole army safely back home and accomplishing it as a routine run with some slight interruption of the service from the irritating habits of German planes swarming across the Channel. These were the golden summer days, when the thunder of battle in France could be heard in England and one officer approaching the Dunkirk beaches saw '. . . what seemed to be vast black shadows on the pale sands,' and could not think what they were. 'As it grew lighter he saw that the blacknesses were enormous formations of men, standing, waiting. He saw them thus whenever he entered the pass, coming or going. They did not seem to change; they did not seem to sit, nor to lie down; they stood with the patience of their race, waiting their turn. . . .'

It was a remarkable comment on a situation which involved all the elements of disaster that Churchill had next to warn the strange people he led that we 'must be very careful not to assign to this deliverance the attributes of victory. . . . Wars are not won by evacuation. . . .'

But Churchill's brandished fist and fine new government did not immediately shake off the lethargy which had overtaken Britain. Everyone waited for the new wind to blow the bogus war away. Unbelievably, a large part of the nation still remained comatose. For Bevan and Jennie Lee this appeared to mark the real end of appeasement, the end of their completely country life and the opening of a third phase in Bevan's career which was to lift him dramatically enough from the raffish rôle of back-bench critic into—well, there were vigorously different points of view about the precise place to which he was now carried.

10

WE were in July 1940. Three-quarters of Europe's coastline was manned by the enemy, watching and waiting its opportunity to launch the final onslaught on Britain. The situation was less acute in the days before Trafalgar when Napoleon's Grand Army lay waiting behind Boulogne, or far back in 1588 when the Armada closed magnificently on Britain, for then there were men, arms and ships to spare to meet the attack. But now: what had England ready to pit against the mechanized might of Hitler? One thing perhaps which had not changed its character since the days of Nelson. As Froude said '. . . A combination of curious circumstances, assisted by four and twenty miles of water, had protected England hitherto from sharing the miseries of the rest of Europe,' and there was some reason to believe that the Channel still had powers out of proportion to its size.

Two other and very opposite ideas sustained the British in those incredible months when the Battle of Britain began, and the first was hopelessly fraudulent. The average Britisher might have quailed had he known the flimsiness of the second wall behind which his spirit remained unbroken, the few planes, tanks and guns, so ridiculously inadequate when all the arts of bluff had worked their way. But we had something else, which Phillip Guedalla vividly portrayed in his book, *Mr. Churchill*: a curious sense that we were in this thing alone now, that we had only ourselves left to rely upon, and were at last without the complications of links in the line manned by people whose reaction we could not guarantee. With heroic absurdity, where we should have felt the weakness of isolation, we found strength. It belonged to the days of chivalry and jousting knights, and its ultimate truth was in serious doubt, but whatever its precise characteristics, it worked, and the speeches and behaviour of Winston Churchill at this period epitomized the unflinching dauntlessness of the British people. It is difficult to think logically when the full facts of any situation are not in one's possession, and the British people only knew that they were in a very tight corner, but knowing as little as they did, their behaviour remained heroic and the world gaped as it watched the mad English preparing to wage a battle already lost.

Bevan's part continued unorthodox. In the course of six years' war he was faced with a number of decisions, any one of which could have changed if not wrecked his career, and it was now his vehemence, now eloquence, now hatred, now utterly genuine beliefs which carried him to the brink of disaster. If one drew a picture of a burly man constantly sniping at the Prime Minister, added the ghost of a fat jolly boy, liable to release a gale of laughter, and introduced an eloquence and bitterness belonging to the eighteenth century, the picture would approximate to Aneurin Bevan in the early stages of the war. He could be several people at different times, but the rôle he appeared to enjoy most was that of political bandit waylaying Mr. Churchill.

By July 1940, he was back at the heart of the political scene and beginning to lay about him vigorously. Before the big issues blew up there were many minor ones. Skirmishes with Ernest Thurtle, the Speaker, Winston Churchill and Herbert Morrison developed one after another until it was possible to see these minor storms heading towards something of tropical violence. For the moment even the preliminaries earned him an unenviable reputation. In a Britain now living under the compulsions of war, one-half the country considered it not only the worst of bad form to criticize the Prime Minister, but tantamount to treason. Others did not surrender quite so easily to the critical vacuum and included a number of dauntless spirits who continued to speak their minds vociferously. Since we were living on a knife edge, it was all the more urgent to prevent the slightest sign of slackness, they argued, and even if criticism went the whole way, even if it became highly personal and assumed the characteristics of scurrility, still it could be justified.

The first signs of the gathering storm were really visible right back in 1939, when Bevan began to ask questions about Russia which were explosive. Why, he then asked, had negotiations broken down between Russia and Britain and how was it that Ribbentrop could go to Moscow but no one of equal stature went from Britain? The Prime Minister, Neville Chamberlain, was the person responsible for this. *He was in fact the man on whom Hitler relied.*

Here was a taste of the ultimate criticism Bevan was to use

time and again over the next five years. Immediately it brought cries of "Be British!" Members in the dim recesses of the back benches muttered and registered the strongest disapproval.

Bevan swung on them: 'You talk to us, you Francoites. There is a major-general here who has, in this House, got up over and over again to defend the Government's policy in Spain which would throw away hundreds of thousands of British lives, and you people over there dare to ask us for more!...'

A daily paper appeared a few days later with:

> I'm packed with pep, I burst with bliss,
> I feel that I'm in heaven,
> The reason is I never miss
> My daily dose of Bevan....

In August 1940 came the brush with Ernest Thurtle. Sitting a few paces from Bevan he suggested that some of the questions asked in the House came from members whose attitude to the war was lukewarm. It was dangerous ground.

'Is it not time,' Bevan snapped back, 'that certain hon. Members should cease to act as pimps of the Government....'

Thurtle: 'Is it in order for a member to apply a foul and offensive term to another member?'

A member, pointing at them: '... it's time to restrain one of them....'

Uproar drowned the rest. It was some seconds before the Speaker restored order. Then someone rose to make an announcement about the war agricultural committees, but the explosion was not quite spent. A loud whisper was said to have come up at the back of the hon. Member's words, bringing him to a stop....

'I say, Bevan, if you would like to come and say that to me outside....'

Ernest Thurtle could not, at this stage, be said to revere Aneurin Bevan. They were temperamental incompatibles. Several times over the next few years Thurtle was to attack him, and repeated in his book *Time's Winged Chariot*, Louis Fischer's story of Bevan in the early stages of the war, thumping a table top in the Café Royal and yelling, 'I'll bet you a quid this bloody war will be over by Christmas. The Chamberlains will sell us out again....'

The Thurtle episode didn't really amount to much. The next skirmish with the Speaker was less spectacular but more significant. Early in 1941 Bevan wanted to know the precise scope of a debate covering the use of school endowments, the Speaker said it was a very narrow subject and Bevan came back with some acid comments on endowment exploitation.

MR. SPEAKER: 'That is a very back-handed way of getting into the Debate some expression of dislike of the public school system. I cannot allow it in this debate. . . .'

BEVAN: 'The Minister said . . . that unless the House passed this Measure it might happen that some public schools would be closed, wholly or partially. I am making the contention that in the interests of the war, it is desirable that that should happen. Is that out of order?'

SPEAKER: 'I do not think it has very much sense.'

BEVAN: 'You and I have been in conflict, on many occasions, Mr. Speaker, and I respectfully ask you to withdraw the remark you have just made. You have no business to say that.'

SPEAKER: 'I am sure that we can sometimes chaff one another in the House without losing our tempers.'

BEVAN: 'I submit that I have kept my temper.'

SPEAKER: 'I do not propose to be dictated to by the Hon. Member. I have told the House my ruling with regard to the debate, and I stick to that ruling.'

BEVAN: 'And I shall stick to my point.'

The Speaker threatened to ask the Hon. Member to resume his seat. Bevan said: '. . . I shall if I get any support, divide the House against the Bill at the end of the Debate,' and sat down.

In August of the same year he rocked the House with the remark: '. . . the Government are the only enemy up to now, which the generals have been able to defeat. . . .' If the element of truth was not as strong as the element of wit it went home deeply.

In October he demanded: How far was Lord Halifax's statement that we did not intend to land on the Continent 'removed from high treason.' Had we given a gratuitous assurance to the enemy that they would not be attacked anywhere? And in December . . . 'The Government have degenerated so far as to become a little caucus communicating between themselves . . .' derogating 'democratic institutions for the sake of their own private reputation.'

In the background the old enmity between the Communists and the Labour Party had flared up afresh and quickly involved Bevan. At the outset, for two short weeks, the Communists had backed the war, and then with an acrobatic *volte-face*, had swung round to peace by negotiation. Here, suddenly, was another example of Imperialism at large, of predatory Right-wing politicians duping the people to die for a cause in which they had no real stake, and the *Daily Worker* came out with flaming criticisms of war and warmongering, flaying Chamberlain, Churchill, the Generals and the Admirals, and—said the Conservatives—faithfully reproducing the Word as whispered in its ear by some spirit from the Kremlin. If it had shown the slightest dash of individuality the Communist Party might have won greater sympathy, but when, with Russia in the war, it performed another split-second somersault and was back where it started, the whole performance so closely resembled a piece of puppetry—distinguished by the fact that the puppet in this case animated its own strings since the Kremlin showed little interest in its protégé —that it was difficult to take it very seriously. 'Communist opposition to the war in 1939 split and ultimately destroyed the Left Book Club,' wrote R. H. S. Crossman later.[1] It also helped to revive the old-fashioned Fabian approach which flowered so strongly in 1945.

About this time came the Home Secretary's warning to the *Daily Worker*. Undermining public morale must stop. The *Daily Worker* took not the slightest notice and when, a few months later, Morrison threatened to ban the paper, Bevan at once sprang to its defence. In those days the shadow of Fascism loomed so much larger than Communism that Communism was granted the tolerance of a crank religion, and it seemed unlikely that it would ever grow to dominate Eastern Europe or become for many people a threat more overwhelming than Fascism itself.

It fell to Herbert Morrison's lot as Home Secretary to contain the *Daily Worker*. It was not easy. Bevan put up fierce resistance and unfolded his case against suppression with ruthless logic. Mr. Herbert Morrison might be one of the most powerful figures in the Labour Party, we might be waging a war of life and death, and every circumstance might demand the suppression of subversive elements; there remained the incontrovertible canon of giving every man his say, provided it did not wreck the war effort. In any community, whether in peace or war, the amount of liberty accorded to any minority must necessarily be under some restraint. The restraint was greater in war than in peace, and

[1] *New Fabian Essays, 1952.*

Bevan was not concerned to argue the abstract principle that anyone has a right to absolute liberty, even though he said that the society which makes the most progress with the least restraint is the most virile and successful society. He was concerned to argue that we could well afford not to suppress the *Daily Worker*, that it should in any case have been challenged judicially in the open courts, and not by legislative sleight of hand. He put it this way:

Last Tuesday, I understood from information which has been brought to me, the Home Secretary met the Newspaper Proprietors' Association, and informed that Association that he proposed to suppress the *Daily Worker* and the *Week*. At two o'clock on the same day, the Home Secretary met editors of the national newspapers, and that evening these two newspapers were suppressed. Members of the House of Commons had no knowledge of the intentions of the Home Secretary until the following day, and it was clear from the newspapers on the Wednesday morning that with one or two exceptions the newspapers were agreed with the Home Secretary to suppress one of their members; and now we have an opportunity, one week later, of discussing this unprecedented action of the Home Secretary on a Motion by a private Member. I submit that that story by itself shows an extraordinary deterioration in democratic standards in Great Britain. It does not seem to me to have been necessary, if the Home Secretary intended to take action of the kind he did, to secure the connivance of the other newspapers in order to do so. My Hon. Friends and myself have made it quite clear in our Motion that we do not share the views of the *Daily Worker*. . . . What I am contending is that it was not expedient to suppress the *Daily Worker* because we could still afford the amount of liberty which the newspaper was enjoying. . . . It seems to me quite unnecessary, in circumstances of that description, to take away a liberty which can be shown not to have affected the national war effort. . . . I should like to ask next why the Right Hon. Gentleman did not make specific charges against the paper and take the paper into court? This House is not the place in which to discuss matters of this kind. . . . Why have we a judiciary which is independent of the House? Because that judiciary can, after a decent lapse of time, discuss an issue calmly in the austere rooms of a court of law, as little influenced as possible by political bias and prejudice, and declare upon the facts without having any political aim in view. That is why it would be so much more desirable to take this matter to a court than to discuss it here. And the Right Hon. Gentleman is the very last person to have charge of this matter, because I am afraid that he has been fighting the Communist Party for so long that he looks under his bed every night to see whether they are there. He is entirely unfit to discharge his duty judicially in this matter. . . . I do not say that without some justification. It was only a few months ago that some newspaper proprietors, not after an official meeting of newspaper proprietors, but, I imagine, after conversations with members of the Government, approached the proprietors of two very important newspapers in Great Britain with very large circulations. The Government, they were told, were very worried about the line they were taking. The proprietors of those two papers said, 'If that be so, we should like to discuss the matter with the Government,' and they saw a member of the War Cabinet. That member of the War Cabinet said—mark his words—that in his view the line taken by those newspapers was subversive— (Interruption) . . . and the Cabinet Minister was the Lord Privy Seal. . . .

Bevan pressed on to argue that powers of suppression were only given to the Government for use in the extreme emergency of invasion, and that emergency had not arisen. There was only one explanation of the Home Secretary's action; that he intended to use his powers as an instrument of intimidation against the whole Press. The Home Secretary and his Government had broken faith with the House. They obtained these powers by 'what now appears a trick.' The Right Hon. Gentleman had violated the pledge given by his predecessor.

Eloquence, invective and gross exaggeration—all of no avail. There were only six voters in support of Bevan's case and not all the pressure of certain shop stewards and a number of near-fanatical demonstrations could get the ban lifted in the next eighteen months. Those eighteen months were one of the blackest and most depressing periods of the war. Civilized susceptibilities, chilled by memories of Guernica and Rotterdam, had found the nightly bombing of London less horrifying than had been expected and Churchill's calculation, on a law of diminishing returns, that it would take 'ten years to wipe out London at this rate' gave a wry twist of encouragement, but the ghastly routine of all-night air raids quickly reduced London to a monstrous rabbit warren where thousands of people went to earth every night, and thousands more steeled themselves to sleep in their own beds. The high mood of Dunkirk was long past; the nerve-breaking business of sheer endurance beginning to take its toll. It was not any longer the Army, the Navy or even the Air Force which did the fighting. The initiative had passed to the common people. It was a curious initiative which permitted little possibility of hitting back, yet the shivering fear which assailed millions of people as the air-raid siren wailed its nightly warning, never ran wild and the sense of death waiting at the end of every street seemed to rouse a deeper level of consciousness which brought classes and creeds together in a camaraderie unknown for a generation.

It led to the most fulsome, and for Jennie Lee the most irritating stories in the Press about the heroism of Londoners who appeared to suffer the torments of hell without a sign of fear and smiled ceaselessly in the face of exploding bombs. In one breath the journalists caught the spirit of endurance which sustained the worst blitzed areas of the East End, so that 'somehow they kept going,' and in another told isolated stories to the point of farcical exaggeration. Jennie Lee, now deeply involved in the practical side of the war, found some of the "blitz stories" repellent. She knew the courage and endurance of the average Cockney. But the quality said to distinguish Londoners from many another Continental city was not, in fact, exclusively British. It was the quality of picking up the threads of routine out of the ruins and carrying on with gloomy tenacity relieved by a certain macabre humour.

One morning Jennie Lee hurried through the blitzed areas by taxi, carrying a special talisman, set on a new task. She was the freshly appointed emissary of the Ministry of Aircraft Production intent on counteracting the confusion brought into factory life by all-night raids, and the talisman consisted of nothing more than a slip of paper with a single typewritten sentence. It was for her what the rosary is to the Catholic, the lucky charm to the superstitious, and its effect on the factories she visited proved remarkable. The slip of paper came originally from Bevan. He had brought it back from the pits of South Wales in the early days of the blitz. Running across the top was the letter heading 'South Wales Miners' Federation,' and then followed these words: 'All key men must stand by their posts throughout air raids or until relieved.'[1]

It was only one of a dozen such orders issued as the towns of Britain took the full brunt of the blitz, but this order was not an autocratic edict from any military H.Q., or even an official Government statement; it was an order issued by the ordinary

[1] *This Great Journey*—Jennie Lee.

miners in the valleys of South Wales after endless lodges had met and decided what action the situation demanded.

So Jennie Lee sallied out in the grey, grim mornings, picking her way between the bomb craters and the delayed action bombs, and was astonished to find a quick response to her talisman and her talks. She saw it all from two angles. There was the humanist in her responding to the ageing mother who worked with desperate concentration over her sewing machine the night after her home had been bombed, in order to make sure that her son —somewhere away in the forces—had a coat to keep him warm. And there was the politician who heard the song 'There'll always be an England,' with a quite new chorus running through it— 'Will there always be an England with a job in it for me?'—and realized that the worker of 1941 was a far more disillusioned person than his or her counterpart in 1916.

The raw young Scots girl who once sold papers outside Pringle's Palace had achieved maturity without middle age and her personality was considerable. Many a shop steward had to keep a hard grip on his senses under the spell of the burring Scots cadences, the brilliant eyes and the sheer vivacity of the young lady who, with her talisman from Wales, won her way into the strongholds of crusty Tory directors.

Presently, she graduated from this job into another with the curious title "balloonatic-in-chief." That was the label given by Lord Beaverbrook, still the erratic power behind the great production drive as Minister of Supply, but now regarded as rather less of a genius than the first flush of enthusiasm had led people to believe.[1] She had in fact become part of the executive staff controlling balloon production. Once again it did not last very long. She swept out of the Ministry of Aircraft Production into Fleet Street, where the *Daily Mirror* invited her to become its political correspondent. She was promised complete freedom of expression, until one day a letter arrived from the Prime Minister addressed to the *Daily Mirror* complaining of the paper's attacks, and the *Daily Mirror*, with the death cries of the *Daily Worker* still in its ears had little choice in the matter.

The personal ascendancy of Churchill was now absolute. He could issue what Bevan regarded as alarmingly authoritarian edicts over the whole field of service and civilian affairs—the

[1] 'In the summer and autumn of 1940 Lord Beaverbrook had done wonders,' wrote Jennie Lee ' . . . But now he was lagging behind.'

inevitable corollary of wartime premiership—and it was partly this which now brought Bevan to the first of his three big wartime steps.

It could easily be supposed that he was primarily set on destroying the "idolatrous worship" of Churchill, or on showing his limitations as a military strategist, when he began his attacks in 1941/1942. Yet Churchill epitomized for him the anti-Socialist forces of Britain, he was the personification of the capitalist freebooter Bevan so much loathed, and although events had thrown Churchill into power that did not make him any more acceptable to Bevan, or indeed to the Labour Party in which, at root, Bevan genuinely believed. Yet the Party accepted a wartime truce where Bevan could not.

The difference was revealing. Some Labour Party members accused him of "swaggering it as a lone wolf." He seemed to love notoriety as well as limelight. But far more complicated characteristics became apparent as the war advanced.

He administered his first shock to an already war-weary public early in 1942 when Singapore had fallen, the Japanese were sweeping everything before them, Hitler and Mussolini were forecasting the downfall of Britain, and the survival of the nation had become so closely identified with the rugged arrogance of Churchill that not even the Communists raised their voices very strongly against him. Once again, the *Tribune* was the chosen instrument for attack. Bevan was now editor. George Strauss, his co-editor, had become Stafford Cripps's Parliamentary Secretary which meant severing all connections with the *Tribune*. Bevan ran it with people like Jon Kimche and the charming Evelyn Anderson, and very soon the imprint of their personalities became clear. One Friday the *Tribune* appeared with the first of a series of articles which shocked the Labour Party as well as the Conservatives.

"Irresponsible cad"—"political stunter"—"the man who would confuse the war"—the abuse flowed thick and fast, and if there was a thin line of intellectuals which welcomed cold-blooded criticism amongst the heady rush of hero worship for the Prime Minister, they were hard put to it to survive the general hubbub. The *Tribune* articles set out, in the first place, to assess Churchill's military strategy, and half of Fleet Street immediately assumed that they were written by Bevan himself. Later it was in some doubt. But that they were inspired by editor Bevan seemed axiomatic. Amongst people who knew him, the clue lay in the pseudonym which the articles carried—Colonel Rainbro'. Bevan was, and is, a great admirer of the original Colonel Rainbro', a Cromwellian leader amongst the Levellers, who challenged Cromwell's interpretation of the new social order far back in 1647. It was Colonel Rainbro' who opened one of the most memorable debates in British history with the words 'The poorest he that is in England has a life to live as well as the richest he. . . .' There followed a tremendous clash between Cromwell and Rainbro'. In the end it nearly cost Rainbro' his head. Now, three hundred years later, another Rainbro' was daring to challenge another Cromwell and this time it looked as though it would cost him his political life.

The first of the *Tribune* articles carried the title 'Why Churchill?' In those days, with the world ablaze from end to end, Britain the one spot in Europe which refused to succumb, and Churchill the chief inspiration of Britain, it was almost equivalent to saying—Why God?

The article opened:

There is something to be said for Mr. Churchill's Government and it has been exhaustively said. The eager Parliamentary Private Secretaries, the brackenised B.B.C., and the 2D-ed press raise a symphony of praise to the head of the least successful War Administration in Britain for 170 years. Lest the trumpets should falter and give forth an uncertain note, there is every Saturday afternoon a blast from that indefatigable First Lord of the Orchestra, Mr. A. V. Alexander. The Master himself now speaks less frequently, though often enough. For he has little new to communicate. A Churchill oration today is not a tonic to the public, but a hangover. . . .

It went on . . .

What is to be said *against* the Churchill Government? Quite a lot also, though little will be published if Churchill has his way. . . .

I make these open charges: (1) that it was Churchill, the then First Lord of the Admiralty, who by his wirelessed orders sent the British warships off on a fool's errand to the north while the German warships forced the south Norway fiords; and (2) it was Churchill who held back the British Admirals from breaking into Trondheim while there was still time to eject the newly-landed Germans. No wonder Churchill, on the dramatic Norway debate which killed Chamberlain, defended the British Government with all his fire and skill. No wonder that Churchill has ever since discouraged recriminations about Norway and refused all other inquiries into our naval and military reverses. This Chief Constable does not want too many investigations, for he is conscious whose finger-prints might be discovered. In the last Great War, when we also suffered fearful set-backs, we also had inquiries. One was into the Mespot horror, so vividly retold in Lloyd George's War Memoirs. Another was into Gallipoli. But Mr. Churchill, as well as the rest of us, learned a lesson from Gallipoli. No inquiries! . . .

I come to the Great Premiership. . . . It cannot be charged that Churchill took the final decision to send the British Army entrenched in Flanders forward into Belgium on the morning of May 10th 1940. When power fell to him later that day the British troops were already marching out of their prepared positions into the German trap. But Churchill had participated in the previous agreement by the Chamberlain Cabinet to perpetrate this cardinal military folly. French politicians and French generals are today standing their trial for their share in it. Am I making plain why Churchill, on succeeding Chamberlain, said magnanimously, 'No recriminations against the Guilty Men!' and included so many in his own Cabinet?

Churchill always had a ludicrously romantic conception of the real value of the French Army. The fellow's head is stuffed with the same nonsense about Napoleon and his tradition as it is about Marlborough. Churchill, the Modern War Lord, has never yet grasped the elementary fact that an army is just as good (or bad) as the social foundations on which it rests. The shrilling bugles go to his head! He hears the deep drums—and he is drunk! He sees the proud fluttering flags—and he could weep! He often does! About the solid industrial base of modern armies and the inter-relation of those economic forces which comprise it the British War Premier and Minister of Defence knows less than his Minister of Information. . . .

The article ran on for several more paragraphs. Towards the end, qualifications crept in. It was absurd to underestimate Churchill's courage as a great war leader. He had rallied Britain magnificently in its most desperate plight, his words and spirit had inspired these islands in their darkest hour. Nothing could belittle his four-square courage or his moments of greatness. But after nine months in office the *Tribune* believed he had still done nothing to give Britain the necessary arms to translate his thundering messages into action, and he remained little more than a magnificent figure-head.

The rage which overtook the Tory Press does not need to be re-called. Anyone who lived through those days will know the effect

136

such words had on the public generally. They were regarded as treasonable. A second article followed close on the heels of the first. Once again it concentrated on military strategy and was murderously critical. A few months before the Italian Marshal Graziani had crawled cautiously towards the Suez Canal instead of making the all-out dash which might have carried him through our weak defences, and now British troops and supplies were alleged to be pouring into Egypt ready for the big counter push. "Pouring into" turned out to be hyperbole of the worst kind, inspired by a certain military gentleman later to become a legendary figure by reason of the remarkable consistency with which he ate his own words. None the less, in the following few weeks General Wavell struck, rolled up the entire Italian front and went on to perform the incredible feat of pushing a vastly superior army right back to Benghazi before he paused. The prospects were suddenly, for the first time in many dreary months, bright indeed. By pushing the Italians out of Libya and reaching Tunis, the face of the war in the West could have been transfigured, but Wavell's 40,000 were already stretched far beyond their limits and without fresh battalions and supplies the tenuous lines reaching across half a continent would certainly snap. And at this critical moment, the situation in Greece suddenly demanded British reinforcements on a large scale, and now

. . . Mr. Winston Churchill thrust in his blade. In five weeks his interference had thrown away the full fruits of Wavell's brilliant effort and had furthermore committed Britain to the disastrous Balkan campaign of April–May 1941. . . . It was repeatedly urged upon Churchill at this critical time, by the most serious military opinion, that the Libyan engagement must take priority in any Mediterranean programme and the Italian power in North Africa [be] destroyed. The strategical objections to any commitment on the Balkan mainland were stressed.

. . . I say that Churchill insisted on it—in the same way that he insisted on sending the *Repulse* and *Prince of Wales* to Malaya, getting Admiralty consent to his demands. The tanks and troops which should have been in Tripolitania went to Greece. After 22 days the Balkan War was over and 15,000 British and Imperial troops were prisoners or dead. The equipment of as many more remained in the hands of the enemy. . . .

So, concluded Rainbro', at one stroke the modern Marlborough threw away his country's finest opportunity in three years of war, caused Wavell to retreat in confusion back to his base, and sacrificed half an army to a hopeless struggle in Greece.

What had begun as an intellectual exercise for the 30,000 people who read the *Tribune* each week now reached out to a wider public and set it astir. The national dailies attacked the *Tribune*, Rainbro' came under fire in the House of Commons, reporters tried feverishly to establish his identity beyond question, at least one future Field-Marshal was on M.I.5's suspect list, and abusive and admiring correspondence flowed in from every corner of Britain. Inevitably abuse overwhelmed praise. For large numbers of people there was something scurrilous as well as sacrilegious about these attacks. Some regarded them as the work of a guttersnipe. Even one of Bevan's devotees complained that it was time the *Tribune* praised somebody. 'My dear,' said Bevan, 'perhaps I cannot find anyone to praise. . . .'

About this time, according to Frank Owen, someone suddenly recognized the style in which the Rainbro' articles were written and privately identified him. By now, Rainbro' said, M.I.5 had begun to open letters entering the *Tribune* office. Mr. X, as I must call the man who guessed his identity, decided to warn him. No further off than Salisbury Plain, where thousands of Armoured Corps troops were training for battle, was Trooper Owen (alias Frank Owen, alias Colonel Rainbro'). Mysteriously one night, a man appeared in a pub on the corner of Salisbury Plain to pass on the warning. 'I then handed him the last chapter of Colonel Rainbro'—except one,' Owen wrote to me. The penultimate article said:

> . . . they intervene in my correspondence opening my letters and scrutinizing their contents. These enquirers are hired by Mr. Churchill's government, and paid for, of course, out of the public taxes. They may be either police, Military Intelligence, or they may be members of that remarkable Gestapo set up by the leader of our British democracy in arms to spy on the sayings and doings of any "deemed hostile" to his own ascendancy, steaming open their mail, tapping their telephones, and generally snooping on their expressed opinions. I cannot believe that these latter gentry have failed to discover the identity of Thomas Rainbro'. Their apparatus would be more flat-footed than usual if they fell down on such a simple constabulary task. . . .

What did it all amount to in the end? There were outraged people who savagely defended Churchill, sacred symbol of the

British way of life. Besmirching him was sacrilege, typical of a ruffianly editor like Bevan. There were some less vociferous and on the whole less articulate, who were inclined to suspend judgment. A mere handful came into the open to support him, a few M.P.s amongst them. 'There were some Generals in his camp,' Frank Owen says, 'and in retrospect they are still there!' The Conservatives shunned Bevan in the House, and some even of his Party friends did their best to persuade him out of habits which they said reduced him to the level of the swashbuckler. Bevan had a tendency to greet their warnings with a gale of laughter or eloquent argument. Nothing satisfied him so much as total war in debate, and now he carried his battle with Churchill out of the *Tribune* into the House of Commons.

It was said that these "outrages" enforced a certain isolation on him. It was said that, at root, Bevan became a lonely man. But a handful of kindred spirits continued to surround him, he found time for swopping poetry declamations with friends, and he was still likely to give a handful of the Chosen a reading of next week's leader from the *Tribune*, in the vinous shadows of Elvinos, the Fleet Street bar.

II

CHURCHILL and Bevan represent opposite poles of the British political scene but there are threads running through their careers, and qualities of personality which reveal curious identities. No one questions the gulf which divides one creed from another, no one questions that they were children of different ages. One born to the settled Mid-Victorian era, when lack of foreign competition laid half the world at Britain's feet, when middle-aged men talked of Gladstone and Disraeli and the English unfalteringly, and with some evidence, believed that they were the chosen people. One born to Omdurman, the flying pennants, the lances and thunder of the cavalry charge, which imprinted itself indelibly on his mind so that these things always moved him deeply thereafter. The other a child of the far more self-assertive late Victorian age with Mr. Gladstone gone, a few cracks appearing in the social façade, young Bernard Shaw preaching high heresies, and signs of organized resistance from the working class assuming alarming proportions. But early differences did not destroy identities. In his schooldays the classics presented difficulties to Churchill as lessons held little enlightenment for Bevan, and Churchill, busy in the hot afternoons of Bangalore, absorbing the things which Harrow and Sandhurst omitted to teach him, reading *The Decline and Fall*, Plato's *Republic* and Aristotle's *Politics*, had a counterpart in Bevan reading equivalent works far into the night in his cottage bedroom at Tredegar. Both, emerging from conventional restrictions, began to talk brilliantly, Churchill revealing a base tendency to trade English essays for Latin translations, and Bevan ready to swop his eloquence for a good argument.

As fully adult persons, they were both at the centre of whatever storms were brewing and soon in full flood of impressive speeches. They were, in the beginning, essentially thinkers whose every other phrase had an emotional undertow capable of pulling an audience off its feet, but if there was a dash of the demagogue in both, one was a very different demagogue from the other, and if they were capable of sharing deep experiences with the common people, one was saved from sentimentality by cold, clear wit.

They were both *bons vivants*, convinced that life should be lived to the full at all costs. They were both rebels, and rebels capable of standing alone against half the world. It was this quality which made them the black sheep of their respective parties at different times. Churchill's constant campaigning for increased military expenditure had always embarrassed the Tory leaders, the unmistakable meaning of his speeches consistently exposed the shambling evasions of the Chamberlains and Baldwins. And if there was one thing the Labour Party felt it could guarantee about Bevan it was that they never quite knew what he would do or say next.

Other identities in personal habits, in energy, even in appearance —both powerfully built men with personal magnetism—were clear. Why then did Bevan single out Churchill for attack? Obviously the man was the demi-god of capitalism, the implacable opponent of the Labour Party, and as such a constant challenge to Bevan. Self-evident explanations rarely encompass the whole truth, but psychological speculation is fraught with danger and should be kept within iron bounds. Yet the temptation to ask certain questions about a feud which had several counterparts down history based upon something more than ideological differences, is strong. Was this the final and magnificent symbol of Orchard the schoolmaster, an Orchard Churchill bringing his rod to bear on the backs of millions of workers? Or in its far more subtle implications was it that Bevan became far too aware of his own shortcomings reproduced in Churchill, and conveniently punished them at one remove?

No such subtleties bothered the Conservative and Labour Parties, assessing Churchill's and Bevan's respective merits. Characteristically each party considered its own champion the better man, seeing a greater intellectual range and eloquence in one, accusing the other of partisan hatred and distortion. Characteristically one was driven by the inner necessity of his nature, the other a party politician, prey to every specious wind which blew.

The battle between them was fully joined in July 1942 with a motion of 'no confidence in the general direction of the war,' put by Sir John Wardlaw-Milne. Bevan rose and addressed the House.

... It seems to me that there are three things wrong [with the direction of the war today]. First, the main strategy has been wrong;

second, the wrong weapons have been produced; and third, those weapons are being managed by men who are not trained in the use of them and who have not studied the use of modern weapons. . . . The Government have conceived the war wrongly from the very beginning, and no one has more misconceived it than the Prime Minister himself.

. . . Why is the strategy wrong? I say, first, that it is because the Prime Minister, although possessing many other qualities, sometimes conceives of the war, it seems to me, in mediæval terms, because he talks of it as if it were a tourney. But the strategy is wrong because the Prime Minister has a wrong instrument of government. . . .

. . . Furthermore—and I said I was going to be quite frank—if the Prime Minister wants to restore confidence in the British Army, he will have to change his Secretary of State for War. Why on earth he appointed him I do not know. I am not trying to be offensive; the . . . Hon. Gentleman has been in the War Office for five years, and he is picked out of a respectable obscurity and is pushed into an office. Nobody, no soldier in the British Army knows him. All they know is that he has been at the War Office for five years, and they have no confidence in the War Office. They do not believe in the War Office, and the Prime Minister's political sagacity is so great that he picks out an official from the War Office and makes him Secretary of State for War. I say that the Prime Minister has great qualities, but obviously picking men is not one of them. . . .

. . . . Do not on these high matters speak with a twisted tongue; do not use words with double meanings; do not use sentences with hidden purposes. On these high matters, speak truthfully and simply, so that the people can understand and trust. Let the Government, for Heaven's sake, make their political dispositions. In the meantime, let them change the direction of the war. Purge the Army and the Air Force of the elements which are not trusted at the moment. Get at the enemy where he really is—21 miles away, not 14,000 miles away. Get him by the throat. . . .

Taken as a whole it was a rousing speech. He even asked for politicians to be sent into battle. Churchill sat throughout glowering. Once or twice he barked an interruption. Once he broke his sphinx-like posture, arms folded, chin sunk on his chest, and started up as though about to say something at length. When he did reply he said he was preoccupied with matters far removed from the realm of Aneurin Bevan.

Although I have done my best, my utmost, to prepare a full and considered statement for the House, I must confess that I have found it very difficult, even during the bitter animosity of the diatribe of the Hon. Member for Ebbw Vale [Mr. Bevan], with all its carefully aimed and calculated hostility, to concentrate my thoughts upon this Debate and to withdraw them from the tremendous and most critical battle now raging in Egypt. At any moment we may receive news of grave importance. . . .

Bevan returned to the attack in September of the same year.

'. . . I wish he [Mr. Churchill] would recognize that he is the civilian head of a civilian government, and not go parading around in ridiculous uniforms. It would be very much more dignified if he . . . went around in ordinary fustian. . . .'

He had just described Churchill's latest war report as 'turgid, wordy, dull,' and 'prosaic. . . .' This shattering indictment followed: '. . . the Prime Minister's continuance in office is a major national disaster. He is no longer able to summon the spirit of the British people, because he represents policies that they deeply distrust. . . .'

The Press and the House of Commons rose to Churchill's defence almost without exception. To make a solemn complaint because the Prime Minister wore, 'or someone told Bevan that he wore, an unspecified uniform on some informal occasion,' belonged to the schoolroom and was bad enough, but to describe the Prime Minister's continuance in office as a major national disaster was 'outrageous falsehood.' 'These sour snarling attacks,' wrote Cummings in the *News Chronicle*, 'must tend to destroy whatever status Mr. Bevan may have acquired as an honest Parliamentary critic. I do not suggest that he should follow Mr. Hore Belisha's inspiring example and enter a Cistercian monastery . . . but if he were to return to some quiet Welsh village for a spell of hard thinking, he might be less apt to talk so violently through his hat.'

Almost simultaneously Churchill flashed at Bevan: 'The Hon. Gentleman is a merchant of discourtesy. . . .' In private Bevan was said to have retorted, 'Better than being a wholesaler of disaster.'

In March of the following year Bevan attacked not Churchill, but Churchill's son, Randolph, then serving with the Army. It was the occasion of the famous letter written by Major Randolph Churchill to the London *Evening Standard* in which he deplored 'a widespread tendency to assume that any Frenchman who has occupied any official position under the government of Vichy . . . must naturally be a traitor, or possessed of a Fascist mentality . . .'

and referred to the 'pharasaical attitude' of 'certain French elements in London.' General Eisenhower had just appointed Admiral Darlan, General Giraud and Peyrouton in North Africa, and the Left wing was aghast at what appeared to be the substitution of another row of Fascists for the row just annihilated. Major Randolph Churchill saw it all very differently.

Bevan asked Churchill whether his son's letter had been censored and Churchill replied '. . . This question should normally have been addressed to the Secretary of State for War, but since the Hon. Member, no doubt from those motives of delicacy in personal matters which are characteristic of him, has preferred to put it to me, I will answer it myself. . . . It was not passed by any senior officer. The base censorship deals with matters of security, which in this case are not involved. . . .'

This small storm might have blown itself out quickly enough but Bevan's blood was up. A week later he raised the question again. He was now at some pains to explain that technically, the question had to be put to the Prime Minister in his capacity as Minister of Defence and that he had, in any case, sent a personal letter to the Prime Minister, warning him in advance. The fact that there was some confusion about the date on which Churchill actually received the letter, obscured Bevan's attempts to clarify his motives. In the next half-hour Prime Minister and back-bencher settled down to a steady bout of bickering.

Bevan argued that if Major Randolph Churchill could write to the *Evening Standard* in this cavalier fashion, then the privilege should be extended to all other serving officers. 'I have friends serving with the Eighth Army . . . sharing the same point of view as I do who would like to have the right to write to the British Press and disagree with General Eisenhower.' 'I am deeply distressed that the Prime Minister is personally involved. . . .' (Churchill smiled.) 'He . . . must not imagine that I have yet yielded to the same political cynicism which has obviously overtaken him. . . .' Remembering the origin of the Rainbro' articles all this was doubly interesting.

Churchill's defence of his son's behaviour was adroit. . . . 'I wonder whether if this letter . . . had been written by any other Hon. Member of the House it would have attracted the energetic attention of the Hon. Member. . . . There are, of course, elements on both sides of the Atlantic who indulge in these forms of badinage. The President of the United States presents a much larger target than I do, as he has no fewer than four sons serving, whereas I have only one. . . . I therefore leave the personal aspect while expressing all acknowledgments to the Hon. Member for his unfailing courtesy. . . .'

In the end, Churchill made the interesting admission that serving officers or men could write to the Press without censorship on all matters other than military matters 'or literature in furtherance of the purposes of any political organization or party.'

Eleanor Rathbone rounded off the episode. 'I only want to say very bluntly . . . Nobody who has watched Mr. Bevan and his evolutions in this House can doubt that he entertains a malicious and virulent dislike of the Prime Minister. . . .'

Yet there were moments in these exchanges when sheer felicity of phrase softened the harsh reputation Bevan had by now acquired. In December 1943, he described the Allied High Command as having approached the problem of attacking Italy 'like an old man approaching a young bride—fascinated, sluggish and apprehensive.' The House came near to liking him for that and if, within a few weeks, it was quickly out of sympathy with him again, it could not deny the effectiveness of this speech which forced the admiration of his most bitter opponents. The opening passages are worth recalling as a piece of Parliamentary criticism which left Eden the difficult task of attempting a reasoned reply and put the "tempestuous Welshman" in a different perspective for some of the most die-hard members of the House.

. . . It seems to me that our Debates get more and more unreal, and indeed, that the House of Commons itself establishes a more and more remote contact with what is being done by the Government. We did not expect yesterday that the Right Hon. Gentleman would be able to tell us the military proposals and plans which were made at that Conference, but the Right Hon. Gentleman went on to hint that other decisions were taken in international and foreign affairs and upon foreign policy. He told us nothing about these, so we are unable to tell what the Government's decisions are until they have been disclosed to us by Government action. It means therefore that the House of Commons is coming to have less and less control over the policies of the Government.

Then came the story from his childhood:

I have spent now more than a quarter of a century of my life in public affairs, and as I grow older I become more and more pessimistic. I started—if the House will forgive me this personal note

—my career in public affairs in a small colliery town in South Wales. When I was quite a young boy my father took me down the street and showed me one or two portly and complacent-looking gentlemen standing at the shop doors, and, pointing to one, he said, 'Very important man. That's Councillor Jackson. He's a very important man in this town.' I said, 'What's the Council?' 'Oh, that's the place that governs the affairs of this town,' said my father. 'Very important place indeed, and they are very powerful men.' When I got older I said to myself, 'The place to get to is the Council. That's where the power is.' So I worked very hard, and, in association with my fellows, when I was about 20 years of age, I got on to the council. I discovered when I got there that the power had been there, but it had just gone. So I made some inquiries, being an earnest student of social affairs, and I learned that the power had slipped down to the county council. That was where it was, and where it had gone to. So I worked very hard again, and I got there—and it had gone from there too. Then I found out that it had come up here. So I followed it, and sure enough I found that it had been here, but I just saw its coat tails round the corner.

The ordinary man in Great Britain has been spending his life for the last couple of generations in this will-o'-the-wisp pursuit of power, trying to get his hands on the levers of big policy, and trying to find out where it is, and how it was that his life was shaped for him by somebody else. We were convinced by our institutions and representative democracy that the House of Commons itself was that instrument, and that seat of power; but these Debates, and especially the speech of my Right Hon. Friend yesterday, convinced me that the House of Commons is becoming almost irrelevant.

These were the dramatic days when Italy suddenly collapsed and the King of Italy, with Marshal Badoglio, agreed to Armistice terms which were not disclosed. Italy had surrendered and was prepared to become co-belligerent, but very few details were permitted to escape for public consumption. The end of Italy came unexpectedly, and a wave of rumour and excitement spread through the country because in those unwary days there were indications that this was the beginning of the end of the war, and there was much talk of how the Germans would take it. High celebrations were officially endorsed, but the terms of the Armistice remained a close diplomatic secret, and Bevan seized upon the situation to attack Churchill again. He put it on record that when the Armistice terms were published the world would be able to judge whether there was any real need for this elaborate smokescreen. Immediately, he knew of only one reason. That the

Government might continue dealing with King Victor Emmanuel and Marshal Badoglio. . . .

Bevan then quoted from Salvemini, who had written in an American paper:

> The treaty of alliance with Hitler of May, 1939, explicitly forbade a separate armistice and a separate peace, to say nothing of "co-belligerency" with the enemy. That treaty was negotiated, agreed upon, and signed not only by Foreign Minister Ciano, not only by Mussolini as head of the Government, but also by the King [of Italy] as head of the State. By agreeing to the Armistice and then to "co-belligerency," the King committed an overt act of perfidy and treachery. It was treachery even if it was done against a criminal like Hitler. A gangster does not become a gentleman if he betrays, not a gentleman, but another gangster. The King of Italy first forsook his oath to the Constitution of the realm and associated with Mussolini for 20 years in the betrayal of the Italian people; then he associated with Hitler in an attempt to betray all the peoples of Europe; then he betrayed Mussolini; then he betrayed Hitler. Whom will he betray tomorrow?
>
> How on earth [Bevan commented] is it possible to convince Italians of the seriousness of our democratic intention in Europe, when we do our very utmost to support and buttress a man who has so evil, disreputable and venal a reputation as that?

There was much more along similar lines about the King of Greece and the Atlantic Charter, about Colonel Zervas and France, and at every turn the utterance was vivid, and Churchill's name continually crept in. One political commentator said: 'One day Aneurin Bevan may be given the chance to prove that he can run a Government Department as efficiently as he can criticize it.'

The House breathed again, certain for a few short weeks that anyone who could command such powers of Parliamentary criticism would not easily relapse into his 'ruffianly past.' Alas, before the year was out he was at it again. Ernest Thurtle said that the House sensed that Mr. Bevan's attacks were the result of 'twisted malevolence,' not 'honest conviction.' He quoted Pope:

> Destroy his fib, or sophistry—in vain!
> The creature's at his dirty work again.

He went further. . . . The attacks 'were for the most part so charged with spleen and malevolence as to lack any real objective quality: Indeed, in their examination of the actions and motives of the Prime Minister they were about as balanced as the efforts of Dr. Goebbels. . . .'[1] Finally, in a moment of magnificent anger Churchill fixed a basilisk eye on Bevan and thundered that he was—a squalid nuisance.

Tremendous lightnings flashed out of the murk and there was continually an exciting sense of two giants from different ends of the social scale, well matched and equipped, coming to the final grips which a robust democracy encouraged, but the inspiring moments were sometimes overwhelmed by sheer rancour and spite and petty hate.

★   ★   ★

Presently the war reached a quite new stage. Everything was ready poised to strike at Nazi-occupied Europe. Gigantic preparations had built a great armada of ships waiting in camouflaged harbours, fleets of planes flew daring sorties over France, armies were massed round the coasts of Britain equipped with weapons quite unknown in history before. An electric atmosphere charged with rumour and counter-rumour enforced fierce disciplines of silence on anyone unfortunate enough to share the slightest shred of official truth. It was a situation where nerves threatened to overwhelm common sense, a casual word might set off an explosion; a situation with terrifying responsibilities involving the possible collapse of four long years of preparation, and somewhere in the background a dim idea that greater things than victory or defeat hinged on this operation, that we were liable to drop back into the Dark Ages if by some diabolical accident it misfired now. The very word "strike" in such a situation was treasonable to the High Command, but now a series of strikes sent an outraged shudder through the Cabinet, and let loose a stream of vituperation from the Tory back-benchers. If this war machine forged with such minute care over all these years was suddenly left in mid-career without sufficient fuel, it would constitute a major act of sabotage. If the flow of arms and ammunition broke down because a handful of miners not directly engaged in war, saw fit to strike for another few shillings a shift, nothing could excuse them.

Ernest Bevin announced, with his unfailing flair for the dramatic, that the stoppage in the Yorkshire coalfield was far worse than if Sheffield had been bombed—as indeed it might have

[1] *Time's Winged Chariot*—Ernest Thurtle. (Chaterson, 1945.)

been—but the miners had their case too, which received scant attention. A dramatic pronouncement of new powers to deal with "industrial agitators" followed.

Anyone starting an unofficial strike was liable to a maximum penalty of five years' penal servitude, a fine of £500 or both. Although these powers applied to unofficial strikes alone, they sent a wave of consternation through the trade union movement, undermining as they did the biggest democratic privilege in the industrial life of Britain—the right to strike whenever and wherever men chose—a right now restrained and largely held in reserve, but still jealously guarded as a final prerogative.

Bevan put together his case against what he considered an abrogation of time-honoured privilege, fast becoming the talk of the country under the peculiar cipher 1AA. Already he had headed a deputation which visited Bevin as Minister of Labour and roundly abused another aspect of his manpower policy. That meeting had developed into something resembling a quarrel when Bevan suddenly threw back his head, released a roar of laughter and said: 'Chuck it boys. He's too downy a bird for us to pull that particular wool over his eyes. I'll tell him what we really must have. And I'll show you how you can give it us, Bevin, and why you ought to.' 'And,' said Bevin, 'he did . . .' he 'put up a case that I could meet and had to meet.' And Bevin reflected: 'There's some stuffin' in that fellow. . . . Me and him can do business.' [1]

But the business with 1AA was not of his choosing. Bevan began his counter attack in the House of Commons on 28 April 1944.

I am bound to ask the House to consider, in the beginning, the way in which this Order [1AA] was made. The House will forgive me if I sound a somewhat personal note. I think Members will agree that, on many occasions, I and some of my Hon. Friends have done our utmost to maintain the dignity of Parliament. I have protested, on more than one occasion, about the Government going behind the back of Parliament, and reaching understandings with outside bodies, and then presenting Parliament with a *fait accompli*. The circumstances in which this Order was made were peculiarly vicious. . . .

. . . I come to the actual nature of the Regulation itself. . . . Take the position of two men going to a factory. They arrive at the

[1] *The Triple Challenge*—Francis Williams. (Wm. Heinemann Ltd.)

factory gates and the foreman says that the rate on the job has altered. Perhaps there is a reduction of 2d. a piece, or 3d. an hour. The employer is all right because he has not locked them out. All he says is, 'Take it or leave it.' In the definition under this Regulation, that is not a lock-out, and, therefore, no penalties are inflicted upon the employer. But if one man says to the other, 'Let us go home,' he gets five years' penal servitude for fomenting a stoppage. . . . Do Hon. Members consider that that is a just and reasonable position in which to put people? . . . The worker has his hands tied behind his back, but the employer is perfectly free.

. . . What is to happen if the Minister's Regulation becomes law? We shall all become "cock-eyed" watching each other. That is, unfortunately, the situation which will arise, that people will have to be careful where they say a thing, and what they say. They will have to speak two languages, one for the street and the other for the trade union meeting. There never was a more absurd law framed than that. Its constitutional implications are shocking.

. . . I have had threats this week that if I went on with this Motion, action would be taken against me, not by my own members but by the big bosses at the top. Well, I do not represent the big bosses at the top; I represent the people at the bottom, the individual men and women, and I say that this Regulation is the enfranchisement of the corporate society and the disfranchisement of the individual. It gives status to the organized body, and destroys the status of the individual citizens. It elevates the irresponsible trade union official— and I use the word "irresponsible" in the constitutional sense of the term, because a trade union official is irresponsible; he is not subject to election, as we are; he is not exposed to pressure, as we are. George Bernard Shaw said, in 'The Apple Cart,' that the person in this country who is in the most strongly entrenched position, next to the King, is the trade union official. Between 7,000,000 and 8,000,000 organized workers and trade union officials are protected under this Regulation, but 13,000,000 unorganized workers have no protection at all.

. . . I, therefore, suggest to the House and to the Government that they ought to take back this Regulation. If they want any special powers, they ought to come to Parliament for them and let us discuss them properly. But the Government, in circumstances of this sort, ought not to put penalties upon the British people which will have the effect, not of minimizing but of aggravating stoppages, and will undermine the morale and courage of the people of Great Britain at a moment when they are needed more than ever. . . .

It was not Ernest Bevin but Arthur Greenwood, Parliamentary Leader of the Labour Party, who came to his feet to answer this speech in one of the most spirited and, for Greenwood, the most abusive outbursts he had launched in many a year. . . . It was a speech, Greenwood said, 'the like of which I have never heard from the most die-hard Tory, in this House or outside. . . . My Hon. Friend gibbeted the trade union movement, gibbeted its leaders, frowned upon its officials and even said that the elected representatives of the people were nobody. . . .'

Then came Ernest Bevin. 'Making catchphrases,' he said, 'is an easier job than directing 24,000,000 people in a war of this character.' To say that he, Mr. Bevin, had influenced the Press to create an atmosphere favourable to the Regulation was a lie. 'Some members would rather that the working class went to hell through chaos than that they won a victory through organization.' He castigated 'the tiny little semi-legal rhetorical minority in the Labour Party,' of which Bevan was uncrowned king. As for the complaint that he had consulted the trade unions and the employers before introducing the Regulation, he asked Parliament to imagine the outcry if he had attempted some piece of legal reform without consulting the Law Society, or if the Minister of Health, envisaging a new National Health Scheme, had refused to consult the doctors.

One of the most dramatic and bitter debates of the war finished heavily in Bevin's favour, but the end of the debate was only the beginning of serious trouble. Bevan had roused the full fury of the trade union empire, there were those amongst the elders of the Labour Party very tired of his heresies, and even some of the small group of M.P.s who backed him, quailed at the derision he had poured on the Olympian figures of the Left. Opposition was one thing; abuse another.

Bevin returned to the attack at Bristol the following week and was answered within a few days. . . . 'Mr. Bevin says I attacked the trade unions in opposing his new order in the House of Commons,' Bevan said. . . . 'Who are my associates in my action? Mr. David Kirkwood, a life-long leader of the Amalgamated Engineering Union, Mr. George Buchanan, Chairman of the pattern workers, Mr. S. O. Davies, for many years a miners' agent and miners' M.P., as I am. . . . We are [also] supported by the South Wales Miners' Federation, the Executive of the National Union of Distributive and Allied Workers, and a whole lot of trade union branches and shop stewards all over the country. . . .'

Mr. Bevin, Bevan went on, won the vote and lost the argument in the House of Commons—a not unusual spectacle. IAA was aimed not at the people who fomented strikes but at those members of the trade unions who were challenging the entrenched position of bureaucrats. It was an Act made to protect trade union officials from their rivals. Mr. Bevin raved, blustered and threatened, to conceal the blunder he had made. Why did he rage so? After all he had 314 votes to Bevan's 23. Why should he worry? 'I suspect because he knows that my 23 represents more trade unionists in the country than his 314.' This conclusion had all the air of a debating conjuring trick, but little substance of established fact.

In the Labour Party the storm was growing, and now came an exhumation of Bevan's war record. Performed with full rites it emphasized his consistent refusal to accept the ruling that Party strife must be suspended in wartime. Back in 1941 Attlee, then leader of the Parliamentary Labour Party, had said: 'National unity does not mean the acceptance by one Party of the views and policy of another. It does not mean that Socialists must accept everything that Conservatives believe. . . . The essence of Democracy is that, although disagreeing, we are able to work together for a common end. . . .'

First splendid renunciations had shown signs of wear by 1942, and counsels were threatening to divide, but Morrison gave his support to this addendum at the 1942 Conference. . . . 'That the participation of the Labour Party in the Government for the purpose of taking its full part in the prosecution of the war, carries with it both the maintenance of the Electoral Truce and general co-operation with other Parties participating in the Government, in promoting the return of Government Candidates at Parliamentary By-Elections. . . .'

By 1943, Party delegates were performing subtle somersaults which reconciled being both in and out of the Coalition, and made supporting the war consonant with not supporting the Government. Vansittartism was backed by a majority vote at the 1943 Conference and sent Bevan off in tremendous anger to address a special delegates' meeting which carried a resolution that the decision misrepresented the views of the rank and file. . . . 'We therefore conceive it our duty to place on record our surprise and indignation that the Labour Movement of this country should be made to appear to share the detestable views which have come to be known as Vansittartism.' By 1944 Bevan was openly flaunting the Executive's desire to preserve the dignity of the Coalition and now—final heresy—had challenged the wisdom of 1AA and incited rebellion amongst M.P.s and rank and file alike, in such a way as to outrage the Party Executive.

The familiar ritual of a belligerent Bevan trying to swing the whole Labour Party back into the path which he believed was its true heritage, and an infuriated Executive making plans to bring to heel once and for all this irrepressible "revolutionary" in their midst, needs closer examination to be seen in perspective. Before the war the Party machine in the House of Commons had become steadily more rigid and doctrinaire, overwhelming one rebel M.P. after another, until the already complicated issue between personal and Party loyalties had developed into a major parliamentary problem. The Party hack was a familiar figure. His vote had all the appearance of a reflex action. Whatever its precise mechanism a three-line whip never failed to produce the requisite result at any given time. Under these conditions, when the Parliamentary Party decided by a majority vote to endorse certain policies, it expected all M.P.s to conform, but there was a danger of any Party ossifying if the pressure became too crushing. The stimulus of debate was the life-blood of political parties, and yet, in a Coalition wartime government, Party members were expected to constrain their more savage outbursts in the interests not only of party but national unity. Bevan had flagrantly violated this understanding with such consistency that now, not even the special dispensations granted the individual dissident—always shown a romantic toleration against the merciless distaste for the organized group in the Labour Party—were any longer his.

Dramatically Arthur Greenwood brought four charges against Bevan and proposed his expulsion. He was a persistent obstructor of the Party, he did not carry out Party decisions, he used exaggerated language about trade unions, and he was a non-co-operator. But to expel him would involve the fifteen other M.P.s who had voted with him, amongst them D. R. Grenfell, former Secretary of the Mines and a member of the Labour Party's own Administrative Committee. It was now clear that the voting on 1AA had been very unsatisfactory inside the Party, despite a three-line whip. Only one-third of Labour's strength voted for the Government with 116 back benchers abstaining. Greenwood's motion for expulsion started a long and heated debate in the

Parliamentary Labour Party which revealed a cleavage even deeper than had been suspected, and it became clear that there was little hope of a substantial majority against Bevan—abstentions, once again, were more likely to be the order of the day. But the air was loud with demands to rid the Labour Party of the perfervid Welshman.

At the next Parliamentary Labour Party meeting Bevan was said to have made a less intransigent speech, Shinwell carried a compromise motion of "censure without expulsion" by 71 votes to 60—there were a number of abstentions—and in the end some leaders of the Party withdrew in a huff, protesting that their position was becoming intolerable. The whole inquiry grew more and more delicate. Mr. George Hall, the Under Secretary for Foreign Affairs, and Arthur Jenkins, Mr. Attlee's Parliamentary Private Secretary, were both members of the South Wales Miners Group in the House of Commons which backed Bevan, the number of rank and file trade unionists who set their faces against 1AA grew every week and these long-drawn-out negotiations threatened to weaken the position of the Executive itself. In desperation the Party called a joint meeting of the National Executive and Administrative Committee. It was a full-dress meeting with forty members present, including Attlee, Dalton and Morrison. It wrangled for two hours. In the end it 'profoundly deplored the action of Aneurin Bevan in deliberately flouting decisions of the Parliamentary Party, and thereby causing disunity in the ranks,' and asked for a written assurance within seven days that he would in future observe Standing Orders. It is an understandable frailty of many politicians that confronted with anything resembling an ultimatum, they usually do what is best for their careers. It can be argued that Bevan was no exception, that he would never have faced a second expulsion from the Labour Party. Certainly he compromised and agreed to their terms.

But Mr. Greenwood and many others were out for blood, and the T.U.C. refused to be satisfied with any motion of censure or polite withdrawal. They reported Bevan to the Mineworkers' Federation and in the process Mr. Charles Dukes opined that some Labour Party members were 'opposition minded.' 'Of course,' Bevan retorted, 'we are opposition minded and we shall continue to be so until the working classes have got power.' It was another debating point easily won, and it served to outrage still more the susceptibilities of those in the Labour Party who normally recoiled from Bevan as from the devil. Even so, he had considerable backing within the individual unions, and on 5 June 1944, he threw down another gauntlet. He was, he said, prepared to resign his seat and contest it again on the issue of 1AA. Here was the final bravado or the final challenge. Of course, Bevan knew that whatever happened in this dispute the South Wales miners would return him once more with an overwhelming majority, and to that extent he could burn his boats with complete impunity, but it was a rare challenge to issue and nobody seemed prepared to take him up. All this turned out to be a dress rehearsal for an equally fierce struggle only eight years away, when Bevan once again cast himself in the rôle of saviour of the Party's soul, and fought another long-drawn-out battle, which from one point of view proved equally disrupting, and from another highly stimulating. Outbreaks of violence when he cast off Party discipline, Standing Orders, traditions of loyalty and half a dozen restraining hands, at one breath, were undeniably ambivalent. They brought down fire on his head, they gave him notoriety, but they also quickened the pulses of the Party and overcame any ossification. Yet there were some to argue that stimulus without disruption was the ideal, an ideal, they believed, beyond the reach of what they referred to as Bevan's braggadocio.

There followed in 1944 one of those incalculable reactions in public life which make the shrewdest politician feel like Sisyphus, for the street urchin of the Labour Party who had threatened to desecrate its most sacred altars, should have been led stonily away into the wilderness. Instead, at the 1944 Labour Party Annual Conference he was suddenly elected to the National Executive against fierce competition. He stood alone no longer; a considerable part of the rank and file was at his back.

*   *   *

The whole long history of the war suddenly raced to a new climax in midsummer of 1944. Shortly before midnight on 5 June, waves of Allied bombers opened the assault on Nazi-occupied Europe, Le Havre was shelled by the Navy, tanks went ashore at Arromanches and within twenty-four hours had pushed far inland. Bayeux and Caen became familiar words to people who did not know how to pronounce them. Six hundred Allied warships escorted great armadas across the Channel and within a short time Churchill, with an indestructible delight in great battles,

155

slipped over for a seven-hour visit to the Normandy beaches. The liberation of Europe had begun. Simultaneously a sinister new bomb which flew under its own power and seemed, at first, uncannily accurate, had begun to fall day and night on a London quite unable to retaliate. The two events vied with one another in the public eye, and there was optimistic talk of General Montgomery rooting the flying bombs out of their lairs on the Continent, although the gap between our point of landing and the apparent origin of the bombs was dismayingly wide. And then, as General Montgomery ran into stronger resistance, the advance slowed up and the queer, inhuman stutter of the bombs became a familiar sound in the life of every Londoner, the first rush of heightened living—as though a dam had burst after all those years of waiting—lost its impetus and people settled down less heroically, to yet another spell of endurance, enlivened by the knowledge that we were at last fighting on the soil of France.

The rockets followed. Mysterious projectiles, carrying a ton of explosive, they began their journey in France, reached into the stratosphere and crashed down at stupendous velocity upon some quite unknown and quite unprepared target. War had reached a new level of mechanical barbarism. The man who touched a switch eighty miles away had no certain knowledge where his weapon struck or whom it killed. Attacker and attacked were now totally divorced. Against this peculiar background, cheerful fatalism was the common reaction to the new threat of death and mutilation, prefaced every hour in London by the wailing siren, but the House of Commons continued to meet and debate in the heart of the capital and the deep flow of habit gradually absorbed this new nightmare, even to the point of renewing the clash between Churchill and Bevan.

Towards the end of June, Emanuel Shinwell asked the Prime Minister if he could assure the House that 'the financial arrangements in France and the recognition of the French Committee of National Liberation . . . [are] now being discussed with General de Gaulle and the French Committee. . . ?'

Bevan developed the question: 'It is not consistent with the authority or dignity of the House of Commons, that financial transactions of this sort should be entered into, without consulting it.' Did the Prime Minister know of 'the very grave anxiety which exists in very many parts of this country that American and British lives may be endangered in France as a consequence of the political handling of this question by the Government, and that, although we are all delighted with the military successes on the Continent ... the Government does not in fact receive the full confidence of all the peoples' in its broad handling of the war? ... In fact, did the Prime Minister realize 'that certain observations by him ... have been deeply resented by millions of people in this country and elsewhere? ...'

Churchill simply answered: 'I am afraid the Hon. Gentleman's question was so long that I have forgotten what was the point of it. ...'

In July Bevan returned to the Armistice issue, this time for Germany, and argued that the Government was failing to reinforce our armies with the most important political and moral weapon by not revealing the terms on which an armistice would be granted. The enemy would resist to the last man faced with the savagery of unconditional surrender, but given terms, thousands might lay down their arms. To withhold terms was to slaughter our own soldiers without any benefit whatever, other than satisfying some mediæval notion that an enemy must be humiliated before he was defeated.

A vote of thanks to the Prime Minister was in the air. Bevan said: 'If this House of Commons is to achieve that last abomination of hypocrisy, it will be necessary for some of us to oppose it. ...'

So the struggle ran on. Every other week throughout the rest of the war period some new clash occurred with the House waiting for one or the other to take the initiative as the circus waits for its star turn.

There followed the surprising reception at the Labour Party Annual Conference of December 1944 when Bevan, the rebel who had 'venomously attacked' Bevin, Morrison, the trade unions and half the sacred idols of the Left, was cheered by the delegates and loosed off another broadside at Churchill: 'I am rather astonished at the bad language used about him. The man has not changed. All that has happened is that people are now finding out the realities they should have seen before.' And later. ... 'As the Labour Party enters the lists in the next few months they should watch the Prime Minister very carefully. ... During the interregnum between a dissolution and an election there should be some constitutional device to keep the Prime Minister under executive control. ... Lloyd George once told me that when Mr. Churchill has made a speech he has won a battle. The act of expression is for him the final fulfilment. The task of concerting his phrases into action is a burden to his soul. For this reason he is the last person to entrust with problems of economic reconstruction.'

An undercurrent of reconstruction talk was now beginning to make itself felt and the Labour Party, so long forced to constrain party politics in a cloud of patriotism, showed signs of restiveness. With the end of the war and a swift election looming ahead, the Executive fulminated that it would be an unworthy thing for so great an adventure to end in squalid bickerings, but Bevan began to agitate for a clear-cut break with the Coalition which would leave the Labour Party free to 'face the future' and he found a new readiness to listen.

Late in 1944 he published his first book, a book directed at the coming election and a further terrific onslaught on Churchill— *Why Not Trust the Tories?* His writing did not match up to his oratory, but *Why Not Trust the Tories?* was a stimulating book in the political convention, if there were moments when the phrases seemed to hang on the air, awaiting applause. 'The first consideration is to see to it that the dominant role in society is played by public ownership. Once that is accomplished we might be able to afford the luxury of some controlled private enterprise. Once you break the back of the big Tories it might be safe to allow a few of the smaller ones to crawl around.' The book has another interest here. It set out to expose "the duplicity" with which the Tory Party won the support of millions of workers who were caught on the crest of the khaki wave after the 1918 war. It showed the striking resemblance between the situation then and in 1944–45; it repeated a number of resounding promises from Churchill, which, it said, were never fulfilled.

Certainly there were many resemblances between the two after-war periods. In 1918 Britain was sweeping towards victory under a Coalition Government, and as in the Second World War, the country had changed Prime Ministers in mid-career, Lloyd George replacing Asquith in 1916 as Winston Churchill had replaced Chamberlain in 1940. Lloyd George had become the nation's idol closely identified with the glories of victory, as Winston Churchill became its idol in 1945. The Lloyd George Parliament had run for eight years instead of its constitutional five; the Chamberlain-Churchill Government was nine years old.

In both periods 'the unity and fighting morale of the nation had been sustained through years of unimaginable suffering by lavish promises of a better Britain, a fairer distribution of the nation's wealth, a more generous provision for the social services, better wages and more secure employment, and a crusade against slums and insufficient houses. The war leaders knew the people were expecting the fulfilment of these promises. . . .' 'But,' wrote Bevan, 'what concerned them principally was how to exploit the situation in order to secure a Parliamentary majority for the Tory Party. . . .'

On all sides, he said, the Tories went through the motions of backing social reform to keep the electorate sufficiently drugged to vote for its shadow instead of its substance. Bevan quoted a speech Churchill made at Dundee on 11 December 1918. . . . 'We have got to do something on a bigger scale than ever before. The three great factors are land, communications and power and the three children, food, housing and manufacture. So long as the railways are in private hands they may be used for private profit. We cannot organize the great questions of land settlement, new industries and the extension of production unless the State has the control of transportation. . . .' Bevan commented. . . . 'A quarter of a century has gone by since then and in that period Winston Churchill has held high office, including four years as a Prime Minister. . . . But the railways are still in private hands. So is power and land. . . .'

And now in 1944–45, he said, exactly the same preparations were being laid for an even more magnificent deception.

Why Not Trust the Tories? marked another climax in Bevan's vendetta with Churchill, but still by no means exhausted it. Throughout 1945, the General Election and on into 1947, when the high and low places were reversed, the battle continued and Bevan's last critical blast in that year . . . 'Mr. Churchill . . . one of the chief architects of our misery . . .' was the beginning of yet another phase.

★   ★   ★

Did it all, from Bevan's point of view, carry any real conviction? Was it just another piece of political manœuvring made outrageous for the simple reason that no one can overlook the person who commits an outrage, and that the man who commits it consistently enough against the idol of the people, cannot prevent his own notoriety if not fame? And was Churchill still the eighteenth-century romantic in love with the past to such a pitch that he would rather go back to the days of the cavalry charge and intolerant British imperialism, where he must always remain a giant, than go forward to 'one world and a federation of free peoples'?

It is not so simple. For his part Churchill might be a man who desired above all things a dramatic world full of villains continually in process of subjection by Winston Churchill, but his devotion to Britain was more than romantic. It reverted to the episode in 1929 when he sought out Jennie Lee in the House of Commons and tried to explain that he did not like a sordid Britain any better than she did. He was just as anxious to have a fully employed, richly living, diversified people in Britain. Yet Bevan, looking at the Britain Churchill envisaged, saw some mystical personification of a great island shrouded in flags and traditions, and that was not the way he chose to interpret whatever national consciousness might mean. There are those amongst his close friends who say that much of his attack was sustained by genuine conviction. Certainly he saw Britain in very different terms from Churchill.[1]

In the late summer of 1947 I asked Aneurin Bevan what he really thought of the late Prime Minister. 'He is a man suffering from petrified adolescence,' he said. . . . 'He is an extrovert, a picture thinker. He has intelligence but no intellect. . . . He really has the values of a boy of seventeen to eighteen but he makes them sound like mature judgments by his sophisticated speech. . . .' A close sympathizer with Winston Churchill said that was an admirable description of Bevan. I failed to persuade Churchill to tell me what he personally thought of Bevan.

If it hopelessly over-simplifies something reaching deep into British history, it comes back in the end to the same platitude. These two men personified the opposite philosophies of Capitalism and Socialism. Attacking one another they were attacking the system of ideas for which each stood. They were part of the occasion, the contemporary instrument, through which the steadily mounting clash between Socialism and Capitalism expressed itself. The next two years were to bring the two systems head on.

[1] It would misrepresent Bevan's wartime speeches to say that they were purely attacks. There were many fine pieces of Parliamentary criticism.

12

FOR the first time in many years it smacked of Tammany Hall and the knuckleduster with no quarter asked or given. The most lurid scares trailed across the newspaper headlines should have stirred the British public to fever pitch, but whether from inertia or intuitive good sense, it refused to believe that the Gestapo crept the streets at night, that Professor Laski was the evil genius of bloody revolution, or even that Churchill by divine right must remain Prime Minister of England. Disillusion with war, and an uneasy sense that one could not emerge from such a catastrophe unscathed, did not entirely dim the glories of victory, and if the newspapers of the day had any validity it seemed that the Conservative Party could not escape another term of office. And then, against all persuasions, the British electorate astonished the world by sweeping into power the "dangerous, colourless, plan-ridden" Socialists.

On 27 July 1945, the *Daily Herald* ran a streamer headline "Labour in Power." Bonfires were set burning in London streets, dancing took place amongst the blitzed sites of the East End, and hundreds of people crowded the People's Palace and demanded a glimpse of their triumphant candidate, Clement Attlee. There followed a procession up The Mall to Buckingham Palace, a procession not unlike thousands which had preceded it, but said to be impelled by a very different purpose. 'We want the Prime Minister,' it chanted, aware that something very remarkable had happened in the political history of Britain.

The final count gave the Labour Party 394 seats against the Tories' 197 and the Liberals' 12. For the first time in its brief history —only forty-five years ago it was a persecuted minority—the Labour Party had indisputable power. A curious reorientation had taken place in the process. For this was not necessarily the upsurge of one class challenging and overpowering another. There were large numbers of middle-class voters amongst the Labour majority, and the composition of Labour's 394 M.P.s reflected the new alignment in the most interesting way. On one side stood 44 lawyers, 49 university and school teachers, 26 journalists, 15 doctors and dentists, 16 managers and technicians; on the other 150 manual workers, 8 working housewives and 39 miners.

Perhaps that was where Churchill made his biggest mistake. Romantically, he still saw a clear-cut division between one class and another, and looked down on the mass of people with a benevolent paternalism approximately a century out of date. But that was only half the story.

Against the better judgment of many Labour Party leaders, who counselled caution, convinced that Churchill's personal prestige must stop any landslide to the Left, Bevan had boldly announced that the Labour Party could and would gain power. He swept aside the suggestion that the Coalition should remain intact until the war with Japan was won, he jeered at the Jeremiahs who doubted the strength of Socialism and his editorials in the *Tribune*—outfacing any suggestion of compromise—set a spanking pace. 'It will not be merely sufficient to get a Parliamentary majority. We want the complete political extinction of the Tory Party and 25 years of Labour Government . . .' he said at the Blackpool Conference in 1945.

In the election which followed so rapidly and unexpectedly on the Blackpool Conference, Bevan and Jennie Lee journeyed up and down the country laying about them vigorously. At large amongst the electorate, they were in their element. Both brilliant speakers, they were convinced that this was the Labour Party's greatest opportunity. Here, for the first time, was a real chance to replace the improvident system which put the people at the mercy of economic environment, here was a chance to replace the hereditary ruling class, to make public interest the real test of public policy, to bring economic environment under control. They both attacked Churchill, as the personification of all that was old, outworn and privileged. More vigorous than his wife, Bevan's attacks followed the same general line. . . . 'People,' said Bevan, 'are thinking too much in terms of personalities when they should be thinking of principles. We see the personality of Winston Churchill paraded on the radio, in the press, built up to gigantic dimensions, until everybody around him looks like a Lilliputian. . . . When a man is in a very big position, the bigness of his position sometimes comes to be described as the bigness of the man. . . .'

There followed the great Laski scare when for ten dramatic

days this slight, bespectacled professor with a remarkable command of language, was accused of being the power behind the Labour Party throne, the hidden hand which would eventually control the Government in the most unconstitutional manner. A ten-day myth was created around one of the biggest brains in the Labour Party, a man capable of noble utterance, inordinate vanity and considerable tactlessness, and a mass of editorials attacked the Labour Party. It looked, at the time, as though this barrage of invective, ridicule and insinuation, released in a hundred newspapers throughout the country, could not possibly be politically impotent. That it was so, seemed to throw a new light on the power of the Press. In 1939 one of our leading daily newspapers published the categorical statement that there would be no war, and now the same paper announced with the same air of omniscience that there would be no Labour Government, yet when both these statements proved utterly false, the paper's circulation continued to progress monotonously towards the third million.

So it came about in the face of all the scares and stunts, the attacks upon "street urchin Bevan" and his "beautifully wrong-headed wife," that the Socialists were returned to power and amongst them, once again, was Bevan, and for the first time in fourteen years, Jennie Lee. There remained one chastening consideration. Cold statistics threw a shadow over the great Socialist triumph. From roughly 24,000,000 votes 12,008,512 were in favour of the Labour Party and 11,942,632 against. Seen in these terms the Socialist majority stood at 65,880.

In the broader world perspective, the Labour Party triumph was part of a gigantic new pattern now unfolding across many continents, with Socialism already established in Scandinavian countries, Communism trying to force its way into Western Europe, and Russia gathering new disciples in Eastern Europe. Great historical forces were not pressing inevitably towards Socialism or one universal brand of Socialism, as some people in Britain believed. What these forces rendered inevitable was large-scale organization and planning, as was reflected in America where its trusts, corporations and cartels recoiled from Socialism as from the devil. But as Professor G. D. H. Cole pointed out, large-scale organization and planning could be as consistent with *democratic Socialism* where responsibility was diffused right down to the roots of a society and the least person had a vote and a say, as with totalitarian autocracy where authority was closely concentrated at the centre and organization became ruthless. Whether one or the other, or something quite different emerged, depended not so much upon the impersonal march of events, as upon men and women remembering that mass-living and planning should not overwhelm that infinitely precious thing personal liberty, that it was not something begotten of bourgeois privilege which died at the Socialist meridian. Men must not only be freed from unemployment, want and fear; they must as much be freed from servility to the mass.

Whatever the ideological niceties, the Labour Party was now completely and solidly in power, perhaps to its own astonishment. Recovered from the shock, Attlee began a rapid search for his first Cabinet and was quickly embarrassed by a wealth of contradictions. Here were many types of skill and mind in profusion, yet these things could not count alone. Traditional elements in the Party held suspect a growing number of new M.P.s who were thought to be careerists willing to join any band waggon on the high road to power. Long years of service must be given due weight. Attlee, Ernest Bevin and Herbert Morrison, combined roots in the movement with more than a modicum of talent and could be relied upon to behave according to the approved code. Cripps, once a rebel, had a streak of idealism which saved him from commonplace censure, and his ability was immense. The rugged Emanuel Shinwell remained quite safe from excommunication. But Aneurin Bevan, who drank at so many perilous pools, and Jennie Lee, who had remained faithful so long to the simple verities of the I.L.P.—what would happen to these, now that Labour at last had staked its first serious claim?

Paradoxically it was said to be Bevin who directly recommended Bevan as a Minister in the new Labour Cabinet. Discussing possible people with Attlee one day Bevin said: 'You ought to give Nye housing. He may be awkward sometimes but he's got his head screwed on right and he's got guts. He'll not let our people down.'[1] Attlee was looking for someone who would remain faithful to a Socialist policy whatever attacks were made on him. Privately Attlee denied this story and said he "found" Bevan for himself.

Whichever way it went the news broke. Bevan was to become Minister of Health. There were many in the trade unions and the

[1] *The Triple Challenge*—Francis Williams.

164

Labour Party who heard the appointment with high trepidation, and cynics said Bevan had to be in the Cabinet, since the Executive could not possibly allow a critic with his devastating potential to remain on the back benches. Even some amongst those who congratulated him could not quite see "the buccaneer" steeped in the tradition of irreverence and attack, becoming a solid Minister of the Crown, without some ghost of his former self breaking through outrageously; and not only a Minister of the Crown. Aneurin Bevan now had the twin giants of Health and Housing under his control.

The strictures were many. Elderly trade unionists clucked their alarm, at least one member of the Labour Party Executive said it was madness, but Bevan's appointment was confirmed and now began the biggest job he had yet undertaken in his whole career. Almost at once, he rose to the occasion in a manner which annoyed the malevolent amongst his critics and reassured the sceptics. Aneurin Bevan had his heart in this huge task. The rôle of rebel had suited him well enough in the past. Now he had the power to set moving his own concept of a great new health scheme, which would offer a continuous "free" service to everyone, irrespective of the fees they could afford to pay.

His ability to read, absorb and sift a mass of facts and papers with immense facility stood him in good stead. He grasped not only the outlines but the details of the workings of health and housing in a way which surprised highly bred civil servants, once aware of his accession to power as an Admiral might regard a boarding pirate. Perhaps after all he would not be so intolerable. There were heresies, but his feats of memory and debate were surprising, his robust humanity pleasing, and if some of their hearts missed a beat to think what he might do next, they continued to turn out speech after speech for him. Bevan did not use them. The reasons were many and complicated. Pocketing one such speech, addressing an audience of doctors, he said . . . 'Although I persist in not delivering these speeches, my most excellent Department insists on giving them to me to deliver. . . . The trouble is, if I used this prepared speech, it would be a pretence of knowledge that I cannot possibly possess and it would give you a quite wrong impression. . . .'

His Private Secretary in the Ministry of Health, a man of considerable perspicacity, given to poetry in spare moments, said he liked him, and another highly placed civil servant—'All right of course—but he's on his best behaviour—he has to be.' I suppose anyone loathing him would not have told me so. There is a vested interest in silence in certain branches of the Civil Service. For the rest, Francis Williams went to see him a few weeks after he became Minister of Health. 'He seized me by the arm as I went into his large, sedate office, led me behind a screen at one end of the room and showed me, spread out on the floor, what looked like the contents of a small ironmonger's shop. "There you are, my boy!" he said. "Have you ever seen a better bath than that in your life? The Royal Ordnance Factories can produce them by the thousand. That's practical politics for you."'

In broad outline, the Health Bill which Bevan presently prepared for the House of Commons, set out to revolutionize the health services through three chosen instruments, the hospitals, the general practitioners and the larger local authorities. The Socialist Party believed that hospitals had sprung up in the most haphazard fashion, until Britain was confronted with an indiscriminate hotch-potch of buildings, in all shapes and sizes, which often failed to provide the most extensive service where it was most needed. Some of the hospitals were hopelessly small with less than thirty beds and Bevan said: 'No one can possibly pretend that hospitals so small can provide general hospital treatment. . . . Although I am not myself a devotee of bigness for bigness' sake, I would rather be kept alive in the efficient if cold altruism of a large hospital than expire in a gush of sympathy in a small one. . . .'

The ideal hospital unit was said to involve at least 1,000 beds and this was impossible while hospitals remained independent units or while so many local authorities could not or would not bear the cost. Bevan set out to merge all the multifarious parts of the hospital system into one co-ordinated service. It meant creating fourteen regions each with its own medical school. Planning and overall administration would be placed in the hands of Regional Boards. Although the Boards were to be appointed by the Minister he would consult every interest concerned. The responsibility for appointing hospital management committees for each large hospital or group of hospitals would devolve on its boards, and the day-to-day administration would pass in turn into the hands of the Committees.

It did not need any very high imagination to see that there might be a case for this, but when Bevan turned to the position of the general practitioners the way became treacherous. Bevan proposed setting up local executive councils in each county and county borough, the members of the councils to be equally divided between men from the professional bodies and men nominated partly by the local authority and partly by the Ministry. All the G.P. had to do if he wanted to join the scheme, was to put himself on the council's list. If he did not want to join, nobody would complain. That seemed dangerously fair. Anyone joining the service was to receive an immediate basic salary—its minute proportions were later to cause an outcry—plus capitation fees. It meant that any young doctor could begin earning a salary of sorts at once instead of borrowing money to buy himself off until he was firmly established. Bevan put it in his usual colourful way: turning to the usurer was what the Opposition called a sense of adventure in medicine.

The Bill next turned to another trouble. The distribution of doctors throughout the country was hopelessly uneven, the Socialists said, and it was proposed to create a Medical Practices Committee which would decide whether or not doctors should be permitted to set up practice in an area already well staffed. Its powers were negative rather than positive. It could say "no" only on the grounds that any particular area was already over-doctored, although just how the term over-doctored was to be defined, remained obscure.

The Health Centres were something of an experiment, and it was proposed that they should be controlled by the larger local authorities, in conjunction with executive councils. There were to be two types of centre, the larger intended to bring together six or ten doctors with all the up-to-date equipment said to be outside the resources of one general practitioner, and open to any patient in the region; the smaller intended to play the part of surgeries.

The Bill had a curious ancestry. Its provisions were not produced in their entirety out of the dusty pigeon-holes of the Ministry of Health, although there were signs of Civil Service temperance at every turn, nor were they solely the result of endless consultations between Bevan and all the fixed stars and satellites of the medical profession. The lately deceased Coalition Government had itself made some contribution, the "professional bodies" played a big part and some inspiration sprang from the 1937 P.E.P. report on Health.

There were many skirmishes in the second, and third readings of the Bill, which Bevan said certainly took from members opposite one of their chief sources of social patronage. Even so it was astonishing to him that the leaders of the medical profession had identified themselves in such a spirit of partisanship with the Conservatives. The spokesmen of some elements of the profession had become the most reactionary politicians in Great Britain. When he revealed that he proposed taking over the endowments of the voluntary hospitals to the extent of £32,000,000, it was described as . . . 'a very carefully prepared measure of highway robbery. . . .' Someone added: 'You can't delegate your conscience to a Minister—even if he is a Welshman.'

Bevan came back grandiloquently: 'Is the intelligent planning of the modern world to be prevented by the endowments of the dead?'

'I believe it is repugnant to a civilized community for hospitals to have to rely on private charity. I believe we ought to have left hospital flag days behind. . . .'

'The only voluntary part of the hospital service destroyed by this Bill is the necessity to sell flags and collect money. . . .'

'It is well established . . . that one of the chief qualifications of some of the ornaments of the profession is the fact that they are able to attract money to the hospitals from rich individuals.'

A dramatic statement from Dr. Dain, Chairman of the B.M.A. Council, said that Aneurin Bevan would become 'complete Medical Services dictator'[1] under the scheme. Either Mr. Bevan or the B.M.A. must give way and a full-scale battle seemed inevitable. Over the next few months it was fully joined.

The Opposition dealt vigorously with the proposal to abolish the sale and purchase of practices and was answered bitterly. . . . 'It is tantamount to the sale and purchase of patients. . . . Indeed, every argument advanced about the value of the practice is itself an argument against freedom of choice, because the assumption underlying the high value of a practice is that the patient passes from the old doctor to the new. If they did not pass there would be no value in it. . . .'

One of Mr. Bevan's lieutenants in the House developed the theme. If it was right for doctors to sell their practices why not medical officers of health, school teachers and sanitary inspectors, and if the doctor had the right to go just where he pleased to practise, why restrict the schoolmaster or dustman?

[1] *British Medical Journal*, 16.11.46.

Under close examination these analogies revealed suspicious divergences but no one in the House pressed analysis too far.

Presently came Bevan's summing up. . . . 'Now that we are reaching the conclusion, let me hope that the echoes of controversy will die down, and that what will reach our ears will not be the declamations of partisans, but . . . the piteous appeals of sick people all over the country . . . who are reaching out their hands to this House of Commons to give them succour and assistance in their difficulties. I believe that, eventually, it will be that small voice that will be heard, and that will be most influential, and not the raucous declamations of controversialism.' In cold print it reads sentimentally but in the House it carried a lofty ring. Bevan has always been genuinely moved by the plight of old and sick people unable to pay for medical attention.

The third reading of the Bill saw Bevan triumphantly through with few words out of place, never a buccaneering scene, and at least two surveys of the medical situation delivered at the level of statesmanship. The repartee when it came was beautifully controlled. Asked what he meant by 'intellectually lonely doctors' he replied: 'Doctors in intellectual purdah.' For the rest he adroitly ignored every bait offered his back bench ghost. But the fire in Aneurin Bevan had not gone out. He was now approaching forty-nine, there were signs of stoutness and lusty living had left its mark, but the diminution of drive which accompanies the middle years for most men was not evident in him.

As the nature of the Health Service gradually unfolded, Bevan's battle with the doctors brought bitter diatribes from some of their leaders directed personally at him all over again. He was accused of his old buccaneering habits, he was accused of intransigence and verbal violence, and some who took part recall moments when metaphorically the big fist descended on the table and Bevan spoke with the finality of a person who believed the moral gods to be immutably on his side. Others just as flatly declare him a model of patience and reasoning. The evidence achieves a high consistency of contradiction but Bevan was not alone in his belief that lofty commotions created by certain sections of the medical profession, down the centuries, about the sanctity of the patient and the inviolability of human life, sometimes bore the likeness of magnificently sustained shams which could, in their worst moments, conceal as rabid a piece of money-grubbing as any concocted in the temples of finance.

It was said that he brought forthright tactics from the House of Commons into the hallowed places of medicine and solemn gentlemen bred in the immaculate hush of the consulting room interpreted his words as vulgar.

From their point of view there were moments of near insolence. For some he was too clever by half. When one distinguished member of the profession protested, 'But, Minister, that is a clever piece of misrepresentation,' Bevan swept back, 'It couldn't be so clever for you to see through it so quickly.' And when a still more distinguished gynæcologist began, 'Minister, speaking for those responsible for women of child-bearing years,' Bevan interrupted, 'Is that a boast?' 'There were times when he made circles round us,' one highly placed member said, 'but he could never resist the witty retort, the lure of the glittering phrase.'

The same person said in the end, 'But he's a great man, you know. Make no mistake about that. It isn't true that he wanted a graduated capitation system as he later claimed, he hasn't always stuck to the facts retrospectively, but he took the hospitals out of local authority hands—immensely courageous with certain gentlemen in the L.C.C. only too anxious to stop him.'

Sometimes one-syllabled Anglo-Saxon words crept into the talks between Bevan and members of the profession he knew well. With Dr. Charles Hill, then Secretary of the B.M.A., there were blunt exchanges in a forthright vernacular both understood, Hill enjoying them as much as Bevan. And Dr. Hill once said: 'There's no doubt whatever about his ability, and he *can* be the most charming man in the world.'

It has to be remembered that the demands made on a modern Cabinet Minister far exceed anything known to their forbears in the romantic individualist past, and anyone familiar with the relentless round of committees, interviews and deputations, the constant need for consultation with civil servants, the sudden jump from a Ministry already involved in enormous local government complexities to Cabinet meetings concerned with half the world, would hesitate to expect a consistent imperturbability from any Minister. Certainly Bevan revealed remarkable powers of compromise, and he showed, on many occasions, restraint and patience through wearying deserts of consultation, which any statesman might envy. And it was not surprising that from his point of view he occasionally found in certain doctors a tempestuousness at least a match for his own. He wrote: 'I usually met its [the B.M.A.'s] representatives when they had come hot from a conference at which the wildest speeches had been made, frequently by the very men who then had to try to come to terms with the people they had been so immoderately denouncing. . . . I enjoyed the challenge. . . .'

He said he found it easy to win victories because they usually expended immense energy on defeating proposals which had never been made. 'Thus they would never become civil servants. As I never intended they should, I was able to concede the point without difficulty. . . Then there must be "free choice of doctor." I myself was most anxious to insist on this . . . Then there was the demand for full rights of free expression of opinion. . . . To this again I was most ready to respond. And so it went on from one blown out slogan to another. . . .' According to his book, *In Place of Fear*, Bevan suggested graduated capitation fees . . . 'highest in the medium ranges, lower in the higher. This would have discouraged big lists by lessening the financial inducement,' and made a reasonable living commensurate with good doctoring. The B.M.A. rejected it, he said. They wanted a uniform capitation fee irrespective of the number of patients. Later the principle was in serious doubt.

As the Health Service swung into its stride it revealed serious flaws and it was a pity that Bevan did not remain Minister of Health long enough to attempt to put them right. He was by no means blind to many shortcomings. The sheer cost of the Service —on a side issue of which he eventually resigned—haunted Treasury officials almost from the very beginning, and yet the offer made to the fledgling G.P. rendered survival dubious. Pay beds as against amenity beds and complications in the ophthalmic services were equally controversial.

For the rest, several years after the Health Service began people still did not realize that it was financed almost entirely from general taxation and not from direct contributions to National Insurance.

That was one of Bevan's main contributions. He examined many methods of paying for the service and rejected everything in favour of general taxation. American friends wanted him to fix an income limit below which treatment would be free while those above paid. He rejected this because it created a two standard health service. He rejected the flat compulsory contribution because it was merely a poll tax with all its disagreeable features.

Since the means of collecting revenues for the Health Service, the normal system of taxation, was already available, it seemed absurd to devise another. So the Health Service was financed from taxes and the contributions to National Insurance covered sickness benefit, unemployment and old age pensions. Apart from this, Bevan himself added some new characteristics to the actual plan of the Health Service.

In the end his worst critics turned out to be silent ones in the Labour Party. He had made too many concessions, they said, this was a bastard Service with the Socialist strains heavily recessive and the Coalition strains dominant, and if they did not put it quite that way in the House, Bevan was left in little doubt as to just what they meant.[1]

With housing it was different. Here he was not under the same tactical compulsion to compromise. Considered dispassionately as an exercise in logistics, the housing problem resolved itself into building over 750,000 new houses in the shortest possible time. Bevan put it differently. 'The housing shortage,' he said, 'is responsible for a greater volume of human misery than nearly any other single source, but I cannot look into the crystal and tell you just how many houses will be built in the next year. . . . We have had too many programmes. It is time we had some houses. If you tie yourselves to figures you become a victim of the importunities of undesirable elements. These are the building contractors who want to hold the public up to racketeer prices and if they know the Minister has committed himself to a certain number of houses in a particular time, they will use that as a lever against him. . . .'

The Opposition fastened on this and drew encouragement from what they at once described as disingenuous evasion. A housing programme without a target, they said, was a ship without a rudder, but they reserved their more savage attacks. The whole conception of Bevan's building policy began with the belief that the housing problem had largely been solved for the middle classes before 1939, but the problem for the lower income groups had remained materially untouched since the industrial revolution. . . . 'Of the houses built by private builders between the wars less than one-twelfth were for letting and just

[1] This, of course, was reflected generally in the policy of the Labour Party which had swung away from the teachings of the Marxist group to Fabian gradualism.

under a quarter were for working-class people.' Now the situation must be reversed. Need would govern priority, not money. He intended to do this by concentrating on houses to let and by using the local authorities as his main planning instrument.

The intervention of the local authority was no doctrinaire decision, the Socialist Party argued. Houses would be built for sale or under contract to private purchasers only by permission of the local authority, to avoid destroying the balance of the programme and to stop manpower and materials satisfying those who could buy houses when their need and hardship was less than those who could only afford to pay rent. It was as necessary to control the flow of building material to the sites according to an agreed system of priorities and the number of men working on the sites, as it was to distribute the material evenly to avoid a forest of half-finished houses springing up in widely scattered places; all of which meant planning, and the Socialists believed that "speculative builders" from their very nature were about as well fitted to planning as ships were to railway lines. To them the local authority was an obvious choice, but defining the instrument was simple enough; making it work quite a different matter.

Any attempt to put into operation a bold housing plan quickly confronted a forest of trouble. Building labour was short, bricks and timber scarce, people of all classes clamouring for houses, builders determined to keep their independence, and a fertile black market draining away men and materials with an ingenuity only matched by the stage magician. If the medical situation had been delicate to handle, housing had all the elements of disaster. Bevan tried to master it with three big bills, the first of which, the Building Materials and Housing Bill, made it clear that the Government intended to go into the building trade in a big way. It horrified the Opposition. They had hardly expected Bevan to come quite so bluntly into the open. The Bill proposed creating a Building Materials and Housing Fund with a first advance from the Treasury amounting to £100,000,000, and from registering varying degrees of amazement and insult, the Opposition pressed on to demand a public profit and loss account to keep check of this "fabulous sum." The demand was sidestepped. The Opposition returned to the attack. Amendment after amendment pressed for the concession until at last Bevan leant threateningly over the dispatch box and burst out. . . . 'What did the last Government spend on prefabricated houses? . . . The House has never been told!' His eyebrows rose to their full extent—a sign of extreme fun or fury. 'Over £2,000,000 wasted on steel houses,' he roared, thumping the dispatch box. 'Therefore it does not lie in the mouths of the Opposition to talk about commercial probity. They should be silent about it otherwise some other putrefying corpses will be exhumed. . . .' But they were not silent. Once or twice they made things decidedly awkward for Bevan and drove him to fresh attacks. Nothing appeared to please him more. In these debates his lightning dialectic skill sometimes dazzled the Opposition. Equipped with what appeared an irrefutable case they would challenge him, suddenly find he had riddled their arguments, and go away wondering why their speakers had let them down. It was the same when anyone dared to interrupt. A lightning and often brilliant retort met every interruption.

The second Bill set out to remove the delays and confusions which overtook local authorities whenever they tried to acquire land for housing, and touched off another explosion from the Opposition which might have created far more havoc if the standard set by one or two members had been maintained. Under this Bill, local authorities could temporarily, under certain conditions, serve fourteen days' notice on the owner of a site, and unless he made representations to the Minister within that time, the Minister could authorize the local authority to take possession. This seemed to stun the Opposition. Here was the final Socialist sacrilege. Traditional rights of property which had taken three centuries to mature would now be dissolved in fourteen days. Before they had quite recovered from the first shock Bevan told a personal story drawn from Wales: 'Although we are classed as a first priority, on two occasions we have failed to obtain a factory because the landlord has refused to release sites. It is an area from which the landlord, who is a coal owner, has sucked riches for the last hundred years. It has created millionaires and now part of it has been rendered derelict. The orange is almost dry. The sites are in possession of the colliery owners, but, like vultures, they will not desert the carrion for fear there might be the slightest bit of nutrition left. The result is that the poor people of the neighbourhood are reduced to impoverishment while they wait for the factory to be established. . . .'

Quite unmoved, Derek Walker-Smith retorted: 'Land was not the concern exclusively of men with broad acres and narrow views, but as much involved men with small houses and small plots. That man would be given half or quarter of the time taken by a Government Department to answer a letter, in which to consider his notice, take advice, instruct his lawyers and draft his objections. The Englishman's home might be his castle, but under this Bill it would be a sandcastle blown hither and thither by the winds that blew from Whitehall. . . .'

Then came the Housing (Financial and Miscellaneous Provisions) Bill, the third and last of the housing trinity. It was intended to close the gap between the "ideal rent" (10s. a week in urban areas and 7s. 6d. a week in rural areas) and the actual rents necessary to cover the high costs of building. The annual loss on a three-bedroomed house with a modern bathroom, lavatory and kitchen was put at £22 for sixty years, and this loss under the Financial and Miscellaneous Provision, was to be divided between national and local funds in the proportion of three to one. It rallied the last remaining reserves of the Opposition who plunged in to prove that this would keep building costs at a viciously high level, and give no inducement whatever for building more houses. Derek Walker-Smith capped it with—'It may be that in some moment of extreme indiscipline and unparalleled iniquity they [the builders] would be the sort of people who would sneak off and build some houses. . . .'

In the end, Bevan's still growing Parliamentary skill and his devastating brilliance in debate piloted the Bills through but now once again came the far more difficult problem of performance. Supplementary to permanent house building a plan for prefabricated houses was developed by the Ministry of Housing and the Ministry of Supply, the Ministry of Works launched its £100,000,000 capital into bulk purchase and the mass production of housing components, Royal Ordnance factories were turned over to cookers, baths and kitchen units, local authorities given power to requisition big houses, and a programme to repair war-damaged houses set moving. None of which revealed the "cracks" which the Opposition confidently anticipated until October 1946, and even then the Labour Government vociferously rejected anything resembling the word "cracks." It brought the first full-scale attack on Aneurin Bevan.

Manningham-Buller opened the debate. No one, he said, would have expected the number of permanent houses built to approach the pre-war monthly average of 30,000, but at least they were entitled to expect that the Socialist housing programme in full flood would have built more than 5,000 permanent houses in each of the summer months. The Minister of Health was gaining an unenviable reputation for secrecy, but the country was entitled to know the reason for this sorry figure. Several other Opposition speakers followed.

Bevan at once pointed out that Lord Woolton, lately Reconstruction Minister, had done precious little to prepare for a housing programme in his brief, inglorious months of office, except to talk glibly about 500,000 houses a year. There was only one flaw in this figure, Bevan said. With five tons of steel in each house it represented more than twice the capacity of the whole sheet steel industry.

The Tories were trying to belittle the achievements of the Labour Government. Had they forgotten their own? Had they forgotten what happened with a Tory-led Coalition in 1919? One year after the end of the First World War, the great slogan "Homes Fit for Heroes" finally produced the housing equivalent of a mouse. Just 124 houses had been built in that year. The Labour Government in its first year of office had built 55,000.[1] And in any case every attack made on the Government for lack of finished houses was actually an attack on the late Government for not having started them. It had taken private enterprise seventeen years to make any serious inroads into the housing problem after the last war. . . .

> Are we to wait 17 years before we get the houses? Apparently I have been able to stimulate private enterprise without a subsidy more than the Tories did with a subsidy. If it is suggested that the Government cannot claim credit for the houses built by speculative builders under licence, is it also suggested that I should make no provision either in manpower or building materials for private enterprise building ?
>
> The Government have accepted the solemn obligation that we should use our building materials and labour first for the production of houses for those who need houses and not for those who can buy them. The Opposition come forward with the old Tory claptrap. The only remedy they have for every social problem is to enable private enterprise to suck at the teats of the State—that we should pour out public money to private enterprise in order to build houses to sell. If I accepted that, the consequences would be inflated housing prices. Housing prices went up 200 per cent. between 1919 and 1922 because no controls of any sort were exercised over the industry.

[1] 55,000 was the round figure of permanent and temporary houses.

I have said that for every four houses built by the local authorities one should be built by private enterprise because four out of every five people in Great Britain need houses to let and cannot afford to buy them. . . . What a venal, specious, tawdry point has been made. . . . I would have expected any real Opposition to challenge me not because I permitted houses to be let, but because I permitted any houses *at all* to be sold. . . .

Bevan was in fine fettle. Yet despite his brilliant handling of the housing debates, a paternal pat on the head administered by *The Times*, and the immense propaganda value of comparisons between 1919 and 1946, an undercurrent of criticism grew both inside and outside the House, until presently, in the very heart of the Labour Party, there were highly placed members who wondered whether the two jobs weren't too big for any one man and whether housing was Bevan's job anyway. It is difficult to see just where it began. Perhaps it was the newspapers who saw in housing something which did not need elaborate white papers before the man in the street could grasp its realities, and seized upon this oasis in a desert of economic theory, certain that here at least they could bring the situation home to their readers. Or perhaps it was straightforward pressure of public opinion which saw a clinically exact row of figures offered it in place of houses. But that falsifies; for in the beginning Bevan did distinctly well against a starved background, and repeatedly refused to reduce the size of houses although he could easily have increased the number built and his own prestige in the process. Yet opposition grew. Public opinion believed, it seemed, that the blood which a stone refused to yield could be got out of bricks. And although the introduction of a state medical service in a relatively short space of time was by far the most arduous of Bevan's two undertakings, it now looked as though he would be judged not on the Medical Bill but on the housing programme.

By the middle of 1946, Bevan spoke in terms which were equivalent to targets. 'I confidently expect that before the next election, every family in Great Britain will have a separate home.' It was perhaps a little rash. Forces were gathering which threatened to wreck not only his housing programme but the very economy of the country.

★   ★   ★

The fates were not kind to the Labour Government in its first two years of office. Close on the heels of Bevan's housing announcement came a quite unexpected débâcle. At the end of the war, Britain was totally mobilized as she had never before been mobilized. Every available man, woman and sometimes child, every available factory and machine, every penny of our gold reserves, and all our vast economic resources in this country and abroad had been canalized for the war effort with a thoroughness unequalled in history. The war had overrun vast areas of the world untouched by the war of 1914–18, farming was thrown into confusion, harvests swept away before they could be reaped and into this barren and bewildered scene a third force struck— drought. Unprecedented droughts overtook Europe, New Zealand, French North Africa, India and South Africa, and what was expected to be a serious food shortage very soon became a disastrous food shortage.

John Strachey suddenly introduced bread rationing for the first time in British history. There followed an Arctic winter without parallel since 1881, until, one Friday afternoon, it was announced that all major industries must cease work, domestic gas and electricity would be cut from nine till twelve and two till four, and nothing short of a "continuous process" could claim exemption from the ban. It was difficult to define just how far responsibility for this paralysis of industrial life rested with the Labour Government generally, how far what the Opposition referred to as "ineptitude and bungling" sprang from the shortcomings of certain Labour Ministers, and to what degree both of these were pawns in the grip of natural forces. But the situation shifted attention from Bevan and the troubles which threatened his housing programme, to Emanuel Shinwell, Minister of Fuel and Power. The Opposition set up a howl for his head. For its part the country, shocked into silence at first, quickly adjusted itself to yet another hardship, even though it was soon very clear that the temporary shut-down of power would reach into the remote corners of industry, into foreign trade and in time into housing. So the great fuel crisis followed close on the heels of Bevan's first publicly announced housing target, and its consequences were not easily foreseeable. The Opposition jeered at Shinwell with the words of Aneurin Bevan: 'This island is almost made of coal and surrounded by fish. Only an organizing genius could produce a shortage of coal and fish in Great Britain at the same time. . . .'

If no small part of the history of Britain had been built on coal, it looked now as though the miners were oddly disinterested in the fate of the very government for which they had clamoured over fifty years, a government[1] including thirty-nine of their own kind which, within a year of taking office, had made real their age-old claim that the mines should be nationally owned. For in 1938 each mining manshift produced 1·14 tons of coal and in 1946 it had fallen to 1·03 tons. There were qualifications to these figures. The proportion of miners under forty fell from 65 per cent. to 56 per cent. between 1937 and 1945, and technical conditions in the pits had become steadily worse over the last twenty years. Flags had been run up to many masts, colliers throughout the country had held high celebration on the day the mines passed into national ownership, but it was uneasy victory and there was no sudden upsurge of production. The spirit of public ownership permeated slowly, if at all. It was difficult to find tangible evidence to show that the mineral called coal, indiscriminately scattered under the surface of the British Isles, now belonged to the people. Life went on much the same, the shifts for all the five-day week were still hard, and a new engine of bureaucracy, the Coal Board, appeared remote, unsympathetic. No one could find a satisfactory way of translating nationalization into physical reality. Yet presently production per manshift showed a small but steady increase and at last it looked as though the vast adventure which began with such high inspiration was not after all to end in anti-climax.

Meanwhile the general situation was becoming still more acute. Britain, artificially shored up by a dollar loan from America, strained to close the gap between imports and exports, which had widened to alarming proportions, "Work or Want" posters went up on hoardings throughout the land, vain efforts were made to reduce the economic complexities to easily assimilable terms, and if few amongst the public clearly understood the deep-seated roots of the trouble—some placed it in the 1931 slump—the sense of crisis became very real.

The day was rich in paradox. A strike at Grimethorpe showed a minority of men who felt themselves social outcasts, without opportunity for reasonable leisure or adult education, prepared to hold the community to ransom, and constrained Bevan to address his own breed in terms which might have come from a very different quarter. If coal nationalization had been entrusted to the

[1] Strictly, a *Party* including thirty-nine of their own kind.

1914–18 generation of miners, he said, they would not be experiencing the strikes which were ... occurring throughout the country. ...

Coming from someone with no mean record of strike incitement himself, it struck an odd note, but there were diametric differences in the two situations. It was one thing, the Socialist Party believed, to incite unofficial strikes against a Conservative Government out of sympathy with the more revolutionary of the miners' demands, and quite another to strike against a Labour Government which had already passed the mines into public ownership. There remained the undisputable fact that the target of 200,000,000 tons of coal a year had to be reached if Britain was to escape an austerity unknown for several generations.

Next came the Enabling Act (Supplies and Services Extended Powers) rushed through the House of Commons to meet the crisis and once more jeered at by the Opposition in the words of Bevan—words disinterred from the great 1AA battle. If Parliament needed special powers it should go to the House and have reasonable discussion. It should not take them out of hand.

We were now in August 1947. The dramatic announcement that the American loan, which should have given us breathing space for recovery, was practically exhausted with recovery still remote, revealed a situation which threatened to suck Britain down into a vortex of depression. Drastic Cabinet and policy changes followed in an effort to check the mounting tide of public wrath and this produced a spectacular paradox. Bevan— the rumour of whose resignation reached certainty—was left untouched as Minister of Health, but Cripps was appointed Economic Controller of the country's destiny, and G. R. Strauss became Minister of Supply. The very trio once ostracized and unceremoniously ejected from the Party for its Popular Front agitation was now ensconced in the high places, the trio which had drifted apart after 1939, was now re-united by the hand of their late opponent Mr. Attlee. If their view had remained intransigent in the interval it might have spelt a spectacular swing to the Left in the Cabinet, but Cripps at least was not the same person who had "raised a clenched fist" in 1936, Bevan had more administrative ballast if iron and steel remained a lynch-pin in his Socialism, and Strauss ... Strauss was then something of an enigma.

Political theorists of the day saw the new alignment as a struggle inside the Labour Party between the claims of the technocrats represented by Cripps and the totalitarians led by Bevan. It was a convenient but highly inaccurate simplification. W. J. Brown now produced his picturesque description of Bevan as a 'man who suffers from some confusion of identity with Danton and from afar off smells the barricades.'

Inside the Party there were other divisions on the House of Lords, the powers of which it was generally agreed, should be curbed. They aimed to reduce its two-year veto to one year. In a sense neither Bevan—who thought the House of Lords weaker unreformed[1]—nor slavish devotion to dogma produced the compromise, but sheer political necessity, because if the nationalization of iron and steel were delayed until the last of the five years' allotted span, and the Lords still held a two-year veto, it might not get through at all. The 1947 Report of the Local Government Boundary Commission, virtually its swan song, brought to a head fierce debate about the future of local government. Later, the situation drove W. A. Robson to write[2] '. . . It discloses . . . an attitude of neglect and indifference towards local government characteristic of the Labour Party as a whole since 1945. . . . The . . . indifference with which he [Bevan] viewed the problem was revealed by his attitude towards a resolution before the Conference [of the Association of Municipal Corporations] asking for an investigation into the structure of local government. He simply dismissed this with the statement that it would have to be preceded by an investigation into the kind of society in which local government must find its place.'

The House of Lords, gold reserves, dollars and gaps figured large in the talk of the crisis towards the autumn of 1947, but coal was still the key to the economic situation. The great fuel crisis continued to dominate everything. It escaped general notice that the 782,000 wage earners in the pits in 1938 had fallen to 697,000 in 1946, which explained no small part of the difficulties. It was more spectacular to attack Mr. Shinwell's unbelievable gamble with the weather and revile him as the supreme example of the political punter ready to risk the nation's shirt on nothing more reliable than the English climate; to accuse the Grimethorpe men

[1] On 6 May 1953 he said that the House of Lords as a revising chamber 'might have to go.'

[2] *The Political Quarterly*—Jan./March 1953.

of treason, the Coal Board of bungling ineptitude, and Bevan—well you could accuse Bevan of any old thing. So the miners were once more at the heart of British history, and a curious twist had crept into the situation. It would be bitter indeed if coal should confuse the housing programme and pull down Aneurin Bevan, the biggest figure who had yet emerged from the coalfields. In the middle months of 1947 that seemed possible.

13

SOMETIMES in repose Bevan's face now wore a brooding look. The lines from nose to chin had deepened, the brow furrowed, the hair admitted patches of silver, but he was still likely to release a gale of laughter into any argument, as a devilishly eloquent boy. Pride sometimes rode the rugged features but whenever the head lifted, it now carried as much authority as challenge, maturity giving a depth to what had once resembled aggressiveness. The cheeks were fuller and pinker, the body bulkier. In private he could still be the good fellow, talking common talk, playing billiards, drinking beer, exploding into working-man's vernacular, witty, sometimes coarse, always very much himself.

In the smoking-room of the House of Commons he sometimes delivered himself of extreme pronouncements as though he enjoyed shocking people. 'If I were Prime Minister . . .' prefaced some remark not calculated to appeal to Left or Right, but "free-wheeling" in this way he said things about the Press, trade unions, and individuals never repeated in soberer moods. There were times when he seemed surprised that others took some of his words more seriously than he did. He would launch an attack on a trade union leader in his presence, become savagely eloquent, and then walk out with his arm round the subject of his attack, his most charming smile in full flower. Yet he did not appear to like it very much if he got as good as he gave. Some people said that he could get very worked up about the T.U.C. There was that in his public utterance, which seemed to see the T.U.C. as the only organized body capable of challenging the sovereign power of Parliament, and in moments it was almost as if he were jealous of that capacity. The whole psychology of power still deeply interested him. But power involved philosophy and his interest in philosophy had not decreased.

Nor had his ability—when he chose to dispense with pure dialectic—to pierce to the depths whatever was under discussion, and reveal the underlying realities normally obscured in the froth of argument. Nor was there any slackening in the infinite richness and variety of his character, so elaborately interested in every-thing, and so capable of complete charm as to make him, on many occasions, an enchanting companion. That side of him was con-tinuously obscured in the press. There was never a dull moment in his, or his wife's company, and they could draw upon immense wealth of personality to divert or enlighten. Their sheer "rich-ness" was a joy to their friends. Intellectually, socially, politically, their lives abounded. Bevan gave the appearance of having read everything, of knowing everyone, and even those gentlemen who regarded him as they might Robespierre were forced, on rare occasions, to admit how fascinating his protean personality could be whenever he chose to brim over with ideas and good talk. In these moods he had an easy, friendly manner, genuine warmth of heart, magnanimity.

He was fully aware of the great problem of the day: "how far can planning go without too much mutilation of personal liberty?" Whenever philosophic reflections entered his talk in those private circles where he gave full rein to his rococo vocabulary, his bent for intellectual speculation continued to reveal a mind capable of thinking beyond the range of most politicians, and he could write:

> The corruption of thought which has accompanied the steepening decline of the existing social order has infected even the Left with its deep distrust of the efficacy of rational thinking. Towards the end of a definite type of society the defenders of it are unable to discover a rational justification for its continuance. This naturally occurs first, in the most sensitive and gifted of them, and these have to make a hard choice. They must either accept that reason has condemned their society to extinction and work for the new one, or cast doubt on the instrument of reason itself. The strain of this crisis produces many strange phenomena, usually of a semi-religious nature like Buchmanism, which is essentially a disease of the declining middle class. Thus the material crisis which is taking place in society outside them is staged within the minds and hearts of the more aware of the ruling class as a spiritual and intellectual torment.[1]

Such moments in history called for the appearance of leaders whose 'imaginative sympathy with the drama of mankind' lifted them far above preoccupations with their own small fate and tuned them 'in, as it were, to the contemporary purpose of which from then on' they became 'the historical instrument.'

[1] *Tribune*, 1948.

Perhaps there was some reason for the conceit of which he was sometimes accused. His utterance could be very remarkable. And if he was a fiercely ambitious man, these philosophic abstractions seemed to justify the belief of some amongst his intimate friends that 'His driving force derives from a deep and unquestionably sincere sense of a missionary avocation to provide politically and socially appropriate interpretation and expression of the needs and ideals of his own class' (Malcolm MacMillan M.P.).

The spirit informing his mission seemed at this point to fuse a revised version of Marx—because Marx and Engels, unlike Lenin, took some account of the intervention of social democracy but did not take enough—a Bevanite interpretation of the emergent social classes, and the philosophy of an obscure South American philosopher, José Rodó. Whatever variations on a theme by Marx and Hegel wove itself into his thinking, he continued from time to time to blackguard the Communist Party—'Its relationship to democratic institutions is that of the death watch beetle—it is not a Party, it is a conspiracy'[1]—and his regard for American capitalism was hardly less hostile.

His Revisions of Marx were not exclusively his own. Several intellectuals of the Left now questioned the Communist Master severely. The principle of greater and greater misery for the working class, as productivity increased and its share in the national income decreased, which was inbuilt into Marx's economic theory, had not come true. The wage-earners' share in the national income was estimated at 39 per cent. in 1911, 42 per cent. in 1924, 40 per cent. in 1935 and probably 50 per cent. in 1950. This was due to the intervention on a massive scale of trade union agitation, political action and the persistent pressure of social democracy at many levels. The powerful effect of this intervention had been badly underestimated by Marx. 'Marx's error,' wrote John Strachey, 'was not in his strictly economic analysis. Marx's error lay in a profound underestimate of the economic consequences which trade union and political pressure, *in a democracy*, could have in modifying the basic economic tendencies of the system, which he had, on the whole, so well apprehended. His was essentially a *political* error, and it is still being committed every day by contemporary Communists.'

José Rodó needs closer attention. I remember Bevan's wife handing me *The Motives of Proteus*. 'That's one of the keys

[1] *Tribune*, 1952.

185

to him,' she said, meaning her husband. Rodó was a Castilian writer who dominated the culture of the whole South American continent in the early 1900's, without possessing sufficient intellectual drive to break through the pragmatic pall eternally surrounding the mental life of the British Isles. Nobody had heard much of him then; few know him now. But Rodó was the most charming, the most erudite exponent of democracy we have had in many a century, and there was something in his Castilian soul which found an immediate echo in men like Havelock Ellis who did his best to make the English aware of his message. It is ungracious—even foolhardy—of the English not to know Rodó. He took the earthy thing we call democracy and converted it into something all light and grace, and full of finely spiritual overtones. In his hands it was not merely a way of government, or way of life. It became a way of spirit.

His excellent essay *Ariel* gives the essence of his creed: 'Ariel symbolizes the rule of reason and of feeling, generous enthusiasm, high and disinterested motives for action, the spirituality of culture, the vivacity and grace of intelligence, the ideal goal to which human selection tends, eliminating with the patient chisel of life the tenacious vestiges of Caliban, symbol of sensuality and torpor. . . .'

Rodó believed that a process of natural selection went on amongst the birds, flowers and insects which led to the survival of the superior and the most beautiful. The same process should animate democracy, bringing to the surface by common consent, the most superior, the best able to govern, the most æsthetically satisfying. . . . 'Democratic equality,' he wrote, 'is the most efficacious instrument of spiritual selection.'

Havelock Ellis in a brilliant foreword to *The Motives of Proteus*, elaborates. . . . 'Democracy alone can conciliate equality at the outset with an inequality at the end which gives full scope for the best and most apt to work towards the good of the whole. So considered democracy becomes a struggle, not to reduce all to the lowest common level, but to raise all towards the highest degree of possible culture. . . .'

Rodó went further. He derived from Renan and Guyau and like them he wanted to fuse the sweetness and light commonly accorded to Christianity with the spirit of Athens, and the capacity which marked men out for the final reach of his new Jerusalem was fundamentally the capacity for love. Not the ecstasy of the young overtaken with visionary beauty, but compassion, an all-embracing humanity.

Next to love came toleration. Rodó loathed intolerance. But toleration for him was a spiritual quality emerging from a long process of inner education, and when he looked around the world he did not easily find it. It was absent from American civilization where material aggrandizement was saved from vulgarity by its sweeping proportions, he looked for it amongst English utilitarianism with its bright stream of idealism running somewhere deep, but for some reason he came closest to that "æsthetic of conduct" which for him lay at the root of spiritual tolerance and moral law, in France, which he considered his intellectual home.

The harsh realities of modern politics and the rugged figure of Aneurin Bevan seem remote from all this. Spirituality, sweetness, light, invite ribald comment when brought into association with the Tory vermin-killer. But there is no doubt that Bevan treasured *The Motives of Proteus* and the writings of Rodó. In one sense this is intelligible. Rodó put forward some concepts not dissimilar from those which inspired the early influential French Socialists. Havelock Ellis recast part of Rodó with a grace at least equal to the original: 'Democracy, in this sense, retains within itself an imprescriptible element of aristocracy, which lies in establishing the superiority of the best with the consent of all; but on this basis it becomes essential that the qualities regarded as superior are really the best, and not merely qualities immobilized in a special class or caste and protected by special privileges.' . . . Bevan quoted this at his 1950 Fabian lecture. Rodó believed with Shaftesbury that 'virtue is a kind of art, a divine art,' and the moral law an 'æsthetic of conduct.'

Whether Bevan believes this I do not know. Later he wrote a book, *In Place of Fear*, which was a more comprehensive statement of his beliefs. For the moment he was preoccupied with other things.

*　　*　　*

The enforced amity of the Allies—America, Britain and Russia, had deteriorated since the war until the great Nazi monster had been replaced by the Russian bear, and an hysterical wave of Communist witch-hunting, with origins which seemed pathological, split and disrupted American life until no one quite knew where the Terror would strike next. The intransigence of Russia at the councils of the United Nations, her stubborn application of

187

the veto, undiminished military strength and violent propaganda, certainly gave cause for alarm in Western Europe, and it looked as though a war of such proportions as the world had never seen was once again threatening Europe and more particularly Britain. Professor Arnold Toynbee, pressing British claims for more say in the affairs of UNO, coined the phrase—"No annihilation without representation." And now the attempts to recover from war were disrupted by American stockpiling, by inflated prices for raw materials, by a resurgence of rearmament, and a dollar gap which one moment showed signs of closing and the next yawned across an even worse abyss.

The long-drawn-out struggle of *homo sapiens* to adapt himself to the planet on which he lived had become a struggle to adapt himself to different ideologies, and the clash between Fascism and Democracy had given place to Communism and Capitalism. In Britain a gentler, less doctrinaire brand of Socialism was trying to blend the best characteristics of both, but the weather had become inexplicably heavy.

Bevan's Health Service was over its Parliamentary troubles and now approaching its inaugural day. Some grudging credit went to him for the comparatively swift establishment of a very complicated piece of national machinery, now a big land-mark in the history of the British Social Services. It was a considerable feat. By December 1947 well over 500,000 homes had been provided out of the 750,000 which it was estimated would be needed to give a separate home to each family in urgent need. In 1948 Bevan announced that the September figure would reach the Coalition target of 750,000. An intimidating number of Acts had been carried through Parliament and the Bank of England, Coal, Transport and Gas were all nationalized, with Iron and Steel under close surveillance. Most people had jobs, the price of basic foods remained reasonable, social security was reaching new proportions, the gap between the very rich and very poor narrowing, but mysteriously the weather had become heavy and the *Daily Express* recorded: 'Mr. Bevan's contribution to the debate . . . was a gross, flagrant and wicked misrepresentation of the truth about Britain. . . . Whom does Mr. Bevan imagine he is fooling with his talk of having "brought the nation back to a more favourable situation than it was left in in 1935?" '

The *Daily Mail* went one better. . . . 'Mr. Aneurin Bevan threw bricks as usual when he spoke to a housing conference yesterday.

No wonder he is called a "dirt mouth" in America and a "twisted mind" in Britain. His trouble is that he hates so many and so much. . . .'

Perhaps they could not forgive him for the most dramatic statement of his whole career. On 4 July 1948, speaking at Manchester he was reported as saying: 'In my early life I had to live on the earnings of an elder sister and was told to emigrate. That is why no amount of cajolery and no attempt at ethical or social seduction can eradicate from my heart a deep burning hatred for the Tory Party that inflicted those bitter experiences on me. So far as I am concerned they are lower than vermin. They condemned millions of first-class people to semi-starvation. . . . They have not changed, or if they have, they are slightly worse than they were. . . .'

It could be demonstrated that there were some amongst the employers in the embittered past of South Wales who fully deserved these epithets, but to imply that all Tories past, present and not yet conceived, were lower than vermin, was to submit once again to that extravagance which could so easily sweep him from a particular truth to a general distortion. The Press set up a hue and cry. In private Bevan, I am told, said he had been misrepresented. It could be argued that his speech had an historical context and referred specifically to those Tories who had ruthlessly exploited the working classes. But the young Tories went into action. Vermin Clubs were formed up and down Britain, the words "Vermin Villa, home of a loud-mouthed rat," materialized one night in black paint on his door in Cliveden Place. Later, bricks were thrown through his windows. Harold Laski opined that Mr. Bevan was 'often brilliant, but there can be little doubt that the unhappy phrase Vermin, has done Labour great harm and it will be a long time before it is forgotten.'

Churchill on the inauguration of the Health Service, added his diapason:

All the more do I regret that this important reform should have been marred and prejudiced in its initiation by the clumsy and ill natured hands of the Minister of Health to whom it was confided. Needless antagonisms have been raised largely by bad manners . . . with the medical profession, and the whole process of imposing this new contribution has been rendered more painful by the spirit of spite and class hatred of which Aneurin Bevan has made himself the expression. . . . He has chosen this very moment to speak of at least half the British nation as lower than vermin. . . . We speak of the Minister of Health but ought we not rather to say the Minister of Disease for is not morbid hatred a form of mental disease . . . and indeed a highly infectious form? Indeed I can think of no better step to signalize the inauguration of the National Health Service than that a person who so obviously needs psychiatrical attention should be amongst the first of its patients. . . .

Presently Bevan went one better. He described the Press of Britain as the most prostituted in the world. Again there might be elements of prostitution in some sections of the Press and there were moments when these elements seemed to abuse every principle by which they lived, but to describe it as the most prostituted in the world! . . . No one commented on his courage. Public men of many brands find some meeting place with the Press a pre-requisite of popularity and success. Deliberate cultivation is commonplace. Deeply embroiled with Churchill, the Tory Party, America and elements of his own people, Bevan did not hesitate to take on the Press as well.

*　　*　　*

The inner recesses of the Labour Party echoed now to many battles. Satellite sub-committees of the Policy Committee were busy formulating the new programme. Bevan wanted more nationalization than eventually emerged. Beyond insurance, sugar and cement, he was interested in chemicals and flour milling and strongly resisted what became the "mutualization" of insurance, a compromise suggested by the then Research Secretary of the Labour Party, Michael Young.

Extraordinarily Bevan had achieved, or been given, the Chairmanship of the Private Enterprise Sub-Committee. That, everyone thought, would sufficiently inhibit even his rugged spirit. He rose to the occasion with considerable *savoir-faire*. He spoke in committee—with a smile as near wry as his cast of countenance could achieve—of distributing the surplus heat from nationalized generating stations to supply steam to conservatories for private enterprise market gardeners! Public enterprise it seemed would compete with private enterprise in many more fields if Bevan had his way, but it was very interesting that he appeared to accept private enterprise as the arbiter of a large area of industry, subject to certain tests of public interest. The man who would nationalize everything wholesale did not appear in these debates.

In the central Policy Committee the feud between Morrison and Bevan had grown over the years. Morrison strongly opposed insurance nationalization. Bevan wanted nationalization or nothing. Morrison pressed for consolidation of measures already taken, among other reasons because he was afraid that fresh nationalization would alienate the middle-class vote, but consolidation was a bastard word to Bevan. It meant inaction if not retreat and he believed that Labour must remain whole-heartedly Socialist and stand or fall by its "true faith." Sometimes Bevan's sheer rush of eloquence gave his case away to the greater restraint and tactical skills of Herbert Morrison.

At Annual Conference—where Party programmes were endorsed, adjusted or theoretically but rarely in fact, rejected—the vote overwhelmingly carried the day for the Attlee-Morrison-Gaitskell gradualist policy. Bevan astounded everyone by delivering the Conference speech on private enterprise and making away with it as brilliantly as ever.

The General Election followed early in 1950. The final count gave Labour 315, Conservatives 297, Liberals 9, Others 3, the Speaker 1. Labour had a majority of six and a stalemate almost unknown in British history brought startled examination of the whole electoral process. The Whig majority a hundred years before in 1847 had various interpretations ranging from five to eighteen, but the Tories were then leaderless and as Peelites and Protectionists divided against themselves. In 1852 a slender majority fell to the Tories' lot, but the parallel with 1950 was not very exact because they also were dependent on forty Peelites. 'It will be an impossible Parliament,' Graham had said to Gladstone: 'Parties will be found too nicely balanced to render a new line of policy practicable without a fresh appeal to the electors. . . .'

His words re-echoed in 1950. Transport House held a hurried post mortem into their considerable losses which had left them with total responsibility and very little power. Some of Bevan's confederates proclaimed that this was the fruit of compromise, the shrivelled remnant of what might have been a resounding majority, and Morrison simply replied that the majority would have worn a Tory hue if they had followed Bevan's lead.

* * *

191

The new Labour Government was given three months to live. It won the first of three vital divisions arising from the Commons debate on the King's Speech, by religious zeal from the whips, and the punctilious appearance of the halt and the lame amongst Labour M.P.s. The vote ran 300–288, giving Labour a majority of twelve. The division arose from a Tory vote of censure on housing and gave Bevan an opportunity to attack the housing-promised-land which had figured largely in Tory election propaganda.

At the following Labour Party Annual Conference Beverley Baxter wrote [*Evening Standard*]:

> Mr. Sam Watson, the party chairman, was delivering a sound if somewhat lengthy speech, and I had an opportunity to gaze upon the great men on the platform. One's eye was at once caught by Mr. Aneurin Bevan, not only because he is a man of some sort of destiny but for his unusual appearance. He had been to the hairdresser and his tailor. Nor did his sartorial achievements end there. He wore a white shirt with a stiff white collar and two white cuffs showing the exact length for a man about town. His tie was of a reserved, indefinite shade. For reasons of his own he had left behind the homely clothes with which he has for so long graced the Palace and formal receptions. No longer was he the Man of the People but the seaside Beau Bevan, the glass of fashion and the mould of form.

The newspapers seemed preoccupied with the appearance and private life of Bevan in the winter of 1950–51. It was recorded in November that 'during the last election, papers which ignored Attlee sent special men round after Shinwell, Strachey and Bevan, not to report their speeches but in the hope that they would drop bricks. . . . There have been some disgraceful things written about their private lives which would have been shabby even if they were true. Press cameras were trained on the windows of Mr. Bevan's home and shop employees were asked to reveal what Jennie Lee was buying.'

A very industrious gentleman went down to Tredegar in October and observed the not very original sight of Bevan setting out from a red-curtained house in Tredegar, where he sometimes stays with his brother-in-law Mr. Jack Norris. Bevan was muffled against the chill air in a fawn coat, black beret and fur gloves. He drove a 16 h.p. Humber Hawk.

Earlier in the day he had walked into the back garden to talk with some bricklayers at work on a garage. He sometimes arrived at Tredegar when all the garages were shut, and with his brother-in-law that summer, had set to work with pick and shovel to enlarge Mr. Norris's garage into a two-car garage. Later they decided to give the work over to the bricklayers and at once the question of a licence arose. Licence No. 8/LA/121/783 dated 30 September was found, after inordinate examination, to be in order but for one thing. It bore the name of Aneurin Bevan instead of John Norris. It was too slight a divergence to demand further investigation and the Press abandoned the trail.

Far more dramatic was the assault on Bevan at White's Club. The Hon. Hugh Stanley, brother of the Earl of Derby, and some friends were at White's Club one night in January 1951 when they heard that Marshal of the R.A.F. Sir John Slessor had arrived with Mr. Bevan as a guest. Some members of the club were angry. Later a rumour ran round that Mr. Bevan had been kicked in the posterior as he was about to descend the last of the six steps into St. James's Street. 'No one I know saw the incident except Sir John,' Hugh Stanley later said. 'Mr. Bevan, who conducted himself with great dignity and restraint, is the only one who comes out of the affair with credit. Although I don't like him, I must say that. . . . I don't think the Minister of Labour could have been hurt very much. . . .' Mr. Bevan's stock rose a little at White's Club. Since it had registered below zero before, the change was not noticeable.

★   ★   ★

In January 1951 Bevan abandoned Health and Housing and became Minister of Labour subject to the same austere disciplines for the moment as every other Labour M.P., because the Party still lived in fear of the snap vote which might bring sudden defeat. It was an exhausting, anxiety-ridden life for the Socialists and the Opposition could not resist the temptation to use the situation for the discomfiture of hated figures like Attlee, Morrison and above all Bevan. The tragedy of Sir Stafford Cripps's withdrawal from public life and his subsequent death made it possible, for a moment, that Bevan might enter the Treasury as Chancellor. Attlee would have committed himself to a policy of no compromise by such a choice. Instead he chose Hugh Gaitskell to replace Sir Stafford Cripps, and at once sowed the seeds for the dramatic developments to follow. Cripps as Chancellor of the Exchequer was tolerable to Bevan, but Hugh Gaitskell represented old-world gradualism, the clinical detachment of the academic, and many other characteristics anathema to him.

As Minister of Labour, Bevan gave a party political broadcast which was a flop; the cold microphone without an audience never inspired him. A brush with the dockers put the ex-agitator Minister in the embarrassing position of trying to quell a new generation of agitators. He was continually interrupted. At last under immense provocation he suddenly shouted: 'Shut up. . . . Do you think the Government should do nothing about it? If your own wife wanted an operation you would damned soon see.' There was more shouting and Bevan declared: 'You are a lot of skulking cowards hiding behind your own anonymity. . . .'

The threat of war had increased alarmingly. The Korean conflict revealed explosive possibilities in the least likely places, and American pressure to increase British rearmament reached a pitch where a perturbed Cabinet decided to bring the original figure of £3,600 millions to its new and fatal level of £4,700 millions. Simultaneously it was agreed to telescope a five-year programme into three years. In the Defence Debate of February 1951 Bevan once more revealed formidable Parliamentary powers. He spoke after Sir David Maxwell Fyfe and dealt with the threat of war. . . .

> I am not frightened by the situation, because, after all, Russia claims —and I think she exaggerates quite considerably here—to have a production of 28 million tons of steel per year. I know she has not got that. She has not got 25 million tons yet. Modern steel power is the best possible expression of arms strength if mobilized, but it is the mobilizing that is the question, because so long as steel is consumed by civil industry the technical basis for armed power is there. I do not believe that a nation, however large its manpower, coldly contemplates launching 25 million tons of steel per annum against the combination of 140 million tons per annum.
>
> For Heaven's sake do not let us have so much bogy man talk. I am speaking about those evil people in many parts of the world who are talking as if the third world war had already begun. We deny that. The fact of the matter is that the Tory Party is as old fashioned as the Communist Party. They are both living in a world that has gone. One has only to read the Communist thesis today to see that it has not changed in the last 100 years since Karl Marx wrote it, and I am a considerable student of Karl Marx.

The Soviet thinking has not adjusted itself to the fact that the most revolutionary power in the world is political democracy. She has not adjusted herself to the fact that progress can only be made in modern complicated industrial civilisation on the basis of peace. She still clings to the notion that war is a revolutionary opportunity, and she does so because the Soviet Union was born in war and because she knows that some nations tried to destroy her by war. Therefore she thinks in those terms. But the fact of the matter is that in the last five years not only has the Soviet Union been able to achieve a number of victories but she has also sustained a number of quite formidable defeats. . . .

He turned to the economics of rearmament . . .

the extent to which stock-piling has already taken place, the extent to which the civil economy is being turned over to defence purposes in other parts of the world, is dragging prices up everywhere. Furthermore, may I remind the Right Hon. Gentleman that if we turn over the complicated machinery of modern industry to war preparation too quickly, or try to do it too quickly, we shall do so in a campaign of hate, in a campaign of hysteria, which may make it very difficult to control that machine when it has been created.

It is all very well to speak about these things in airy terms, but we want to do two things. We want to organize our defence programme in this country in such a fashion as will keep the love of peace as vital as ever it was before. But we have seen in other places that a campaign for increased arms production is accompanied by a campaign of intolerance and hatred and witch-hunting. Therefore, we in this country are not at all anxious to imitate what has been done in other places. . . .

It is a fact, a fact that stands out, that one of the most important contributions that have been made to the pacification of the world at the present time was the behaviour of my Right Hon. Friend the Prime Minister in securing the friendship of India and Pakistan, whereas the Right Hon. Gentleman [Churchill] would have still faced that situation with early nineteenth century conceptions. We think that the things happening in Asia at the present time are not only the consequences of malignant plottings by the Soviet Union. Do not let us get it wrong. It is certain, of course, that the Soviet Union are doing their very best to work these things up, but the events taking place in Asia at the present time are under the influence of historical compulsions which do not have their seat in the Kremlin at all. We shall deal with them. . . .

That is the reason we do beg that we shall not have all these jeers about the re-armament that we are putting under way. We shall carry it out; we shall fulfil our obligations to our friends and allies, and at the same time we shall try to prevent such an exacerbation of the world atmosphere as makes it impossible for nations to come together in peace and harmony and give mankind another breathing space.

Within a few months the speech was to have ironic repercussions. The beginnings of the clash between the Prime Minister (Clement Attlee), the Foreign Secretary (Herbert Morrison), the Chancellor (Hugh Gaitskell), and people like Bevan (Ministry of Labour), Harold Wilson (Board of Trade) and John Freeman (Parliamentary Secretary, Ministry of Supply) presently reached public ears. It was soon to be the opinion of the last triumvirate that the programme was physically impossible in prevailing conditions, except by the use of measures which would do grave—perhaps permanent—damage to our civil economy.

It needs emphazising, in view of what transpired by the following April. Hugh Gaitskell next outlined to the Cabinet possible features of the forthcoming Budget which included a charge for false teeth and spectacles under the Health Service. Any attempt to inhibit what Bevan regarded as the gloriously free and growing child of his Health Service, was not merely repugnant but sacrilegious. The saving to the Treasury would be negligible, he argued, and seemed to imply that this was a political attack upon the Health Service by a fellow Minister whose brand of Socialism and personality were quickly becoming as suspect to him as were far more rugged reactionaries. He argued vociferously inside the Cabinet, he exploded on more than one occasion, chin out-thrust, blue eyes glaring across the table at Morrison. In the past whenever he had protested to Sir Stafford Cripps about cuts in the Social Services, Cripps, as Chancellor of the Exchequer, sympathized with him. Bevan had grown accustomed to winning his way. Now, suddenly, with Gaitskell, it was different. On 3 April, just a week before the Budget, he told a meeting at Bermondsey: 'I will never be a member of a Government which makes charges on the National Health Service for the patient.' Delivered with considerable vehemence it had the ring of another Bevan outburst, but there were those in the Labour Party who saw it as a stratagem, a warning to policy-making members of the Cabinet not to take an irrevocable step which would disrupt Cabinet unity and reveal to the outside world a dangerous division within the hierarchy of the Party.

Manœuvre or not, it failed. Hugh Gaitskell's Budget, when it burst on a tired and disillusioned public, not only kept faithfully to £4,700 millions, but added teeth and spectacle charges. Bevan had been set aside. Indignation now threatened to overwhelm him because he saw this not so much as a serious hardship on the patient, as a willingness on the part of the Cabinet to conspire against the first principles of the Health Service. The sum saved on teeth and spectacles amounted to £13 million. 'I am worth more than £13 million to the Labour Party!' Bevan was said to have exploded at one meeting.

There was considerable coming and going. Bevan saw Attlee four times in eleven days. The Prime Minister failed to understand just why it was Bevan wanted to resign. Their final meeting lasted only a short time.

Oliver Lyttelton had already challenged Bevan to explain why he was still a member of the Government in view of his threat to resign: 'Surely we are entitled . . . to have a full account of the struggles which he has had with his conscience, and to learn the reasons why upon this occasion at least his conscience has not won. . . . This rugged monolith of the Labour movement is now standing precariously balanced on the foundation of a verbal quibble.' Bevan himself joined the laughter.

Francis Williams, lately Public Relations Adviser to the Prime Minister, said:

> The threat to resign has been almost the most persistent single theme in Bevan's ministerial career. I remember calling on him at the Ministry of Health about four months after the Labour Government took office in 1945. His opening words to me were: 'Tell the Prime Minister unless I get backing on this I am going to resign.' "This," was a dispute over material priorities for housing which he was having with the Ministry of Supply. Since then he has threatened to resign on one issue after another—the last time on the eve of last year's Labour Party Conference when for an hour or two his resignation was, I believe, actually in the Prime Minister's hands. He has been like a man who threatens suicide so often that no one believes him until he actually does it. . . .

Bevan rose in his wrath to attack Williams. It was an explosive piece of platform rhetoric and Williams simply said:

> Mr. Bevan, as ever, protests too much, although I am glad to see that a latent caution prevents him from carrying his indignation at my reference to his persistent habit of resignation to the point of denying that it is true.

The *News Chronicle* stated categorically: Mr. Aneurin Bevan and Mr. Harold Wilson are not to resign from the Government. Internal evidence from one M.P. present at the crucial meeting of the Parliamentary Labour Party justified this. Something intervened to produce a new emphasis on rearmament troubles. One of Bevan's henchmen, a very able man we are likely to hear more of in the future, stayed up far into the night discussing the grounds for resignation. It was rumoured that Jennie Lee played a part in these decisions.

On 21 April Bevan wrote to Attlee 'after a prolonged agony of uncertainty':

My dear Clem:

In previous conversations with you, and in my statements to the Cabinet, I have explained my objections to many features of the Budget. Having endeavoured, in vain, to secure modifications of these features, I feel I must ask you to accept my resignation.

The Budget, in my view, is wrongly conceived in that it fails to apportion fairly the burdens of expenditure as between different social classes. It is wrong because it is based upon a scale of military expenditure, in the coming year, which is physically unattainable, without grave extravagance, in its spending.

It is wrong because it envisages rising prices as a means of reducing civilian consumption, with all the consequences of industrial disturbance involved.

It is wrong because it is the beginning of the destruction of those social services in which Labour has taken a special pride and which were giving to Britain the moral leadership of the world.

I am sure you will agree that it is always better that policies should be carried out by those who believe in them. It would be dishonourable for me to allow my name to be associated in the carrying out of policies which are repugnant to my conscience and contrary to my expressed opinion.

I am sorry that I feel it necessary to take this step after so many years of co-operation in a Government which has done so much for the cause of Labour and the progress of mankind.

I need hardly say that my adherence to the cause of Labour and Socialism is stronger than ever and that I believe that renewed efforts by all of us will result in another thrust towards the goal of our hopes.

As is customary, I shall explain my position in greater detail in my speech to the House of Commons. May I conclude by wishing you a speedy return to health and vigour.

Yours sincerely,

(Sgd) Aneurin Bevan.

And Attlee replied:

My dear Nye:

I have your letter of today's date. I note that you have extended the area of disagreement with your colleagues a long way beyond the specific matter to which as I understood you had taken objection.

I had certainly gathered that if the proposal for imposing charges on dentures and spectacles were dropped, you would have been satisfied.

I much regret that you should feel it necessary to offer your resignation, but in these circumstances I have no option but to accept it. I note that you propose to make a statement in the House.

Thank you for the good work that you have done as a member of the Government during these difficult years.

Thank you also for your good wishes for my health.

Yours ever,
(Sgd) Clement R. Attlee.

One phrase is worth repetition: 'I note that you have extended the area of disagreement with your colleagues a long way beyond the specific matter to which as I understood you had taken objection.' Did Attlee mean that Bevan had reinforced his reasons for resigning by introducing a quite new emphasis on rearmament? Later, in private, the Prime Minister confessed himself still baffled by the grounds of Bevan's resignation. Whatever they were, the story echoed through the country.

Having all the appearance at first sight of a shattering blow to Left-wing unity, the Labour Party, far more powerful and resilient than in the days of Ramsay MacDonald, quickly "closed its ranks" and Bevan said he did not want to encourage a split.

John Gordon opined 'Poor Mr. Nye Bevan is in trouble again. You can't help feeling sorry for him. All he wants to do is to convince simpletons like us that he alone of all the medicine men in the market place has the pill to put us right.'

Speaking from the traditional seat of ex-Ministers at the end of the third bench, Bevan in a blue suit and darker blue tie began quietly, with something between diffidence and nervousness, to explain his resignation to a packed House three days later. Mr. Morrison, Mr. Gaitskell, Mr. Dalton and other Ministers on the crowded Government front bench, had their backs to Bevan and remained so without stirring for nearly thirty-five minutes. There were no interruptions from either side of the House. These moments of ritual explanation have a melancholy dignity. The man who has chosen martyrdom, as much expiates as explains a violent rupture in the constitutional fabric.

These occasions are always exceedingly painful, especially to the individual concerned, because no member ought to accept office in a Government without a full consciousness that he ought not to resign it for a frivolous reason.

The House will recall that in the Defence debate . . . I said . . . 'the extent to which stock-piling has already taken place, the extent to which the civil economy is being turned over to defence purposes in other parts of the world, is dragging prices up everywhere. . . .

'If we turn over the complicated machinery of modern industry to war preparation too quickly, or try to do it too quickly, we shall do so in a campaign of hate, in a campaign of hysteria, which may make it very difficult to control that machine when it has been created. . . .'

The failure on the part of the American Government to inject the arms programme into the economy slowly enough [had] already caused a vast inflation of prices all over the world, [and had] disturbed the economy of the western world to such an extent that if it goes on more damage will be done by this unrestrained behaviour than by the behaviour of the nation the arms are intended to restrain. . . .

We are entirely dependent upon other parts of the world for most of our raw materials. The President of the Board of Trade and the Minister of Supply . . . have called the attention of the House to the shortage of absolutely essential raw materials. . . . I say therefore, with the full solemnity of the seriousness of what I am saying, that the £4,700 million arms programme is already dead. It cannot be achieved without irreparable damage to the economy of Great Britain and the world. . . .

It was a remarkable Budget. It united the City, satisfied the Opposition and disunited the Labour Party—all this because we have allowed ourselves to be dragged too far behind the wheels of American diplomacy. This great nation has a message for the world which is distinct from that of America or that of the Soviet Union. . . .

It has never been in my mind that my quarrel with my colleagues was based only upon what they have done to the National Health Service. As they know, over and over again I have said that these figures of arms production are fantastically wrong, and that if we try to spend them we shall get less arms for more money. . . .

He ran his hand through his thick, whitening thatch several times, dabbing his face with a big loose handkerchief. Then leaning forward, finger stabbing, he began the attacks on Gaitskell.

> . . . there are too many economists advising the Treasury, and now we have the added misfortune of having an economist in the Chancellor himself . . . the Government . . . should set up a production department and put the Chancellor in the position where he ought to be now, under modern planning . . . with the function of making an annual statement of accounts. . . .
>
> There was a passage towards the end [of the Chancellor's speech] in which he said that he was now coming to a complicated and technical matter and if members wished they could go to sleep. They did. Whilst they were sleeping he stole £100,000,000 a year from the National Insurance Fund . . . so that rearmament of Britain is financed out of the contributions that the workers have paid into the fund. . . .

At this point there were cries of 'Oh!' and of 'Shame!' to which Mr. Bevan retorted: 'Certainly that is the meaning of it. It is no good my Hon. Friends refusing to face these matters. . . .' Turning to the National Health Service he went on . . .'

> If he [the Chancellor] finds it necessary to mutilate, or begin to mutilate, the Health Services for £13,000,000 out of £4,000,000,000 what will he do next year? Or are you next year going to take your stand on the upper denture? The lower half apparently does not matter, but the top half is sacrosanct. (Laughter) Is that right . . .?
>
> I say this, in conclusion. There is only one hope for mankind—and that is democratic Socialism. There is only one party in Great Britain which can do it—and that is the Labour Party.

Emrys Hughes (Lab. Ayrshire S.) shook hands warmly with Bevan as he finished and the House streamed into the lobbies to take its private measure. In so far as *The Times* can be said to achieve anything resembling anger this speech engendered it.

> Only ten weeks ago Mr. Bevan had not grasped this mortal threat . . . [its editorial ran]. The first quality of a skilful advocate is to found his case upon some element of truth. . . .
>
> . . . to present this as the suicidal state already reached by the rearmament programme, though it may be dramatic is to deny and disfigure the facts. . . .
>
> . . . It is in Mr. Bevan's personal attack upon the Chancellor of the Exchequer that the mood and motive of his departure from the Cabinet most clearly show themselves. . . .

Referring to the 'startling and disgraceful' charge against Gaitskell it said—

> To describe the charges for dentures and spectacles which the Minister of Health will propose today as "throwing away" the health service is entirely irresponsible. . . .[1]

*   *   *

Down in Tredegar on 30 April, Bevan repeated his explanation to his constituents, and men and women who had known him as a boy gave him a tremendous reception. 'Come on Nye,' they roared, waiting for the eloquent thunder which from their point of view had been absent from the valley for too long. It was a big night for Ebbw Vale deep in the shadow of the Monmouthshire hills, aware of unemployment still haunting South Wales, of hardship and the threat of yet another war. It was a big and moving night for Aneurin Bevan. There was much singing before, during and after the meeting, there were tears in many eyes and the deep roar of Welsh voices swallowed up the night with *Land of My Fathers, Guide me, O Thou Great Jehovah* and *Abide With Me*. Bevan rose to their mood. There must be no wild and idle talk about a split in the Labour movement, he said. The very fact that there were differences of opinion made unity all the more essential. If the heritage of our forefathers was used intelligently, it was unnecessary for mankind to walk the way that Russia had walked. In the event, as the year slipped away, there were some signs and portents that Bevan had not entirely mistaken his combined rôle of Jeremiah, Cassandra, and guardian of the holy Socialist tablets.

*   *   *

But Bevan's resignation went deeper. British Labour Party Socialism sprang from the Bible, nonconformist preachers, trade unions and the working-class movement. It was an upsurge which began as far back as John Ball, developed through Tom Paine, involved Robert Owen, and had its modern realization in Keir Hardie and Robert Blatchford. It had no systematized philosophy. The tradition was a radical one. It made more explicit the clash within the Party between widely differing Socialist creeds.

[1] *The Times*, 24 April 1951. There was also, of course, the curious anomaly that Bevan had himself previously introduced a Bill for 1s. charge on prescriptions.

Blatchford and Keir Hardie had little in common with Karl Marx as a professional philosopher. They believed in humanism, in moral values, in the common fellowship of man rather than the philosophic necessity of any internecine war as a class war. Classic phrases in the Marxian catechism were given little prominence in their creed, and science as an instrument of social investigation had too clinical a ring for their warm, sentimental slow-moving temperaments. Attlee and Morrison came closest to sustaining this heritage within the demands of modern economics and a world steadily passing into the hands of applied rather than pure science. They were the direct descendants. They did not desire, see or encourage, class warfare as the underlying force of which they were the expression. They were far more Fabian than Marxist, admitting the inevitability of gradualism, and they wanted all kinds and classes in the Labour Party. There was no definition of Socialism universally acceptable to all gradualists, but broadly they believed that basic economic power should not remain in private hands, that there should be a classless society in which—'no one is so much richer or poorer than his neighbours as to be unable to mix with them on equal terms'[1]—that the status of the average man in society must be increased, and all this achieved without the revolutionary haste which would tear the fabric of society apart. Gaitskell had much in common with this view, but brought a cool, passionless precision to world problems, apparently as much concerned with introducing order into chaos as Socialism into Britain. Bevan, whose roots in the Bible-thumping Socialism of South Wales were deeper than most, who ostentatiously displayed his working-class origins, was a considerable Marxist scholar, and remained constitutionally incapable of championing any but the working class, defining that—or so it seemed—in the narrow, old-world sense. 'One can trace in many of his speeches an emotional fidelity to a concept of the exploited poor which takes hardly any practical account of the alteration in the class structure of British society which war and the Labour Government itself had brought about . . .' Francis Williams wrote. He appeared to believe in class warfare, he wanted to press public ownership into fresh fields far more rapidly, he hated the word consolidation, and saw parliamentary democracy as a revolutionary instrument. It would misrepresent people like Harold Wilson, R. H. S. Crossman, Ian Mikardo,

[1] Professor G. D. H. Cole.

Michael Foot, John Freeman, Barbara Castle and Jennie Lee, now brought into tempestuous unity under the leadership of Bevan, to say that they shared his views, unconditionally. There were many subtle heresies within the group. A wider fringe of thirty other M.P.s who hovered on the brink of conversion one day and turned in revulsion the next, included some more devoted to the pacifist tradition of early Socialism than to Bevan. Ironically, some of Bevan's closer associates were "rootless" intellectuals without any direct heritage from the working class, but Bevan seemed supremely unembarrassed by their support. They considered Herbert Morrison a Liberal not a Socialist. Some looked upon Attlee as the apotheosis of mediocre caution coming close to apostasy. Some wanted more Socialism in a much shorter time.

Many differences were concealed in these generalities. Paradoxically it was Bevan at the 1950 Fabian lectures who referred to new thinking and gave a warning of its dangers:

> I perceive in some curious quarters so many misgivings about the relationship between democracy and public ownership, and so many people who have been doing a lot of curious re-thinking that it is absolutely essential for us to keep our eyes clear on the main destination and not be diverted up the side paths. . . .

He still believed that . . .

> People do not have large fortunes by consultation; it is only after they have got them that they are prepared to consult! Property in the modern world—and when I am speaking about property I must guard myself and say I mean not personal property but social property, that is to say, the ownership of large aggregations of capital that can only be co-operatively useful but can be privately owned—is essentially authoritarian, and therefore it naturally follows that those who believe in it are prepared to hand it over to another lot of authoritarians, but not over to democrats. That is why, so long as large elements of the economic machine are in the hands of private persons, democracy is not safe. . . .
>
> But . . . we are not going to have a monolithic society, we are not going to have a society in which every barber's shop is nationalized. . . .

Richard Crossman's Fabian lecture made this interesting point:

> All the obvious things have been done which were fought for and argued about. And yet, mysteriously enough, though we have carried out all these things, the ideal, the pattern of values, has not

been achieved. We have done them, we have created the means to the good life which they all laid down and said, 'If you do all these things, after that there'll be a classless society.' Well there isn't. . . .

In the *New Fabian Essays*, published eighteen months later, he said that the evolutionary philosophy of progress, as represented in Wells, and the revolutionary philosophy of progress [as represented in Marx?] had both proved false. The first task therefore was to re-define progress. And later. . . .

The planned economy and the centralization of power are no longer Socialist objectives. . . . The main task of Socialism today is to prevent the concentration of power in the hands of *either* industrial management, *or* the State bureaucracy—in brief, to distribute responsibility and so to enlarge freedom of choice. . . .

Nothing was more interesting in the Labour Party than Bevan's growing isolation from those intellectuals who thought that some re-definition of Socialism or Socialist long-term policy, was necessary. His "conservative" devotion to a brand of Socialism conceived years before seemed to cut him off from 'new' thinking among the Fabians. Some considered him still living in the Stone Age.

These were some of the forces underlying Bevan's resignation. Rearmament and Health charges were no more than the occasion. It was a conflict within a party not divided against itself, but capable of containing explosive rebels without disaster. And yet. . . . As the self-appointed Messiah threatening everyone, Bevan could behave outrageously and survive, only so long as he did not challenge the first profound instinct of the Labour Party which said that solidarity in times of crisis was axiomatic, and loyalty the only precept by which it could live.

This was indeed a time of crisis. The dollar gap had widened alarmingly, competition threatened to exclude British goods from many export markets, the depth of rearmament bade fair to disrupt economic life, and it was already evident, to the least amongst the soothsayers, that a further drop in standards of living faced the nation at a point where—six years after war—it would seem utterly baffling if not criminal to the public at large. To resign at such a point, to reveal party disunity to the gloating Conservative gaze was, from the point of view of Transport House, close enough to disloyalty to be indistinguishable from it. There were those amongst the cynics who smiled when one mentioned philosophic differences and said: 'If Bevan hadn't tried to manœuvre at Bermondsey we shouldn't be in this mess. . . .'

Whether Bevan's resignation was fortuitous is irrelevant. The clash of ideology remained. It was a clash which would not only be fought out in the House of Commons, in the Parliamentary Labour Party and the National Executive of the Party. It extended into the wider field of the constituency and local Labour Parties whose vote in the long run deeply influenced which policy or person the Party would follow, and always waiting in the background was the great juggernaut of the trade union, capable of crushing the most spectacular rebel, and not likely to regard with benevolence a man who had once released the full force of his invective against it. By the manner and timing of his resignation and the personal attack launched upon Gaitskell it looked as though Bevan had opened himself to one of three highly dramatic destinies. He was dealing now in ultimates. Minor issues were not of great consequence. He might sink out of sight in the wilderness, a martyr to resignation in the severe and highly puritanical tradition which had claimed some distinguished figures in British politics; he might split the Labour Party irreparably; or close to himself any political future other than that of Prime Minister.

Within a personality so rich and complicated as Bevan's motives may lie hidden in the deepest caverns of the subconscious and it would be presumptuous to assume a knowledge of what must be an infinitely fascinating labyrinth.

*   *   *

The next six months were not less spectacular. Three resignations from the British Cabinet forced the American State Department out of the complacent assumption that what was necessary for military strategy must be politically feasible. Inflation reached a pitch where the 1d. newspaper had to be increased to 1½d. On 3 May, fifty-five Labour Members refused to vote for the key clause of the Government's Health Service Bill and it was revealed that opposition to the charges for dentures and spectacles, now limited to two years, had grown.

July brought the pamphlet *One Way Only*, jointly sponsored by Aneurin Bevan, Harold Wilson and John Freeman. The Press condemned it with 'some consistency.' There were scurrilous references to 'Bevan's attempt to endanger British security.' It deserved a better fate. The preamble in the opening pages revealed once again a preoccupation with matters far removed from immediate troubles, and there was an authentic Bevan ring about the style. . . . 'No one who presumes to influence, or who by the accident of circumstance is in a position to influence, the minds of his fellows, is entitled to stand aside and let the streams of human endeavour meet and leap towards catastrophe without doing his utmost to avert the tragedy. In the language of the incomparable Abraham Lincoln we must "disenthrall ourselves."'

A number of non-sequiturs followed, but the lofty note prevailed. 'They reach down and tap the inexhaustible reservoirs of spiritual sustenance which are never reached by intellectual ingenuity alone. This is why the main argument of this pamphlet insists that the fate of each one of us is bound up with the fate of all of us. . . .'

A grandiose piece of nonsense was now given the air of gospel truth. . . . 'Most of the great decisions in human history are simple. They demand more of courage than of ability.' There were other statements so idealistic that they remained remote from a world driven by power politics, and at many turns the pamphlet was open to devastating answer, but it showed very clearly that the authors were not anti-American, although this was automatically assumed by many newspapers.

Since 1945 some Socialists have sought to trace all the ills from which mankind has suffered to Britain's association with the United States. America was a capitalist country, and any dealings with her amounted to supping with the devil. This notion came most inappositely from those who still like to regard Soviet Russia as somehow the vanguard of the working class and the cause of world Socialism. For the rulers of Soviet Russia have chosen in turn since the Revolution the following associates in political alliance: the Reichswehr-dominated Weimar Republic, Hitler Germany and imperialist Japan. It is ironical that those who can so easily find excuses for all these adventures in diplomacy conducted by the purists of the Kremlin, should at the same time furiously condemn as a patent betrayal the mere fact of association between Truman's America and Labour Britain.

In the opinion of the Bevanite triumvirate foreign policies generally admitted an element of compromise. It was hopelessly unrealistic for a Socialist foreign policy to exclude any but its own kind from higher conclaves. No Socialist in his senses preached co-operation only with other Socialist Governments.

There were many other statements flatly contradicting interpretations put upon Bevanite behaviour by everyone who regarded them as devils incarnate fed with poison direct from the Kremlin.

More immediate matters were translated into what can be summarized under four points:

1. War was not inevitable but would certainly become so if the rearmament race continued unabated.

2. The under-privileged colonial peoples had a right to complete their social revolutions and it was the task of British Socialism to persuade our Western allies to assist those revolutions by economic and technical aid, instead of collaborating with counter-revolutionary forces in order to suppress them, the result being that the under-privileged would be driven into the arms of Soviet Russia.

3. Rearmament should be subordinated to a World Plan for Mutual Aid and the 'degree of rearmament necessary to deter the Russians from military adventures' should be financed under a system of Socialist controls which would maintain some equilibrium between wildly fluctuating costs of living, protect social services, prevent excessive profits and something vaguely described as 'luxury spending.'

4. It was not only possible but desirable to press on with a fresh series of measures designed to carry forward the establishment of a Socialist Britain. These included: The control of financial forces; the rate for the job; the abolition of price rings and rigged markets; more industrial democracy; more efficiency and social responsibility in the nationalized industries; the creation, by compulsion if need be, of Development Councils especially for ship-building and ship-repairing; the provision of buildings and equipment to approved manufacturers; public competition in privately owned industries; the nationalization of some monopoly concerns; the public ownership of sugar, cement and possibly some chemicals; the full use of statutory powers against inefficient farmers; nationalization of food-producing land which is not fully used; the reform of fruit and vegetable marketing; the public ownership of some mineral workings; the mutualization of industrial assurance; reconsideration of the problem of the tied cottage; public responsibility for all water supplies; the reduction of

excessive prices; publicly owned markets; the rationalization of cold stores; public ownership of meat wholesaling; Government bulk buying of consumer goods; the establishment of a Consumer Advice Centre.

Point 4 was largely contained in the Party document, *Let Us Win Through Together*, but, as the pamphlet stressed, 'Some of these measures may now be susceptible to some modification and improvement; they all remain to be carried out. . . .'

Rearmament remained the real core of the pamphlet. Clearly the optimum figure for British rearmament was highly controversial and Bevan looked upon £4,700 millions as the product of someone's intuition, a sort of "psychic bid" best calculated to win American favours. Exactly £4,700 millions, no more, no less was the sacred sum which, placed under the nose of the Russian bear would stop him biting. The pamphlet said: 'On 12 September 1950 the Prime Minister announced an expansion of our armaments programme to a figure of £3,600 millions over three years. "This great expenditure," he said, "represents the maximum that we can do . . . without resorting to the drastic expedients of a war economy." A bare twenty weeks later, on 29 January 1951, he raised the programme to £4,700 millions and proposed to carry it out without resorting to the drastic expedients of a war economy and without explaining how the impossible had suddenly become possible.'

Diplomatic and military calculations were now made 'with the precision of a Euclidean theorem,' but were not nearly so easy to prove. Possibly the Russians had retreated from Azerbaijan, abandoned intransigence in face of the Berlin air-lift, failed to launch an attack on Yugoslavia and shown very little stomach for developing the conflict in Korea, but that might signify concentration of forces for other purposes, and Christopher Mayhew insisted that we must put 'peace before plenty.' 'If,' Bevan's supporters said, 'there is no imminent danger of a Soviet attack, then our scale of rearmament is excessive; but if there *is* imminent danger then it is not enough.' This made the curious assumption that danger existed independently of any measure of defence Britain might take, which was not so. Mayhew said:

if the danger is not imminent now, this is partly due to Western rearmament. And if the West becomes still stronger, the danger will become still less imminent. . . . What will have produced the cease-fire in Korea? The knowledge in the minds of the Russian and Chinese leaders that the West was not merely strong, but becoming rapidly stronger. The cease-fire will have been the first dividend of Western rearmament. . . . The Bevanites' mistake is that they enormously over-estimate the influence for world peace of the amount of aid that Britain can provide in the coming years. No matter how drastic the arms cut, what we can supply cannot possibly produce the grandiose effects suggested in the pamphlet. . . . But as responsible people we simply have to face up to the facts. The facts are that unless the unexpected happens we cannot in the next year or two have peace *and* plenty simultaneously, and that as good citizens we have to put peace first. . . . [*Daily Herald*]

Nevertheless, one section of the pamphlet, instead of grandiose suggestions, put forward a rather more sober scheme for increasing the national income of undeveloped territories by 2 per cent. and commented: 'If it could be achieved it would be at least a sign that the weight of Asian poverty was being lifted very slightly. . . .'

None of which took into account the far more profound question of offering the poverty-stricken masses of the world not merely guns, which epitomized unthinking force, but some living idea, capable of challenging the dynamic of Stalin's Communism, although the instantaneous assumption that poverty meant Communism over-simplified a very complex pattern of widely differing behaviour.

There was another trouble. Darwin, who so seldom crept into political discussion, was capable of putting these dialectical exchanges in their place. A century before he had pointed out that all animals and plants produce more offspring than can survive and a constant struggle for existence occurs. In man, 'two-thirds of all men, women and children on earth today live their lives surrounded by squalor, hunger, disease, starvation, illiteracy and premature death.' (*War on Want*—pamphlet Association for World Peace, June 1952.) If this exaggerated the situation, there was enough truth left to show that surpluses from rich countries were hopelessly inadequate to effect any radical change. Certainly investment to industrialize the wastes of the world might revolutionize them, but industrialization alone was not enough. The great upsurge of people's governments in Asia was said to be dedicated to the control of famine, poverty, squalor and illiteracy. Whether they could achieve it was another thing. By supporting that part of their aims the demands of morality might in the long run, it was argued, coincide with the absolute claims of our own self-interest. On the other hand it could, said certain Conservatives, gratuitously clear up the aftermath of revolution on behalf of Communism.

Amongst it all no one spoke of rooting the trouble out at its source. No one breathed the much abused term birth-control, and it was almost as if Catholic scruples restrained Bevan's group. Yet there were eugenists who would rather export certain of our habits than our surpluses.[1]

Newspaper headlines excelled themselves with Bevan's pamphlet: *Daily Telegraph*—'Bevan Attack on Union Chiefs'; *Daily Mail*—'Bevan Opens Fire—On Attlee'; *Daily Express*—'Bevan Attacks The Lot.'

★   ★   ★

In the summer of 1951 Bevan and his wife went to Yugoslavia. He stayed with Marshal Tito for two days and came back with his regard for the late guerilla leader enhanced. He wrote a series of not very enlightening articles about his visit which seemed so concerned to avoid any breach of confidence that they dwindled away in a desert of historical fact. His picture of Marshal Tito holding conference on the island of Brioni, not in a royal palace, but in a grey stone shelter open to the sea, had a romantic ring. Grouped round the table, wrote Bevan, were the men who helped Tito carry spectacular guerilla war into the heart of enemy country. 'It was clear that here was no personal tyrant with a chasm set between himself and those who served him. They were colleagues together, sharing an immediately heroic past and now engaged in facing the perilous present.'

Tito turned out to be a formidable swimmer. When the trio went swimming together with Tiger, Tito's German police dog, Tito and Jennie enjoyed Bevan's discomfiture because he was no swimmer. 'I explained that there is all the difference in the world in swimming in the Adriatic and learning to swim in a Welsh mountain pond about a thousand feet above sea level under a cloudy sky amidst a number of dead dogs and cats.'

★   ★   ★

In the election which followed the vote ran Tory, etc. 321, Labour 295, Liberal 6, Others 3. The Tories had a clear majority

[1] Michael Young's excellent Labour Party pamphlet on India did in fact deal with birth-control.

of seventeen over all other parties and twenty-six over Labour in a straight division. A Tory majority of any kind was, in one sense, intoxicating to Bevan, and with shoulders squared and hand on his heart he declared one day, three months later in the House of Commons: 'I am not making a party political speech at all.' There was a gust of laughter. He added with a sly smile: 'If it shows signs of a party complexion it is because the facts are so ominous.'

In March 1952 a young and comparatively unknown Tory M.P., Iain Macleod, challenged Bevan: 'I want to deal closely and with relish with the vulgar, crude and intemperate speech to which the House of Commons has just listened,' he said, after Bevan had spoken. '. . . to have a debate on the National Health Service without the Right Hon. Gentleman would be like putting on *Hamlet* with no one in the part of the First Grave-digger. . . .'

Bevan had given an explanation of the difficulties with the School Dental Service, and Macleod said:

I am grateful for that explanation but it is entirely inaccurate. (Interruption) Oh, yes, certainly it is. First the figures of the Right Hon. Gentleman about the School Dental Service are inaccurate. The Right Hon. Gentleman made a great reputation in the previous two Parliaments by always speaking at the end of the health debates and never answering any points. He is much less effective when he comes down into the arena. First, he does not know the figures. In 1939 there were 866 dentists in the School Dental Service. . . . But the figure at the end of 1947 before the pull of the National Health Service drew the dentists and the potential dentists away from the School Dental Service, was about 1,060 and it is from that figure down to the low one of 810 we have now, that is the measure of the failure of the Right Hon. Gentleman to carry out his guarantees. . . .

Mr. A. C. Manuel and Mr. John Baird rose.

MACLEOD: 'Just a moment. I appreciate that the Right Hon. Gentleman is in need of care and protection.'

ANEURIN BEVAN: 'No. Will the Hon. Gentleman give the school population at the same time?' Mr. Macleod answered in detail.

BEVAN: '. . . but the Hon. Gentleman is assuming all the time that the children who were formerly dealt with by the school dental officers were not dealt with. Very large numbers of them were dealt with in the general Health Service itself. . . .'

MACLEOD: 'That is utterly ineffective. (Hon. Members: 'No!') Of course it is. The Right Hon. Gentleman simply does not know what he is talking about. . . .'

BAIRD: 'The Hon. Gentleman is not doing himself justice and he is misleading the House. He knows quite well that the School Dental Service was always the Cinderella of the dental profession and that we have never had an efficient school dental service in this country. He also knows that a large proportion of the children today are being treated by the ordinary dentist in his surgery, and the health of the school children today is higher than it was before.

More speeches followed. It then being seven o'clock, leave was given to move the Adjournment of the House and further proceedings postponed.

The debate re-opened some hours later.

MACLEOD: 'When we interrupted this debate a little more than three hours ago, to discuss the succession to the Bamangwato tribe, I was in the middle of a good-tempered and hard-hitting duel with the Right Hon. Member for Ebbw Vale, but at the moment the Right Hon. Gentleman does not appear to be in the Chamber. . . .'

It was a big day for Macleod. He threw the giant-killer out of his stride. Later, Macleod became Conservative Minister of Health.

★   ★   ★

On 5 March, a stormy debate on defence was followed by open revolt against Attlee's leadership from fifty-seven Labour M.P.s who sat the green benches with Bevan in their midst, silent but smiling. As a result the Labour amendment was defeated by 314–219, the Tory majority swollen to 95. It was described as Bevan's 'first public display of his minority leadership.' When the Government motion was put to the vote what were now known for purposes of newspaper convenience as "Bevanites," marched into the division lobby against the programme which had been planned by their own leaders. This time "Mr. Bevan and his friends" mustered 55 against Mr. Churchill's 313, a majority of 258. It was the final heresy.

The *Herald* editorial ran: 'This is a time for frankness. We must tell Mr. Aneurin Bevan and his supporters that they have set out on a course which will harm the country and imperil the future of the Labour Movement. They are now deliberately bent—as was shown by their conduct in last night's House of Commons divisions—on challenging the democratic decisions of the Parliamentary Labour Party, and advertising their antagonism to its elected leader, Mr. Attlee.'

This appeared to shock Bevan almost as much as his own behaviour shocked the *Daily Herald*. There were many comings and goings. Tom Driberg said it was not the Bevanites who were responsible for the alleged split in the Party but those who insisted on the amendment. 'Why?' Driberg asked with a combined air of injured bewilderment and journalistic frankness:

> Because this amendment, by supporting in principle Churchill's White Paper on Defence, violated the compromise reached at the Labour Party Conference at Scarborough last October. At Scarborough a policy manifesto was agreed by every member of the National Executive Committee and endorsed by Conference—the Party's policy-making body. It was agreed, and endorsed, only because it deliberately avoided committing the Party on the issue on which Bevan, Wilson and Freeman had resigned from the Labour Government. While supporting adequate military defence, it carefully refrained from specifying any particular programme or level of defence; it insisted that the development of the world's backward areas should have equal priority with defence. . . . [*Reynolds News*]

Had the leaders of the Party deliberately chosen this moment for a "showdown" with its rebellious elements and if they had sprung a "trap" had it proved unsuccessful because "so many mice crowded into the trap that it burst, and the mice made off with the cheese?"

All of which brought indignant denials from some of the Ministers involved in the Scarborough "compromise discussions" and set half the Press speculating whether Mr. Bevan was now on the high road to real power, to the leadership of the Socialist Party and beyond that. . . .

The inner story of the crisis ran rather differently. As I have pieced it together from various people, it appeared to go like this. The Drafting Committee which prepared the Scarborough Resolution omitted the £4,700 million figure. Wilfred Fienburgh, then Secretary of the Policy Committee, dealt with the actual wording.[1] Submitted to the Drafting Committee which included Aneurin Bevan and Herbert Morrison, Morrison said he regarded it with some dubiety but understood it as endorsing Labour Party rearmament policy. Some Bevanites denied that Morrison made any such remark at the Drafting Committee; only later at the Executive Committee when Conference was safely over. Bevan,

---

[1] Many people, of course, discussed the advisability of excluding the £4,700 million figure and many M.P.s contributed to the attempted compromise.

they said, would never have endorsed the agreed statement which he supported publicly from the Conference platform because it deliberately left out any specific rearmament figure.

Later came a dramatic close of Conference Executive meeting to discuss the machinery for selecting television stars best calculated to grip the new and far more visual imagination of the television electorate. With the Labour Party in power Attlee, within the Parliamentary Party, had selected broadcasters but in the vacuum of an election there were those—Bevan amongst them—who believed the responsibility should shift to the National Executive. Personalities were discussed.

Christopher Mayhew, already rated high amongst viewers, was automatically first choice, but a suggestion that women should be represented brought forward Miss Barbara Castle's name. She also spoke for the other point of view in the Party. Morrison smacked the election programme lately endorsed by Conference and said—what other point of view?—hadn't they as a Party agreed by a majority vote to accept this programme? Someone said the clause on disarmament was open to two interpretations. Morrison struck back vigorously, and now Bevan rose again in all his might. The outer world knew nothing of this. What began as a pleasant little diversion on television became another eruption on party machinery and policy, not altogether free from the anger generated amongst old world Executive members, confronted by far too many Bevanite successes in the Executive elections. They now held four of the seven constituency party seats, enough seriously to threaten the Old Guard of the N.E.C.

Back in London six months later, matters reached a new head. On the Friday before the fatal Parliamentary Party meeting, the rebels met to discuss what they should do in the House of Commons defence debate, and drew up a resolution which was passed to the Chief Whip who was given to understand that pressure was being brought to bear 'on the leadership.' Certain of compromise in one form or another the Bevanites destroyed all copies of the resolution 'in case it should fall into the malign hands of the Press' (*Observer*, 9 March). At the following Parliamentary Party meeting there seemed to be little attempt to arrive at a compromise resolution and the rebels began to think that the leaders were deliberately working towards a show-down. Six or more speakers, it seems, were called from Mr. Attlee's side and two or three from Bevan's. If this fairly represented the strength of the two points of view, it left dissatisfied at least one important Bevanite. 'Let there be no leaks,' he called as the meeting broke up. It was the opinion of at least one other M.P. present, that the Bevanites had quite a fair showing and there was no question of engineering a show-down.[1]

The real issue from the Party's point of view lay deeper and conditioned what was to follow. Were majority decisions, democratically determined by a total vote inside the Labour Party, to be followed faithfully in the House of Commons or could they be flouted with impunity?

Bevan now announced in public. 'If we are asked to recant I shall say—"No, we won't." If they ask us to promise not to do it again I will say—"No, we can't." As far as I am concerned the battle against Toryism is still on. I shall seek to persuade my colleagues that they should take the most vigorous part in that struggle so that we can go on together, but if we can't go on together we shall go on alone. . . . Who split the Party?' he shouted. 'They knew we could not vote for it. . . . Have we now reached the point where a Socialist is to be expelled from the Labour Party because he won't vote for one thing, and will vote against the Tories?'

These were the words recorded by the newspapers.[2] If they were accurate they seemed remarkably like another spontaneous overflow from the dark places of his Celtic soul which carried Bevan beyond the boundary of his real intent. '*We shall go on alone.*' What did that mean? *Was* he threatening to split the Party after all his protestations that loyalty to the Party precluded any attempt to create a cleavage? Or was he merely saying that we —the Bevanites—would go on fighting the magic figure £4,700 million, which converted a rational defence programme into an irrational ogre?

Some Executive members were now very tired of Bevan. One wit amongst them said he had exclusively reserved to himself the rôle of early Socialist martyr and unlike his Christian forbears could not tolerate anyone else being thrown to the lions. Another complained of a swashbuckling quality not to be regarded in the best democratic tradition. Certainly he could thunder and thump the table when moved by the immutable stupidity of people

---

[1] These meetings fall into many subtleties. Another speaker it seems was called who was against rearmament but was not a Bevanite.

[2] *News Chronicle*, 10.3.52.

unable to see eye to eye with him, and there were moments of aggressive self-assertion labelled as 'fascinating' by some people who witnessed them.

It was also agreed that bringing pressure to bear in association with other M.P.s was different from organized rebellion in a group with an appointed chairman. It remained true that if democracy meant anything within the Labour Party the minority must not only be permitted to have its say but should legitimately attempt to convert itself into a majority. It was differences rather than divisions which kept a Party alive. There were two objections to this. First the danger that democratic resistance could deliberately be used to cloak organized rebellion. Second—as one M.P. put it—that Bevan had gratuitously appointed himself the official Difference Maker on the grounds that True Socialism, the revelation of which had been granted to him and a few disciples alone, must be protected from desecration. Bevan argued that the reverse of the first point might equally be true and fierce differences of opinion suffer premature death by constant appeals to loyalty. For the rest it has to be said that Bevan, the most brilliant personality in the Labour Movement, would attract a following whatever happened.

The Party machine did not concern itself with too many niceties. There were rumours that the fifty-seven rebels would be asked to recant in writing. The fifty-seven included a number of pacifist and traditional Socialists who were not sympathetic to Bevan's general principles. Under searching examination, the threat of expulsion, or even censure, the fifty-seven would probably dwindle to twenty, but those twenty included some of the most able young men in the Labour Party and sheer numbers were not strictly relevant.

There was a horrible familiarity about all this. It was an understatement to say it had happened before. All over again it now looked as though Bevan was about to be cast into outer darkness. He refused to withdraw and the Party insisted on loyalty. In particular I am told that Herbert Morrison, very sick of the turbulent Welshman and his interminable scenes, too familiar with the unending story of one rebellion after another, and acutely aware of a challenge to his own position in the Party, insisted on an intransigence alien to his liberal heritage. At the next Parliamentary Labour Party meeting Attlee sponsored a strong resolution which sought not only to reintroduce Standing

Orders, but to condemn the action of the rebels. Once Standing Orders were accepted Party members could vote against the majority only on issues which invoked the "conscience clause."

Disaster threatened, the two sides becoming more bitter as the debate advanced, and it was only the intervention of moderating influences like Strachey and Strauss, and a dashing speech by another M.P., criticizing the Chairman for tactical mistakes, and saying both sides were equally to blame, which brought some measure of reconciliation. Several other comparatively young M.P.s also played a conciliatory part. The motion of censure was softened. At this point Bevan, gracefully repeating a somersault he had performed at least once before in his career, climbed down to the extent of accepting Standing Orders, and that seemed an enormous concession in the circumstances. But bitterness rankled and the future seemed filled with foreboding. The threat of a split had more substance than anyone cared to admit.

In the wider perspective the rearmament issue would dwindle as more fundamental conflicts between Government and Opposition spread, conflicts where Bevan found the views of his leaders less intolerable, and reconciliation if not co-operation became possible. For the rest it seemed for the moment as if the Labour Party had drifted into this crisis. Personal animosity and mutual suspicion accused Bevan of plotting revolt and Attlee of forcing a crisis. Neither was completely true. Fantastically, in the event, all Bevan's points were granted as much by the Conservatives as anyone else.

*   *   *

An episode on Newport Station was read symbolically. Returning to London from his constituency Bevan, carrying his own luggage as became a democrat, saw an empty first-class compartment, but when he tried the door, it was locked. Asked to open the door a porter pointed to the "Reserved" label on the window. It was departure time, no one had claimed the compartment, and as Bevan explained, 'If you don't unlock it the compartment will be idle. The train doesn't stop between here and London.'

The porter was adamant. 'But . . .' said Bevan and the train began to move.

A ticket inspector swiftly intervened, unlocked the compartment and Bevan climbed in. 'Ridiculous,' he said as the door closed behind him.

★   ★   ★

A Press conference launched *In Place of Fear*,[1] his first serious book, on a well prepared public in the spring of 1952. Some ballyhoo, not of Bevan's making, developed. There, on the dais, beneath a portrait of an early eighteenth-century savant, sat the Terror, in full panoply. He was flanked on either side by two representatives of his publishers, who anticipated any possibility of misunderstanding by beaming upon him as if he were the young find of the spring publishing season.... He looked prosperous, charming, even in moments during his speech, impish, and as the conference finished, journalists flocked round seeking autographs as though he were Clark Gable.

This was a big day. It launched a rather ornate compendium of his beliefs which might set a new seal on his career or incite derision from the intellectual Left or Right. The book itself sounded better read aloud than read in silence. Its style varied between logical argument, pontification and a tumultuous and sometimes poetic imagery. It was not an ordered book unfolding a system of thought. It was a short credo sometimes disappearing in the darker places of Bevan's polysyllabic language. A collection of essays more than a unified book, it presented vigorous and stimulating ideas, some of them clothed in highly original language.

It could be shown from this book that Mr. Bevan was no more the political buccaneer bent on destroying the pillars of society than he was a political philosopher bringing society's unhappy contradictions into a new system of thought. There was in this an element of anticlimax. The red-robed Danton, capable of wrecking democratic institutions, just was not there, and little in the credo would disturb orthodox Left-wing thinkers if one excluded the section on rearmament and foreign policy. But it was difficult to find the precise criterion from which to judge the book because it was not clear what he had set out to do. Examined from the strictly intellectual standpoint the book re-formulated trusted precepts in the Socialist philosophy rather than broke new ground, but there were moments when his brilliant gift for aphoristic exposition gave it an original ring.

[1] A detailed analysis of this book is given in the Appendix.

July 1952 brought a public rebuke from Attlee. Bevan had disclosed part of earlier Cabinet discussions in a House of Commons speech, violating 'a well established rule inhibiting members of a Government from revealing what passes either in Cabinet or in confidential discussions.'

Bevan hotly disputed this. *The Times* was flooded with documented letters producing precedents for and against but the sterility of complete objectivity seemed to invade the correspondence in the end. It was a dramatic move for Clement Attlee and set off reverberations through the whole Labour movement as one M.P. after another turned and savaged the Bevanites. One newspaper alleged that there was now a Party within a Party. It held regular meetings to decide its Party line, organized a travelling circus to tour the constituencies, and even, A. J. Cummings said, had a 'shadow Cabinet.' No one observed certain identities with those far distant days of the Query Club, the small-scale coterie meeting for education, lectures, discussion of aims and concerted action, all quite legitimate democratic instruments for enlarging a following. Certainly Bevan's following had grown in the most unexpected places—the Conservatives had largely carried out his rearmament policy—but no one yet knew its precise extent, or the nature of the shock which waited a few months away.

The climax came in October 1952. A breathless Annual Conference at Morecambe waited for the results of the National Executive Committee Elections, the pulse of feeling in the political wing of the Party proper. A bespectacled Scot from the Union of Post Office Workers read the results in a burr so thick the delegates could hardly believe their ears. A wave of excitement, cheering and boos ran through the hall. The Bevanites had displaced Herbert Morrison and Hugh Dalton, captured another two seats and now held six of the seven constituency party seats. They were jubilant. The vote ran: Mr. Bevan, 965,000; Mrs. Castle, 868,000; Mr. Driberg, 744,000; Mr. Griffiths, 700,000; Mr. Wilson, 632,000; Mr. Mikardo, 630,000; Mr. Crossman, 620,000. The sole survivor of the Old Guard was the warm, lovable Jim Griffiths, a man whose very nature seemed to deny displacement.

On the platform as the news came through Bevan sat, jaw out-thrust, hands clenched, his face impassive. Later he relaxed into a smile. 'Let the facts speak for themselves,' he beamed. 'I don't want to exacerbate feeling.'

It was easy to point out that there were twenty-seven members of the N.E.C. and a large part of the remaining twenty were solid trade unionists, now likely to stiffen their resistance. There was also to be taken into account the real seat of power, the Parliamentary Labour Party, for the moment largely anti-Bevan. Both bodies as constituted in October 1952 could easily hold in check any move which they considered a flagrant violation of policy or tradition. But from sitting in solitary state among the classical gods of Socialism, Bevan had now ousted all but two— Jim Griffiths and Clement Attlee—and taken another step nearer the leadership of the Party.

Arthur Deakin, emperor of vast and sometimes uncharted trade union territory, swiftly counter-attacked. There were people in the Party who had set up a caucus using differences of opinion which no longer had any real significance, such as rearmament. 'Let them get rid of their whips, dismiss their business and campaign managers, conform to the Party constitution. . . .' Uproar threatened to drown even his Brobdingnagian utterance. Continually he was interrupted. At last he got out, 'An organization has been set up—well an organization will be set up, too, to counteract these activities within the movement. . . .' (Cheers and boos.)

Historically, elements of the apache dance—the broken bottle followed by a kiss and final embrace—had distinguished many Labour Party conferences and the latest performance by Bevan and Deakin was not more vociferous or passionate than episodes in the past, but a rift in the relations between trade unions and Party could prove at least as disastrous as any internecine conflict in the Party itself.

*   *   *

Conflict indeed. Late in 1952 Hugh Gaitskell attacked Bevan with that biting coolness which distinguished his donnish outbursts and Clement Attlee emerged from a cloud of Olympian detachment to damn as "quite intolerable" the existence of a party within a party, with separate leadership, separate meetings and supported by its own Press. He next moved a resolution which some Bevanites said was undemocratic and a gross violation of freedom of speech, but Attlee's supporters regarded him as long suffering to the point of martyrdom and turned the accusation of "unconstitutional behaviour" back on the Bevanites.

Characteristically each seemed to use identical weapons whenever they came to final grips. The resolution read: 'This Parliamentary Labour Party accepts and endorses the statement of the Leader of the Party, and calls for the immediate abandonment of all group organizations within the Party, other than those officially recognized. . . .' There was also a clause about personal vilification.

The vote ran 188–51, overwhelmingly supporting Attlee's leadership. For a moment it looked as though Bevan would erupt spectacularly, but wiser counsels prevailed, he accepted the vote, and the group wound up loudly protesting that this was illiberal, based on allegations which were not true and—final irony—prejudicial to Party unity. 'Each one of us . . . will take every legitimate step to persuade the Parliamentary Labour Party to reverse the decision and to restore as soon as possible to Labour M.P.s their full rights of free association.' No one hastily assumed that the forces which Bevan had so skilfully disposed would automatically disintegrate. Indeed the reverse might be true, an overt movement becoming invert and creating fresh neurosis within the Party. Attlee was overwhelmingly re-elected leader of the Party but Bevan challenged Herbert Morrison for deputy leadership and achieved 82 votes to Morrison's 194. Bitterness broke out again when Attlee revised the methods for election to the Shadow Cabinet (a Parliamentary Committee of twelve) to check any group winning places out of proportion to their true support.[1] The Bevanites said it gave the majority a stranglehold over any minority. One member retorted that Bevanism was no longer valid as a separate body of thought—most of its conclusions having been built into Party policy—but was merely a device to manœuvre for power within the Party. Others went further. They said that Bevanism as a carefully enunciated alternative programme had never existed. In the thirties when Bevin attacked Lansbury the issue at stake was clearly pacifism. When Morrison turned on Cripps in the same period, everyone knew precisely what was meant by the Popular Front. But when one attacked Bevanism. . . . 'The Bevanites,' wrote Michael Young, 'have not committed themselves to any detailed declaration in conflict with the N.E.C. . . . On the face of it there is only a small difference of degree over rearmament, over the American

---

[1] Clearly this was done only with majority backing. In the previous year the principle of whether to take a second ballot was discussed *after* the votes were cast. On this occasion the decision to do so was made before.

alliance, over nationalization, and surely so much heat cannot be generated over a little more or a little less. . . .'

Of course, definitions of Bevanism varied according to which section of that immensely complex and diversified organism, the British Left wing, one belonged. In the constituency parties it was one thing, certain trade unions saw it differently from others, the Parliamentary Party differently from local parties or unions. It became gloriously evident in the last murmurings of the struggle that some protagonists were busy destroying what had no existence for others. Trouble over the *Tribune* Brains Trusts re-echoed the confusion and brought the redoubtable Kingsley Martin into vigorous defence of his chief weekly rival. Once again in the end the apache dance came to the conclusive embrace, but this time the embrace resembled a wrestler's and it was not easy to detect the kiss.

Amongst it all one thing was certain. Labour faced a difficult time ahead in which one figure would stand above everyone else in the public interest. Bevan had become the Great Figure of the Left. Everyone asked about him, visiting Americans spoke anxiously of him, on the Continent he was the man of the hour, in Britain hardly a day passed without some reference to him in the newspapers, and the House of Commons was full to overflowing whenever he spoke.

Early doubts and uncertainties were gone forever. The raw young agitator had grown into the councillor, the councillor become the M.P., the bohemian intellectual the rebellious back bencher, the back bencher the Cabinet Minister. And now Bevan was the only fixed star in the political firmament who not merely threatened to extinguish many splendid lights of the Left and challenge even the baleful glare of Churchill, but might himself, one day, become Prime Minister of England.

14

ANEURIN BEVAN has come a long way. It is half a world back to No. 32 Charles Street, the pit heaps and the stuttering boy from the elementary school. Aneurin Bevan has travelled far and the story is by no means finished. It is a long way back to despotic coal-owners, and the unions a prey to legal prosecution, to homes without sanitation, no holidays, a sixty-hour working week, and starvation hovering at the heels of every strike. It is a long way back to victimization, company towns, no secondary education, and the franchise open to men of twenty-one alone. H. G. Wells is no longer read, Queen Victoria an anachronism, Darwin a dim old gentleman who did something with apes, the glories of Liberalism overwhelmed by its imminent death and Marx translated into a world crisis he foresaw in different terms. The mines are nationally owned now, holidays are paid holidays, forty hours are worked in the pits for wages that have crept high in the scale of basic industries. South Wales no longer depends totally upon one coal-mining industry, and the trade unions have grown into a fifth estate in the land with a power capable of challenging Parliament itself. Enlightenment from education is available to all, the Health Service sustains us against illness, and a slow transformation has replaced the employer, in certain basic industries, with gigantic new boards.

The young talk now of nuclear fission, women understand mechanical mysteries once forbidden them, hypnotically people repeat—"standard of living"—and tend to mistake culture for a motor-car. Technicians are more esteemed than artists, planners than poets, the synthetic film star than the man who thinks, and a vast materialism, unlovely by its very totality, sets at naught the private self once a spiritual consolation in the midst of mediocrity, and now translated into psychological mechanisms.

The young talk of atomic energy and the ways of science. The middle-aged remember other things. It is a long way back to the fancies of the *Yellow Book*, to young Mr. Wells whirling in and out of the Fabian Society, to the warm verities of the I.L.P. and the fervour of the early Welsh Socialists, but Aneurin Bevan is middle-aged, and can remember these things. He can remember particularly the Biblical passions which first informed the Left-wing movement, and he remains a child of that age. He has inherited its fire along with a whole generation of mining folk, but he slowly accumulated a wealth of learning Blatchford never knew, canalized his convictions in new philosophies, gave his blessing to plans and planning. Are the times out of joint? Can Bevan born in one age reconcile himself to another? The question is not entirely rhetorical.

Aneurin Bevan has come a long way. Whatever lies in store for him, he remains a magnificent example of the potential in men born to frustration and hardship and the bleak life of the mining valleys, but as the *Observer* remarked at the time of the Party split: 'It is not easy to change basic habits at fifty-three, but there is little doubt that Aneurin Bevan will be able to command and give loyalty—his blind spot—on the scale required of a statesman, only if he can escape from the egocentricity that his life story has induced. He will need to lose his feeling of being unloved. . . . And he will also need to become less of an old-fashioned orator and intriguer, and more of a patient explainer and team-worker, if he is to fit into the modern scene.' In a word it has yet to be seen whether he can control or exorcise those elements in his character which threaten disruption to states-manship and judgment. Whether he himself would consider "statesmanship and judgment," anything more than part of an outworn coinage, remains in doubt. Certainly the words need re-examination in the light of modern values. Whatever secondary characteristics they reveal, both retain an essence universally valid if it is difficult to define.

That Bevan one day may be Prime Minister of England depends upon many things. Obviously the Labour Party must first come back to power. Unless ill health beset Attlee and Morrison they still intervene in the line of ascendancy. After Attlee, the tradition of seniority and long service in the Labour Movement made Herbert Morrison the most likely choice until the October Conference débâcle when he was swept off the Executive after thirty years' service. Bevan's stock was, at that time, very much in the ascendant and he flourished in Opposition. Over the next few years his reputation as a Conservative giant-killer may grow until he dominates the Opposition benches and its leaders. Indeed he is already said to do so. Given the Bevanite majority on the N.E.C.—six out of seven constituency seats—and a crisis atmosphere demanding powerful leadership, he might move into the last sacred circle.

But the trade unions have still to be taken into account. Eighty-two of the T.U.C.'s 183 affiliated unions pay the political levy to the Labour Party. They control a considerable part of the purse strings and exercise deep policy influence. At least four amongst the union leaders can make themselves felt in the Parliamentary Labour Party which, with power to elect the Party leader, in effect appoints a Prime Minister designate. If Arthur Deakin (Transport and General Workers), Sir William Lawther (National Union of Mineworkers), Tom Williamson (National Union of General and Municipal Workers) and Jack Tanner (Amalgamated Engineering Union) united to endorse Bevan's policy it might throw the present balance of the Parliamentary Labour Party into confusion. But Deakin can be said to love Bevan with an intensity matched by Bevan's love of General MacArthur, Sir William Lawther attacked Bevan at the 1951 Labour Party Conference, Tom Williamson is distinctly in sympathy with Attlee, and silver-haired, handsome Jack Tanner . . . well he is no potential revolutionary. Running close in size and influence the Communist-led Electrical Trades Union already backs Bevan, as do U.S.D.A.W.[1] and other lesser unions. One chastening qualification occurs. Within a short time, three if not four of the big bosses, including Deakin, Lawther and Tanner will reach retirement. Whether their successors will sustain Right-wing policies is difficult to calculate. Perhaps Bevan can afford to attack these gentlemen now. He is young. They are all in their sixties, he in his fifties. They will be out of his way in a few years, but others, equally hostile, may take their places.

The forces are infinitely subtle. Nothing quite like this system of check and counter-check exists anywhere else in the world. As it stands at the moment, the massive majority of the trade unions strongly opposes Bevan, reinforcing a similar situation in the Parliamentary Labour Party. It must also be remembered that the great slow-moving pachyderms of Transport House have always sniffed suspiciously at the brilliant intellectual flowers adorning the banks of the Labour Party, aware of death by deadly nightshade. Hard pressed they might prefer a Jim Griffiths as leader of the Party. Jim Griffiths because, as the sole surviving

[1] In 1952 on rearmament only.

member of the Old Guard on the Executive (October 1952) acceptable to trade unions and Bevanites, he might reconcile the two forces and prevent a deepening split.

For the rest Bevan epitomizes the upsurge of mining people who went into the trade unions, local government and House of Commons and formed the spearhead which eventually helped to bring a Labour Government to power and set moving for the first time a Socialist experiment on the grand scale.

The wheel may yet turn full circle in the next six years, a Prime Minister emerging from the men of the mines. If Bevan's book *In Place of Fear* is taken at its face value, what we should then see would be far less revolutionary than the Primrose League leads us to suspect.

He spoke in his book of a radical extension of public ownership. He said that the Labour Party had allowed itself to be frightened away from true nationalization into the "constitutional outrage" of boards. He wanted Ministers who were directly responsible to Parliament. . . . 'It is clear to the serious student of modern politics that a mixed economy [of public and private ownership], is what most people of the West would prefer. . . .' But 'relations between public and private enterprise have not yet reached a condition where they can be stabilized. . . . Before we can dream of consolidation the power relations of public and private property must be drastically altered. . . .' To sustain stability he saw the social scene of the future dominated by public property. . . . 'Private property should yield to the point where social purposes and a decent order of priorities form an easily discernible pattern of life.' Formulating its programme as this was written, the Labour Party spoke of nationalizing water, minerals and key sectors of the engineering industry, the chemical industry to be similarly dealt with. Other fields were under discussion. Beyond water, minerals and engineering, Bevan had pressed strongly for the nationalization of rented agricultural land, and appeared to be interested in the establishment of a Government investment corporation to provide capital for new processes and possibly industries. Somewhere within this appeared the threat of a capital levy. It was not stated whether as Prime Minister he would frown on America or Russia, but the pamphlet *One Way Only* revealed reasonable reactions to both. 'A Socialist foreign policy does not mean that friendship should be sought only with Socialist powers.'

And if books and pamphlets are not necessarily equivalent to political action, Americans can sleep soundly of nights if they take into account the complexity and subtlety of the democratic process as represented in the British Labour Party, which tends to imprison rather than aggrandize any Prime Minister. None of the Liberal and Labour Prime Ministers of Britain in the last fifty years achieved personal ascendancy in absolute terms. Churchill came nearest to it, but he had the advantage of the Conservative Party constitution which leaves immense power in the hands of individual leaders. In the Labour Party it is necessary to win majority backing from the National Executive Committee, the Parliamentary Labour Party, and the trade unions before a Prime Minister can behave with authoritarian bluntness. All three bodies as now constituted are traditionally cautious. They tend to convert Prime Ministers into catalysts, reconciling opposing views, interpreting the majority mood of conferences. Attlee brought the process near to perfection. A natural disposition to distrust display fused with Party tradition and produced the Divine Chairman.

Of course, some say that Bevan will only recognize the present Labour Party constitution so long as he remains a minority leader in the Parliamentary Labour Party and it suits him. The constitutional approach to Party and national problems is Attlee's not Bevan's, they say. I would very much doubt this, but perhaps his critics do not realize the jungle of difficulties which confronts any spirit foolhardy enough to attempt to change the Labour Party constitution. It was tried in 1937 by no less a person than Cripps with limited success after a bitter struggle. The local constituency parties were then granted another two seats on the National Executive Committee which meant that seven out of twenty-seven seats were in Labour Party hands. These seven seats were also turned over to an exclusive Labour Party vote, uninhibited by trade union membership. Another twelve seats are directly elected by the trade unions, five women members depend upon the vote of the whole Party in which the trade unions have an overwhelming majority, and the remaining three are the Leader of the Parliamentary Party, one member from the Socialist societies, and the Treasurer. In a word the unions have a powerful majority on the N.E.C. and although some of them may back Bevan on rearmament, that is very different from taking a general leftward swing. Trade unions in Britain are notoriously staid, cautious bodies not given to the passionate revolutionary embrace. And it is the curious paradox of Bevan that combining 'an extremist programme with stalwart faith in the freedom of parliamentary democracy,'[1] he becomes a bulwark against Communism. '. . . if there were no Bevans in the Labour Party there would be many more votes for the Communists.'[2] Certainly it would need a crisis of far more severe proportions than anything we have seen since the war to break traditional shackles and release any would-be dictator on England's green and pleasant land. And as Woodrow Wyatt wrote of Bevan: 'At heart he is profoundly democratic . . . he may be dictatorial at times in his manner, but never in his policy or in his beliefs.'

[1] *British Politics since 1900*—D. C. Somervell.
[2] *Ibid.*

Appendix

Society presented itself to Bevan in his book *In Place of Fear* as 'an arena of conflicting social forces and not as a plexus of individual striving. . . . These forces are in the main three: private property, poverty and democracy. They are forces in the strict sense of the term, for they are active and positive. Among them no rest is possible. . . .'

The issue in a capitalist democracy thus resolved itself into '. . . either poverty will use democracy to win the struggle against property, or property, in fear of poverty, will destroy democracy. Of course, the issue never appears in such simple terms. Different flags will be waved in the battle in different countries and at different times . . . but poverty, great wealth and democracy are ultimately incompatible elements in any society.'

Applied to the social scene fifty years before, when Bevan was born, these demagogic categories had almost complete validity. Poverty was so extreme, wealth so concentrated in the hands of the few, democracy still so fledgling, that they were indeed incompatibles. Enormous conflicts released into society eventually clothed themselves in the Labour Party, the trade unions and adult enfranchisement. These three forces over fifty years brought far-reaching changes.

The signs of emotional fixation with his boyhood were considerable when Bevan seemed to imply that the conditions of 1897–1926 remained strong enough today to justify continual incompatibility. The Labour Government's three terms of office might have passed for nothing. He sometimes wrote as if there had been no change in the relationship between property and power since 1931. There were pages in the early chapters of the book which attacked a social situation differing so much in degree it hardly existed in kind. There were times in fact when he seemed to commit the very crime of which he complained. . . . The student of history should be on his guard, he wrote, 'against the old words, for the words persist when the reality which lay behind them has changed. It is inherent in our intellectual activity that we seek to imprison reality in our description of it. Soon, long before we realize it, it is we who become the prisoners of the description. . . .'

Reality indeed. The great mass structures of rich and poor which distinguished the early 1900s had gone, the number of people extremely poor and very wealthy had narrowed and considerable redistribution of national income had lifted the lower income groups away from the old poverty line. Men worked less hours for more money under better conditions, and the number of idle rich had declined. But it had to be remembered that widespread unemployment might at any time resurrect the monolithic generalizations woven into Bevan's words. That was the strength of his case. Any society which could not control wholesale unemployment continuously suffered the threat of a throw-back to savagely destructive class differences, although the incidence of millionaires appeared to be permanently crippled by death duties, and surtax. Bevan of course completely understood this. Seen in these terms his generalizations became intelligible.

Examined in detail the situation revealed infinitely subtle characteristics. Where money was once concentrated in a few hands power had now taken its place. Where one wealthy family held all the capital in a given company, it now tended to be distributed as shares amongst the public. Great combines and monopolies traced large parts of their capital into thousands of small homes and gave the illusion of widespread distribution of power as well as ownership. But shareholders played very little part in running the affairs of big business. Power was concentrated in the hands of the directors, of the few owners of massive share-blocks and of the technicians and the managers. Preference shareholders were virtually absent landlords, owning part of the business but never taking part in it. The diffusion of shareholders corresponded with a new concentration of power. Which of the terms: Poverty, Democracy, Private Property expressed these complexities? Which of these terms revealed the tendency to transfer power from ownership to management?

Even the class equivalents of his categories Poverty and Wealth—in Marxian terms the Proletariat and Ruling Class—revealed under close analysis considerable qualifications since the black and white days of the late 1800s and early 1900s. Many working-class children had graduated to universities and become school-teachers or the like. Their children in turn, brought up in middle-class surroundings, sometimes progressed into the professional classes. Over two generations some dilution of class had come about. The old rigid, hierarchical system which made progression from one class to another a rare phenomenon had relaxed as educational opportunities widened. A strong dislike existed among the working classes for those who were ashamed of their origin, but increased wages brought many people in sheer money terms into the middle-class income groups, and they tended to ape the superficial characteristics of the class into which they had "climbed." But money was a small part of class difference. Clothes, codes of conduct, values, accents, interwove to produce the highly complex characteristics of the British class structure, something still undergoing deep examination by research workers trying to pin down the elusive elements of its inner psyche. Class was only a social distinction if regarded traditionally. A hierarchical class structure emerged in the modern university based on ability rather than birth or money. Sometimes it revealed internecine bitterness at least as fierce as Bevan's. By changing the method of discrimination one did not escape emotional tensions. The self-enlarging desire for greater respect from his fellows was one of the most difficult characteristics to combat in highly developed modern man, and with its growth, fresh brands of nepotism and influence automatically emerged. Class revealed itself as discrimination between one level and another which could be made from systems of values so different as to remove the common connotation of the word class today, only to substitute fresh feuds. The classless society at peace with itself might after all be a myth.

Reducing these complexities to vast abstractions like Poverty, Democracy and Private Property had political validity but did not advance our understanding of the class phenomena.

Bevan's final summary of the social scene appeared in the penultimate paragraph of Chapter One and was more accurate. 'From 1929 onwards ... there was wealth, great wealth, concentrated in comparatively few hands, although cushioned by a considerably developed middle class. Second, there was a working class forming the vast majority of the nation and living under conditions which made it deeply conscious of inequality and preventable poverty. Third, there was fully developed political liberty. ...'

Fourth, he should have added, under two Labour Governments the absolute rule of private property had almost vanished, the profit motive suffered a severe inhibition of its sovereignty, and market fluctuations alone no longer governed our whole economic life.

*   *   *

Bevan explained in the second section of his book that 'The classic principles of Marxism were developed when political democracy was as yet in its infancy. The State was a naked instrument of coercion, accompanied by varying degrees of Royal absolutism. ...' Quite early in life he realized that 'Classic Marxism consistently understated the rôle of a political democracy with a fully developed franchise.' In a word, instead of revolution by violence, it was possible, in mature communities, to have revolution by vote. Bevan favoured parliamentary democracy as a method of social progress and looked upon free institutions 'as not only the most desirable of political systems, not only as the one most congenial to the flowering of human genius, but as indispensable in a modern industrial community.'

Chapter Two read like a model apologia for free thinking democrats, except for a cloud no bigger than a man's hand which came and went on the distant horizon. He believed that 'Private property in the main sources of production and distribution endangers political liberty, for it leaves Parliament with responsibility and property with power.'

We have already seen that generalizations like property are no longer so significant as they were; that does not invalidate Bevan's belief that power may still be, in part, at one remove from Parliament.

When the Conservatives were in office, he pointed out, they reduced Parliamentary intervention to a minimum. 'A striking instance of this was Neville Chamberlain's insistence that he had not promised at election time to deal with unemployment....' Snowden and Mac-Donald were not fundamentally different. 'They did not look upon parliamentary power as an instrument for transforming the economic structure of society. For them the rôle of Parliament was to be ameliorative, not revolutionary.'

Revolutionary? Primarily Parliament was a revolutionary instrument for Bevan, and at once the clash between himself, Clement Attlee and Herbert Morrison became clearer. They saw it as an instrument of social change; he revolutionary change. They were prepared to admit the inevitability of gradualism; he the gathering impetus of *real* Socialism. The fact that Parliament 'interprets its own authority and from it there is no appeal ... gives it a revolutionary quality,' he wrote. By reason of this it 'enables us to entertain the hope of bringing about social transformations without the agony and prolonged crises experienced by less fortunate nations.'

Other parties saw Parliament as a means of creating the necessary conditions for the most fruitful operations of private enterprise. They did not use the power of Parliament to its full, Bevan said, they did not 'extend it for collective action.'

'The Socialist dare not invoke the authority of Parliament in meeting economic difficulties unless he is prepared to exhaust its possibilities. If he does not, if he acts nervelessly, without vigour, ingenuity and self-confidence, then it is upon him and his that the consequences will alight.'

For those who held sacred Britain's unwritten constitution there followed the cloud no bigger than a man's hand.... 'He will have played his last card and lost, and in the loss, Parliamentary institutions themselves may be engulfed....'

*   *   *

Under the heading *Modern Man and Society*, Bevan said that science, in trying to make the forces of nature predictable was looking for certainty not adventure. Yet Heisenberg's Principle of Uncertainty in the most scientific of the sciences, physics, remained uncontroverted and indicated that certainty had not been established, if by virtue of the geometrical progression of knowledge it ever could be. Not that Bevan said it had. He simply argued that if individuals were to make a home for themselves in society, they must set out to make the social forces as reasonably predictable as science was making those of nature.

This was in direct contradiction to anti-Socialists who believed that society should be 'a great arena for private economic adventure.' At once, said Bevan, they were revealed as profoundly unscientific, unaware perhaps that some of them would consider the term complimentary.

It is some indication of the unco-ordinated nature of the book that a quotation from the very last chapter on page 151 would have reinforced this argument vividly, but was thrown up in a quite different place. 'Children are taught in our schools to respect Bruno and Galileo and other martyrs of science, and at the same time they are encouraged to close their minds against those who question the assumptions underlying contemporary society.' Scientifically analysed, Bevan saw many falsities in those assumptions. Man was not made to become an item in the price of production, efficiency could never measure personal happiness, slums and disintegrated families were not inevitable, rampant nationalism deserved a minor rôle in human affairs.

There were many fine things in this chapter. Reason thrown into disrepute, doubt questioning the very roots of our methods of thinking, so often sought refuge in the primitive herd emotion of extreme nationalism and we were back in the dark places of ancient man where superstition strove to substitute wisdom. This was highly undesirable, Bevan wrote, as were many other characteristics of modern life.

The chapter ended with the observation that when Popes, Kings, Dukes and Princes had patronized the arts in the past they had done so, very often, with public money raised from taxes, rents or profit. He himself as Minister of Health, was responsible for a Statute which permitted municipal authorities to 'spend public monies on educational, artistic and other allied activities.'

*   *   *

In the chapter Private or Collective Spending Bevan said that capitalist society was impermanent because it represented a hotch-potch of private values unwilling to acknowledge the paramount importance of social values, and suffered under the constant threat of unemployment. He believed that a deliberate change in consumer demand, necessary when slumps threatened industry, could best be brought about by collective action or public investment. He considered it unfortunate that the most successful men in capitalist society, those who became 'the money-owners' decided by their interests and purchasing power 'the character of the economy of the future.' He said that great wealth could not be accumulated by personal qualities or exertions alone. It often derived from the 'power to exploit the exertions of others.' Various forms of "surplus" were analysed, but no fundamental definition of "surplus value" appeared to be given. Roughly it worked like this: The cost of a kettle to the consuming public took into account not only the price of raw materials, a proportion of the cost of capital equipment necessary for production, the price fixed as an adequate reward for a man's labour, management and distribution costs, but the dividend paid by the kettle company to shareholders who may have had no part whatever in the production of the kettle. This was surplus value. It could be re-distributed to those who actually made the kettle. Instead it went into the hands of someone largely disinterested in kettles as such. And if one said that he had risked his capital, it was at once necessary to ask by what means he amassed it. Capital, wealth, and even for that matter income were not necessarily in proportion to effort, ability or moral right. Trace back their roots to early "economies" and it was seen that wealthy overlords and barons had not "produced" the land they owned, and therefore had no natural right to possession. Often they had fought, plundered and possessed by force. Similarly, accumulated capital rarely represented returns given to the community. Social continuity produced laws of inheritance which passed wealth amassed by one person of no special consequence or service, through his descendants to someone who might once again contribute nothing to his day and age. Apart from natural resources, any amassment of capital frequently began by the accumulation of the surplus value of goods produced by others.

At quite another level, if brilliant ideas were any measure of earning capacity, great scientists would have been wealthy men, inventors retired with fabulous riches, yet not these men, but the manipulators 'the financier, the gambler, and those with social pull' tended to emerge as millionaires, wrote Bevan.

If effort as such was any justification for great wealth, a consistent, ingenious and frequently hard-pressed burglar had as much right to it as the millionaire. Not the effort itself but the social utility of the effort was what mattered to Bevan. He put it in his usual aphoristic way. 'The subjective consciousness of exertion is no test of its objective merit.'

It was a grave pity that this chapter should throw out the splendid promise—'Soviet Communism and Socialism are not yet sufficiently distinguished in many minds'—and fail to develop it. But Bevan boldly placed on record his hatred of the police state and all its repressive ancillaries. He gave a balanced picture of the good and bad in Soviet society. There was, he wrote, a spiritual malaise in Western Europe arising from profound lack of confidence in current values and 'a prolonged hesitancy to choose between a number of proffered alternatives.' Yet he did not see democratic Socialism as a middle way between Capitalism and Communism. Principles and energy of its own sustained democratic Socialism.

* * *

Sweeping on to foreign policy he asked, were we to continue living haunted lives, inhibiting social services, undermining economies through swollen rearmament programmes? It was not so much Communism we had to fear, as fear of Communism. . . . ,

'A substantial Budget surplus promised a long awaited reward for the patient and industrious people of Britain,' in 1950, he wrote. 'At no time since the end of the 1914 war was the British Communist Party so weak. We had proved to all, except those too blinded by prejudice to be able to see, how democratic institutions could be used to hold back Communism. . . .'

It was vital to understand that if fear of Communism reached pathological proportions it might induce the very collapse in Western economy desired by Russia, without any resort to arms. Indeed the depth of rearmament already held high promise for long-term complications of the most profound kind. The horrible paradox that by not going to war, Russia could wreak more havoc than by any attempt to overrun Europe, held the seeds of cynical disillusion in the whole world situation. And disarmament following on rearmament threatened even worse disasters, for disarmament could deflate the world boom and create a slump with wider and more shattering results than the Wall Street cataract of 1931.

There was a tragic inevitability about fear. It created conditions in which the ability to contain the outcome of fear was matched by debility in the life-blood of the community. We might remain poised, bristling with arms, looking across Europe at the dark towers of the Kremlin for a whole generation, if the deeper tides of unemployment did not suck us into the vortex. We might submit to a permanent impoverishment of our standards of living. But Bevan's solution appeared to over-simplify the issues. Fear did not decrease in proportion as armaments were cut, indeed it might increase and encourage fresh neuroticism in the national psyche. And in 1952 there was little sign of the rearmament programme really wrecking our economy.

At the purely economic level he was more convincing. 'A recession of only four per cent. in employment in the United States was sufficient to produce a crisis in Europe. A recent report published by the United Nations grimly underlines the danger. . . .' The whole world outside the Eastern block was held in the dollar universe of the United States and economic satellites would be instantaneously subject to any downward drag from the central star. 'If nothing is done to deal with that situation Stalin will not need to lift a finger. The Capitalist system will do the job for him.'

It was Bevan's profound conviction that America was not yet mature enough as a civilization to lead the world. Impulsive, militaristic elements in the U.S.A., threatened international affairs with adolescent outbursts not calculated to preserve the peace. There were those in America who saw his own outbursts in a not dissimilar light. 'I am not anti-American. . . . But I don't believe that the American nation has the experience, sagacity, or the self-restraint necessary for world leadership at this time. . . .' [1]

*   *   *

The book at last broke back into humanist sentiments. Dylan Thomas was quoted 'After the first death, there is no other.' Bevan saw 'The capacity for emotional concern for individual life' as 'the most significant quality of a civilized human being.' Either his vermin speech was the unintentional overflow of a rhetorical moment or what followed became meaningless because he added that—it 'is not achieved when limited to people of a certain colour, race, religion, nation or *class.*' The italics are mine.

It was another of those moments in the book when apparent contradictions confirm the opinion of one close crony that rather than suffer from surfeit of words Bevan's articulation was incapable of expressing the depth and complexity of his thought. And yet . . . and yet. . . . Was it rather that a considerable personal conflict in Bevan expressed itself in different language according to which censor challenged which impulse? Or was it that the manifestations of his mind were greater than the mind itself? Certainly, in the end, a note of finality distinguished far too many statements in the book. It was difficult to believe that a mind so flexible and imaginative as Bevan's did not know that truth was many sided. Renan went further: 'Truth lies in a nuance.'

Yet it would be extravagant to ask for anything resembling detachment from such a born leader as Bevan who probably belongs to Nietzsche's sublime ones, intoxicated with eloquence, brilliant, resourceful, and capable of leaping to gorgeously complete conclusions.

No one else could have written *In Place of Fear*. It was not academically intellectual in the sense that *New Fabian Essays* (1952) were intellectual, but it was a social document of the day, and his genius for aphoristic exposition, his gift of poetic expression illumined many a chapter and marked the book out from others of its kind. For the rest, *In Place of Fear* needs to be read in its entirety to measure its true significance.[2] Anyone who pretends to understand Bevan should at least make the attempt, and the attempt should be made now while the book can be seen in its contemporary setting. This brief analysis is no more than a pointer to the book itself.

[1] Speech at Jarrow, March 1952.
[2] *In Place of Fear*. (Wm. Heinemann Ltd., 1952.)

INDEX

A

ADAMSON, W., 39
Alexander, A. V. (later Viscount), 135
American Industrial Workers of the
World, 29–30
Ammanford, 33
Anderson, Evelyn, 134
Archangel, troops sent to, 40
Ashcroft, Tom, 44
Association for World Peace: *War on
Want*, 210
Asquith. *See* Earl of Oxford and
Asquith
Atlantic Charter, the, 147
Attlee, Clement, 8, 9, 100, 154, 161;
on National Unity, 152; and the
1945 Cabinet, 164; and Bevan's
resignation, 198–9; his Socialist
philosophy, 203, 204; dispute with
Bevan on Cabinet discussions, 220;
criticism of Bevanites, 221–2; as
Prime Minister, 228

B

BADOGLIO, Marshal, 147
Baird, John, 212, 213
Baldwin, Earl, 61, 103–4
Balkan campaign (1941), 137
Bargoed, 33
Baxter, Beverley, 192
Beardsley, Aubrey, 15
Beaverbrook, Lord, 90–2, 133
Beckett, John, 83
Beerbohm, Sir Max, 15
Bevan, Aneurin: Birth, 19; childhood
and early life, 13–14; schooldays,
22–3, 24; family buy Seven, Charles
Street, 24; spare-time butcher's boy,
24; begins work at pits, 26; searching
questions at Sunday School, 27;
arrest and release from Army call-
up, 34–5; Chairman of Miners'
Lodge, 37; scholarship to Labour
College, 41; explorations of London,
44; return to Tredegar and unem-
ployment, 46; elected to Tredegar
Urban District Council, 51; Miners'
Dispute Agent, 52; nominated for
Ebbw Vale, 71; election speeches,
72; maiden speech in House, 72–3;
first impressions of House, 73–4;
early speeches, 74–9; attack on At-
torney General, 75–6; attack on
Lloyd George, 77–8; and the Mosley
party, 84–5; as Lord Beaverbrook's
guest, 91–2; shares flat with Frank
Owen, 93; attack on the Means
Test, 94–5; marries Jennie Lee, 102;
honeymoon in Spain, 102–4; visit to
Russia, 102; suspension from the
House, 112; illnesses, 113, 120; buys
country cottage, 113–14; visit to
Spanish front, 116–19; expelled from
Party, 119; readmitted, 123; attacks
in the House, 126 ff.; editor of
Tribune, 134 ff.; attacks on Churchill in the House, 141 ff.; attacks on
IAA, 149–50; censure from Party
and T.U.C., 153 ff.; Ministry of
Health, 164 ff.; Health Bill, 166 ff.;
housing programme, 172 ff.; debate
on housing, 175–7; Manchester
speech on Tories (1948), 189; Minister of Labour, 193; brush with
dockers, 194; Defence Debate (February 1951), 194–6; resignation,
198–202; visit to Tito, 211; in Opposition, 212; revolt over rearmament, 213 ff.; dispute with Attlee
over Cabinet discussions, 220; success at Morecambe Conference, 220;
challenge for deputy leadership of
Parliamentary Labour Party, 222
His power of invective, 4; effect
on other people, 4; epigrammatic
phrases, 6; breadth of knowledge,
7; alternating moods, 7–8; working
class roots, 7, 8; character, in the
House, 10, 183–4; eloquence, 10;
ambition, 11–12; stuttering, 22, 23,
28, 31–2, 44; width of reading, 26–7,
184; wit and audacity as a speaker,

238

O

P

R

S

T